Praise for *Mapping Experiences*

Mapping Experiences will help both designers and consumers of design services understand how to visualize experiences and the system ecology in which products and services exist with the all-important customer. His approach to the subject is both broad and deep. The analytical and practical/practice chapters speak directly to the current interest in visual artifacts associated with strategy and service design.

—Paul Kahn
Experience Design Director, Mad*Pow
Author of *Mapping Websites*

As designers grapple with ever more complex services and systems, the need to visually map them is paramount. There are hundreds of different ways of mapping and diagramming experiences and they are locked away in hundreds of different books and academic papers. Jim Kalbach has pulled them all together in an excellent book that should be on the desk of everyone involved in UX, service design and business.

—Andy Polaine
Design Director, Fjord

Adopting an outside-in perspective, developing empathy with the people you support, and creating visualizations of these perspectives is the power-trio for the future of your organization. The trio allows you to support people, internally and externally, in a more nuanced, coordinated manner. It also enables you to see new paths ahead, so that you can branch away from your competition. Jim's book is an excellent explanation of this trio, and includes a collection of tools that you can put to immediate use.

—Indi Young
Research consultant and empathy coach
indiyoung.com

With Mapping Experiences, *Jim Kalbach has done a terrific service for anyone tackling complex, systemic design challenges. He not only documents the best approaches to experience mapping, but also pushes the topic forward, by sharing his insights and hard-won experience about this rich, still-evolving area of design practice. Mapping Experiences will be an essential guide for many years to come.*

—Andrew Hinton
Author of *Understanding Context*

We live in an age where images are more powerful than words. Everyone working in the areas of customer experience and strategy will benefit from learning how to express ideas visually, and Mapping Experiences *is a great place to start.*

—Victor Lombardi
Author of *Why We Fail: Learning from Experience Design Failures*

This book offers the right approach to using maps as a tool in experience design and execution, and that is, there is no one-size-fits-all. Instead of offering just one idea around how to best align your teams around the idea of better experiences, Kalbach offers several tips, tricks, and processes to actually get things done. This is the down-to-earth manual that's been missing. Readers will find the right way for their unique challenges, not one unique process to try to make fit for their situation. Everyone can benefit from reading this book!

—Jeannie Walters
CEO and Chief Customer Experience Investigator of 360Connext, writer, and speaker

Our experiences interacting with faceless companies often make us ill. Mapping Experiences, *wielded properly, might actually do something to eliminate the all-too-typical shoulder shrugging and buck passing we face—and help designers and decision-makers alike become customer experience heroes.*

—Lou Rosenfeld
Publisher, Rosenfeld Media
Co-author of *Information Architecture for the Web and Beyond*

Kalbach gives clarity to the growing number of customer-focused visualization—and provides readers with practical guidance for creating their own.

—Kerry Bodine
Coauthor of *Outside In: The Power of Putting Customers at the Center of Your Business*

Thoughtful. Rigorous. Clear. Jim Kalbach's Mapping Experiences *literally creates a new cartography for organizations and innovators to successfully navigate design processes. His essential themes of "designing to align" and "aligning to design" address the key issues I see in enterprises seeking to better organize around UX.*

—Michael Schrage
Research fellow at MIT Sloan School's Initiative on The Digital Economy
Author of *Who Do You Want Your Customers to Become?*

Mapping Experiences

A Guide to Creating Value through Journeys, Blueprints, and Diagrams

Jim Kalbach

Beijing · Boston · Farnham · Sebastopol · Tokyo

Mapping Experiences

by James Kalbach

Copyright © 2016 James Kalbach. All rights reserved.

Printed in Canada.

Published by O'Reilly Media, Inc., 1005 Gravenstein Highway North, Sebastopol, CA 95472.

O'Reilly books may be purchased for educational, business, or sales promotional use. Online editions are also available for most titles (*safaribooksonline.com*). For more information, contact our corporate/institutional sales department: (800) 998-9938 or *corporate@oreilly.com*.

Acquisitions Editor: Nick Lombardi	**Cover Designer:** Ellie Volkhausen
Developmental Editor: Angela Rufino	**Interior Designers:** Ron Bilodeau and Monica Kamsvaag
Production Editor: Melanie Yarbrough	**Illustrator:** Rebecca Demarest and Melanie Yarbrough
Copyeditor: Phil Dangler	**Compositor:** Melanie Yarbrough
Proofreader: Rachel Monaghan	
Indexer: Lucie Haskins	

Revision History for the First Edition:

2016-04-01	First release
2016-05-20	Second release

See *http://oreilly.com/catalog/errata.csp?isbn=0636920038870* for release details.

978-1-491-92353-5

[TI]

For my mother and father

Contents

"Then the Ping-Pong match begins."

That's what a customer told me about his experience with the billing process of the company I was consulting. After digging deeper and having conversations with other customers, it became clear to me what he meant.

Apparently, the company was known for sending incorrect invoices. Finding a resolution often proved difficult for customers. They instinctively called the support hotline first, but agents there weren't empowered to fix problems with invoices. Customers then called their sales representative, who wasn't responsible for billing issues. Relatively quickly, customers fell into an aggravating communication loop with the company.

But it got worse.

The collections department didn't suspend its scheduled warning notices. And they didn't know if a customer may have questioned an incorrect bill. So amidst customers' frustration troubleshooting an incorrect bill, they received a past-due notice.

That not only added insult to injury, it also made the resolution exponentially more complicated: three or four parties were now involved, and the customer was caught in the middle. Ping-Pong, indeed.

This was not rare. I easily uncovered similar stories with just a handful of additional customer interviews. One person I spoke with recalled how absolutely livid she was when this happened. She was ready to cancel a service vital to her business just out of principle.

As a designer, I find it disheartening to hear such stories. But it's not surprising. I've seen it over and over again: in large organizations, one hand does not know what the other is doing.

My research was part of a larger experience mapping project I was conducting. The effort resulted in several diagrams to illustrate customers' current condition: a map of the end-to-end journey and a series of workflow diagrams illustrating their experiences step-by-step.

To conclude the project, I held a workshop with various stakeholders from a variety of functions: sales representatives, marketing specialists, business managers, designers, and developers. Walking through the illustrations allowed us to comprehend the customer experience in detail.

I intentionally put myself in the breakout group examining the billing workflow—just to see what would happen. Everything went fine until we got to the point where an incorrect bill and past-due warnings were sent out. Then came the collective outrage: "How is this possible?" they asked. They were unaware their company was capable of inflicting so much pain on customers.

A clear action item emerged: implement the ability to place a hold on bills that customers have challenged. This would prevent collection notices from being sent out until the issue was resolved. The head of customer care had a draft proposal for this procedure by the end of the day. Initially, this was to be done manually, but eventually an automated hold was needed.

Of course the real problem was sending incorrect invoices in the first place. But even if that were corrected, a larger, more fundamental issue emerged in our team discussion: the organization wasn't able to handle customer complaints and requests across departments.

From this particular incident, the sales manager was easily able to recount additional stories of troubleshooting non-sales–related issues with customers. This distracted him from his sales duties. And the customer care representative described how their team often couldn't help customers on the phone immediately, yet would have to take the brunt of their anger.

By coming together and having a conversation around the actual experience, we were able to reflect on the company's performance as a service provider across functions, beyond this one particular incident. It became obvious: the organization faced larger, systemic issues. These only came to light after we focused on the experience from the customer's point of view.

Aligning for Value

Few organizations deliberately want to create bad experiences for the people they serve. Yet experiences like the one described earlier happen all the time.

I believe the fundamental problem is one of alignment: organizations are out of sync with what the people they serve actually experience.

Misalignment impacts the entire enterprise: teams lack a common purpose, solutions are built that are detached from reality, there is a focus on technology rather than experience, and strategy is shortsighted.

Aligned organizations have a shared mental model of what they are trying to accomplish. They are obsessed with delivering amazing experiences for the people they serve.

More and more, people select products and services based on the total experience they have. To meet market expectations, it's imperative to align around the end-to-end experience.

To achieve alignment, I see three imperatives organizations must follow:

1. **View your offerings from outside-in rather than inside-out.**

   From my work with dozens of companies, I have seen teams with the best intentions focused too much on internal processes. They are wrapped up in a type of organizational navel gazing. Many simply don't know what customers actually go through.

   What's needed is a change in viewpoint—from inside-out to outside-in. Organizations must have a clear understanding of the experiences they create. This is not limited to just frontline personnel. Everyone must empathize with the individuals they serve.

   In this sense, gaining *empathy* isn't only about feeling the same emotions as another person. Instead, it refers to the ability to grasp what others are experiencing, the ability to put yourself in their shoes. Empathy for others comes with the recognition that their perspective is valid even if it's different from your own.

But a little empathy is not enough. Members of the organization must *deeply* care about their customers and what they experience. They need to internalize people's desires and motivations, and advocate on behalf of the people they service in everything they do.

2. **Align internal functions across teams and levels.**

   Organizational silos prevent alignment. Aligned organizations instead work across functional boundaries. They have a relentless focus on doing whatever it takes to ensure their constituents have great experiences.

   Alignment is not just about superficial improvements. It's about the collective actions of the entire group, at all levels. An organization's backstage processes have as much to do with the overall experience as the visible points of interaction that individuals encounter.

   On his TV show, top chef Ramsay Gordon saves failing restaurants by realigning the whole establishment. He usually starts by fixing the kitchen. He'll chastise cooks for improper food storage or for having a dirty exhaust hood above the stove. The actions in the kitchen influence the experience diners have.

> *Misalignment impacts the entire enterprise: teams lack a common purpose, solutions are built that are detached from reality, there is a focus on technology rather than experience, and strategy is shortsighted.*

Aligned organizations have their kitchen in order. They move together in the same direction for the same cause—to create brilliant experiences. And they don't focus on parts of the experience. They consider the end-to-end interaction. The sum of local optimizations does not guarantee optimization at the global level.

Note that "alignment" is already an inherent part of the business strategy vernacular. Typically managers speak of upward alignment—getting everyone in the organization to work toward a stated strategy from above. My interpretation of the term focuses on *value alignment:* looking first at the value an organization needs to create from the individual's perspective, and then figuring out the strategy and technology needed to deliver that value.

3. **Create visualizations as shared references.**

    The challenge of alignment lies in the difficulty of seeing interdependencies across the organization. Each department may be functioning fine on its own. But from the users' perspective, the experience is a patchwork of interactions they have to navigate themselves.

    Visualizations are a key device to break down siloed thinking. A diagram of the individual's experience serves as a tangible model for the teams to rally around. More importantly, visualizations allow the viewer to grasp interlocking relationships at once.

In the story opening this preface, sales managers and customer care agents had separately shared their obstacles and inefficiencies with their managers. But it was not until decision makers could see connected factors that both the problem and the solution became apparent. Reports and slide decks don't have this causal effect. Visualizations do.

But visualizations don't provide answers outright, they foster conversations. Diagrams are compelling artifacts that draw interest and attention from others in the organization. They are a means to engage others in discourse. Visualizations point to opportunities and serve as springboards into innovation.

In a broader sense, visualizations inform strategy. They are a key way of seeing the market from the customer's perspective. Mapping experiences isn't a nice-to-have design tool; it's a must-have for strategic alignment.

Finally, as practices like lean product development take hold in organizations, the need for alignment only increases. Small, empowered teams need to be on the same page as the rest of the organization. A compelling visualization gets everyone moving in the same direction for the same reasons. Your organization's agility depends on shared purpose.

Scope of This Book

This book is about a *type* of tool that provides organizations insight into their broader product and service ecosystems. I call these tools *alignment diagrams*—an umbrella term for any map that seeks to align how individuals in a system engage with that system and its provider. Chapter 1 explains this concept in more detail.

This book deals with various techniques for mapping experiences, not a single method or output. The focus is on the *category* of diagrams that collectively seek to describe the human experience. Many related techniques are included here as well.

These diagrams have already been an implicit part of the design and creative disciplines for decades. In fact, you may have already used alignment diagrams as part of your work.

Reframing these approaches as tools for organizational alignment emphasizes their strategic relevance. They help flip an organization's perspective from inside-out to outside-in. In doing so, they help build empathy and provide a model for decision making that is inclusive of the human condition.

Alignment diagrams also offer a common vision throughout an organization. They aid in creating consistency in thought and action across departmental lines. This type of internal coherency determines success.

To be clear: alignment diagrams are no silver bullet and only part of organizational alignment. However, I believe the story they tell goes a long way in achieving alignment, particularly in larger organizations.

The concept of *mapping* helps us understand complex systems of interaction, particularly when we're dealing with abstract concepts like *experience*. But mapping experiences is not a singular activity limited to one type of diagram over another. There are many possible perspectives and approaches.

In this sense, this book is about *possibilities*. My hope is that the book expands your thinking and approach toward mapping in general.

There are many types of diagrams covered here, each with different names and backgrounds. Don't get hung up on labels. Many of the distinctions are historical and based on which term was coined first. Instead, focus on value alignment, not one specific technique over the other. It's entirely possible to create a new type of diagram that continues to evolve the practice. I encourage you to do so.

> *This book is about possibilities. My hope is that the book expands your thinking and approach toward mapping in general.*

What This Book Is Not About

This book is not about customer experience management, service design, or user experience design. It is about diagrams—key tools that span those fields of practice. The approach I describe here is *not a design process* but rather a process for mapping independent of specific discipline.

This is also not a comprehensive book about formal techniques in graphic design, information design, or illustration. There are volumes of resources about graphic design and illustration that go into much more detail than I can here.

Finally, I realize that there is a technical difference between the words *map* (an illustration of where things are) and *diagram* (an illustration of how things work). However, this book does not distinguish between the two. In practice, terms like *customer journey map* and *experience map* are, in fact, misnomers. But they are so widely used that the distinction between map and diagram becomes irrelevant.

Audience for This Book

This book is intended for anyone involved in the end-to-end planning, design, and development of products and services. It's for people who need a holistic view of the ecosystem in which their offerings are situated. This includes designers, product managers, brand managers, marketing specialists, strategists, entrepreneurs, and business owners.

Regardless of your skill level in mapping, there is something for you in this book. The steps and processes outlined here are basic enough for beginners to start creating diagrams. The related techniques should provide new insights for experts as well.

A Note on the Diagrams

I've taken painstaking care to provide a range of diagrams in this book that reflect different approaches to mapping experiences. My interest is in providing complete, whole examples so you can view them in their entirety. Although I've given the utmost attention to the display and clarity of each diagram, in some cases, not all texts are legible. Please see the references in the image credits and throughout the book to locate the originals online, where available. I also encourage you to find and collect your own examples for inspiration and guidance.

Rapid Techniques

The process I outline in this book comes without a time frame. Informal efforts can be completed in a matter of days, while formal projects may last weeks or months. I describe a more formal process, particularly in Chapters 4–8.

Throughout the book, however, I highlight approaches that can greatly speed up the process. They are indicated with a "Rapid Technique" symbol to help you navigate to them quicker.

Together, these techniques will help you run a mapping effort even within a fast-paced environment.

Book Outline

This book is divided into three parts.

Part 1: Visualizing Value

Part 1 provides an overview and background on the concept of alignment diagrams.

- Chapter 1 introduces the term *alignment diagram* as a class of document that seeks to visually align an individual's experience with the services of an organization. It focuses on the concepts of value alignment and value-centered design.

- Chapter 2 looks at the key elements of *mapping experiences*, breaking them down into individual components.

- Chapter 3 deals broadly with the topic of *strategy* in general and the role of visualization in strategy creation.

Part 2: A General Process for Mapping

Part 2 details a general process for creating alignment diagrams, broken into four phases: initiate, investigate, illustrate, and align. After understanding and empathizing with the current experience, we envision what future experiences can be.

- Chapter 4 details how to *initiate* a mapping project, including the key considerations in effectively framing the effort.

- Chapter 5 outlines how to investigate and perform research before creating a diagram.

- Chapter 6 provides an overview of how to *illustrate* a diagram.

- Chapter 7 deals with how to use diagrams to *align* teams, primarily through a workshop.

- Chapter 8 presents a range of complementary techniques used in conjunction with alignment diagrams to *envision future experiences* and solutions.

Part 3: Types of Diagrams in Detail

The final part of the book looks at some specific types of diagrams in detail, including a brief historical overview of each.

- Chapter 9 starts with *service blueprints*, the oldest type of diagram covered here.

- Chapter 10 focuses on *customer journey maps*, including investigations into decision-making and conversion funnels.

- Chapter 11 deals with *experience maps*. There is also a discussion of "job maps" as well as workflow diagrams.

- Chapter 12 looks at *mental model diagrams*, as pioneered by Indi Young. There are also discussions of grounded theory, information architecture, and related diagrams.

- Chapter 13 discusses *spatial maps* broadly. This is less of a diagram type than a diagram format, but its form has an impact on what it can and can't show.

About the Author

Jim Kalbach is a noted author, speaker, and instructor in user experience design, information architecture, and strategy. He is currently the Head of Customer Success at MURAL, the leading online whiteboard, and has also consulted with large companies such as eBay, Audi, SONY, Citrix, Elsevier Science, Lexis Nexis, and more. Jim holds a master's degree in library and information science and a master's degree in music theory and composition, both from Rutgers University.

Before returning to the United States in 2013 after living for fifteen years in Germany, Jim was the cofounder and long-time organizer of the European Information Architecture conferences. He also cofounded the IA Konferenz, a leading UX design event in Germany. Previously Jim was an assistant editor with *Boxes and Arrows*, a prominent journal for user experience information. He also served on the advisory board of the Information Architecture Institute in 2005 and 2007.

In 2007, Jim published his first full-length book, *Designing Web Navigation* (O'Reilly, 2007). He blogs at *http://www. experiencinginformation.com* and tweets at *@JimKalbach*.

Acknowledgments

Writing is solitary; publishing a book is collaborative. It's amazing just how many people are involved. I thank you all. Hopefully I won't leave anyone out.

First, I'd like to thank the good folks at O'Reilly who made this project possible, in particular Mary Treseler, Angela Rufino, Nick Lombardi, and Melanie Yarbrough.

A special thanks goes out to Paul Kahn for encouraging me to write about alignment diagrams after my talk at the European Information Architecture conference in Paris in 2010. My collaboration with him deepened my understanding and interest in the topic, and I learned a lot from Paul along the way. I'm grateful for his comments on my texts during the writing process.

I'd also indebted to the technical reviewers for their feedback: Leo Frishberg, Austin Govella, Andrew Hinton, Victor Lombardi, Jess McMullin, Chris Risdon, Gene Smith, and Dan Willis. Their expertise and insight was invaluable to me.

I'd also like to thank everyone else who reviewed individual texts and chapters: Amber Brown, Megan Landes, Donna Lichaw, Jim Nieters, and Jen Padilla.

I'd like to thank Professor Michael Schrage for his feedback on early drafts and for in-depth conversations about alignment. His work in general, and in particular the ideas from his book *Who Do You Want Your Customers to Become?* (discussed in Chapter 7), has influenced my thinking and work. Thanks, Michael.

Thank you to all of the contributors of case studies and diagrams. I am very grateful to have such talented people involved in this book:

- Thanks to my former colleagues for the case study in Chapter 2: Jen Padilla, Elizabeth Thapliyal, and Ryan Kasper.

- Thank you to Amber Brown for her case study from Sonos in Chapter 5.

- Thanks to Paul Kahn and Mad*Pow for their excellent case study and beautiful diagrams in Chapter 6.

- Thank you to Christophe Tallec for his case study on Journey Games in Chapter 8.

- Thanks to Susan Spraragen and Carrie Chan for their contribution to Chapter 9. I enjoyed collaborating with you!

- Jim Tincher's input and contribution from his excellent work at Heart of the Customer was particularly helpful. Thanks for the case study in Chapter 10.

- Thanks to Peter Jones for his insight and contribution on Gigamaps in Chapter 13.

A special thanks goes out to Indi Young, who not only contributed a case study to Chapter 11, but also helped shape that chapter greatly. I appreciate your collaboration, Indi.

Thanks to all the creators of example diagrams who gave me permission to include their diagrams in this book:

Part 1: Brandon Schauer and Chris Risdon of Adaptive Path, Paul Kahn, Julia Moisand Egea, Laurent Kling, Booking.com, Tyler Tate, Accelerom, Gianluca Brugnoli, Amber Brown, Elizabeth Thapliyal, Ryan Kasper, Claro Partners, Clive Keyte of Intrafocus, Michael Ensley of PureStone Partners, and Daniel Bartel of Strategyzer.

Part 2: Jim Tincher, the folks at Macadamian, Beth Kyle, Chris Risdon, Eric Berkman, Sofia Hussain, Scott Merrill for his photo, Brandon Schauer, Erik Hanson, Deborah Aoki, Kevin Cheng and the good folks at Rosenfeld Media, Donna Lichaw, and Steve Rogalsky. Thanks also to Jeff Patton for a very informative conversation about user story maps.

Part 3: Pete Abilla, Andy Polaine, Adam Richardson, Effective UI, Jim Tincher, Gene Smith, Yvonne Shek, Adaptive Path, Roger Thomas of LexisNexis, Beth Kyle, Indi Young, Patrick Kovacich, Chiara Diana and Roberta Tassi, Julia Moisand, Mark Simmons and Aaron Lewis, Helen Rogers and the team at Berg, Andy Polaine, Lavrans Løvlie, Ben Reason, Jamie Thomson, and the folks at Mad*Pow.

A special thanks goes to Hennie Farrow for the beautiful diagram in Chapter 6, but also for providing the style for the artwork in this book and consulting with me on many other aspects of it. Thanks for listening to me, Hennie!

I'd also like to thank my wife, Nathalie, for her support and encouragement. And I'd like to thank my father, Donald Kalbach, for reading most of the chapters and providing feedback on the text. Thanks!

Finally, I've been teaching a workshop on diagrams for about five years. Presenting this material and learning from my students has shaped a great deal of this book. To quote the opening lines of composer Arnold Schönberg's book on harmony, "dieses Buch habe ich von meinen Schülern gelernt"— I learned this book from my students. Thank you!

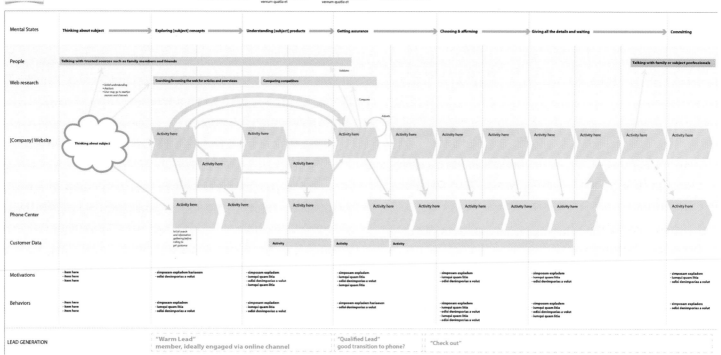

The above diagram is a blank model for a multichannel experience map created by Chris Risdon and the folks at Adaptive Path – leaders in experience mapping techniques (taken with permission from: "Anatomy of an Experience Map" *http://adaptivepath.org/ideas/the-anatomy-of-an-experience-map*).

In this book, we'll look at how to complete this and other illustrations to help you shift team alignment from an inside-in to outside-in perspective.

PART 1
Visualizing Value

I've seen it over and over again: organizations get wrapped up in their own processes and forget to look at the markets they serve. Operational efficiency is prioritized over customer satisfaction. Many simply don't know what their customers go through.

But we're witnessing a shift of Copernican* proportions: nowadays, customers don't revolve around the business; rather, the businesses must figure out how they fit into the lives of their customers. This requires a shift in mindset.

Part 1 covers some of the fundamental aspects of the mapping process.

Alignment diagrams, introduced in Chapter 1, are a category of diagram that reorients organizations. They help move from an inside-out view of the market to an outside-in perspective.

Chapter 2 deals with the overall approach to *mapping experiences*. Although the concept of experience is slippery, there is a systematic way to capture an experience in a diagram.

Diagrams not only help design better experiences, they also inform *strategy*. Chapter 3 looks at how alignment diagrams point to new opportunities. They represent a new way of seeing the market, your organization, and your strategy.

---

* E.g., Denning, Steve. "Why Building a Better Mousetrap Doesn't Work Anymore," *Forbes* (Feb 2014). *http://onforb.es/1SzZdPZ*

"There is only one valid definition of business purpose: to create a customer."

— Peter Drucker
The Practice of Management (1954)

IN THIS CHAPTER

- Introduction to alignment diagrams
- Value-centered design
- Principles and benefits of mapping

CHAPTER 1

Introducing Alignment Diagrams

People expect some benefit when they use the products and services an organization provides. They want to get some job done, solve a problem, or experience a particular emotion. If they then perceive this benefit as valuable, they'll give something in return—money, time, or attention.

To survive, organizations need to capture some worth from their offerings. They need to earn profit, maximize reach, or improve their image. Value creation is bidirectional.

But how do we locate the source of value in such a relationship? Simply put, value creation lies at the intersection of human interaction with the provider of a service. It's where the experiences of individuals intersect with the offerings of an organization (Figure 1-1).

FIGURE 1-1.
Value lies at the intersection of individuals and the offering of an organization.

A number of years ago, I was struggling to determine what type of diagram to use on a project: a customer journey map, mental model diagram, service blueprint, or something else. After some comparison of several examples, a similar set of principles became apparent: these diagrams all represent the value creation equation in some way.

Viewing the commonalities of various diagrams opened up possibilities. I wasn't locked into one prescribed method over another. I realized the focus should not be on a specific technique but rather on the broader concept of value alignment.

More importantly, I was better able to connect the dots between human-centered design and business objectives. Concentrating on *alignment* allowed me to talk with business leaders and stakeholders about the importance of design in reaching their goals. Within a short time, I was running workshops with senior leaders and showing my diagrams to CEOs.

Creating solutions by focusing on the interaction between individuals and organizations represents a perspective referred to as *value-centered design*. In his article "Searching for the Center of Design," service design expert Jess McMullin defines value-centered design as follows:

> *Value-centered design starts a story about an ideal interaction between an individual and an organization and the benefits each realizes from that interaction.*

In this chapter, I introduce the concept of *alignment diagrams* to describe a class of diagrams that visualize the story of interaction between individuals and an organization. By the end you should have a firm grasp of value alignment, the commonalities and key differences between diagram types, and the benefits of value alignment.

Alignment Diagrams

The term *alignment diagram* refers to any map, diagram, or visualization that reveals both sides of value creation in a single overview. It is a *category* of diagram that illustrates the interaction between people and organizations.

Such diagrams are not new and already used in practice. Thus my definition of alignment diagram is less of a proposition for a specific technique than a recognition of how existing approaches can be seen in a new, constructive way.

Logically, alignment diagrams have two parts (Figure 1-2). On the one side, they illustrate aspects of the individual's experience—a depiction of aggregate behavior across archetypal

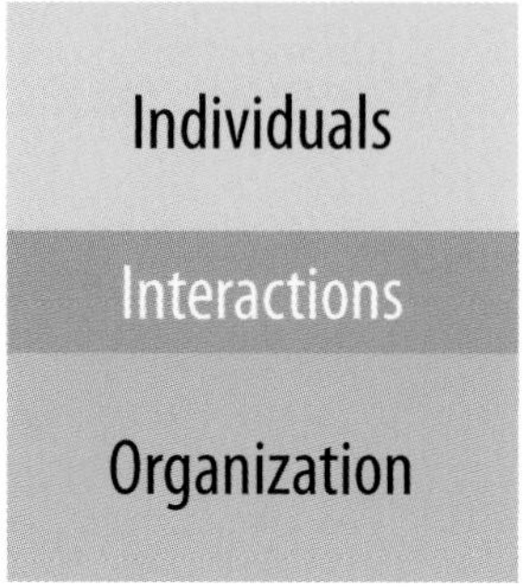

FIGURE 1-2.
Alignment diagrams have two parts: a description of an experience and a description of an organization's offerings, with the interaction between the two.

users. On the other, alignment diagrams reflect an organization's offerings and processes.

The points of interaction between the two are the means of value exchange.

You may have already used them: service blueprints, customer journey maps, experience maps, and mental model diagrams are widespread examples.

The following sections compare common types of diagrams to reveal their similarities. These five examples represent archetypes of diagrams. Most other related diagrams can be categorized against one of these core patterns. Part 3 deals with each of these diagrams, as well as related diagrams.

1. Service Blueprints

Service blueprints diagram a service offering. The technique has the longest history of the examples discussed in the book.

Figure 1-3 shows a service blueprint created by Brandon Schauer, a strategist and business analyst with Adaptive Path, a leading user experience design group. It depicts the experience of a conference attendee.

Service Blueprint for Seeing Tomorrow's Services Panel

find out more: http://upcoming.yahoo.com/event/1768041

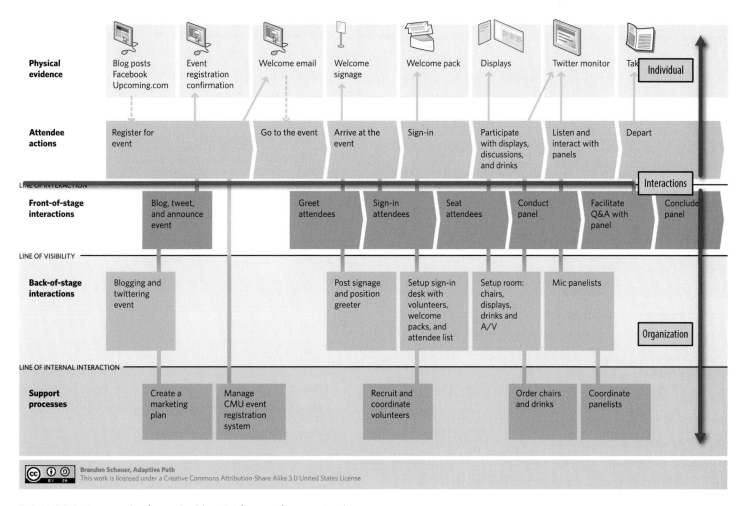

Physical evidence	Blog posts Facebook Upcoming.com	Event registration confirmation	Welcome email	Welcome signage	Welcome pack	Displays	Twitter monitor	Tak...	**Individual**
Attendee actions	Register for event		Go to the event	Arrive at the event	Sign-in	Participate with displays, discussions, and drinks	Listen and interact with panels	Depart	

LINE OF INTERACTION — **Interactions**

Front-of-stage interactions	Blog, tweet, and announce event		Greet attendees	Sign-in attendees	Seat attendees	Conduct panel	Facilitate Q&A with panel	Conclude panel

LINE OF VISIBILITY

Back-of-stage interactions	Blogging and twittering event		Post signage and position greeter	Setup sign-in desk with volunteers, welcome packs, and attendee list	Setup room: chairs, displays, drinks and A/V	Mic panelists	**Organization**

LINE OF INTERNAL INTERACTION

Support processes	Create a marketing plan	Manage CMU event registration system	Recruit and coordinate volunteers	Order chairs and drinks	Coordinate panelists

FIGURE 1-3. An example of a service blueprint for a conference attendee.

The customer actions are indicated at the top and business processes at the bottom. In the middle Schauer indicated the "line of interaction"—the touchpoints where there is an exchange of value.

2. Customer Journey Maps

Customer journey maps illustrate the experiences of an individual as a customer of an organization. They typically include making a choice, such as the decision to buy a product or service, as well as to stay a loyal customer.

Figure 1-4 shows a simple customer journey map of a search service for finding architects internationally. This is a modified version of a diagram I created for a project a number of years ago, concealing the name of the product and company. It describes how a customer interacts with the provider of the search service from beginning to end.

Phases of interaction are listed across the top, starting with "Become Aware" and going to "Renew/Upgrade." The rows show various facets of the customer experience: actions, state of mind and feelings, desired outcomes, and pain points.

The bottom half shows key departmental activities to support or respond to the customer. An analysis of strengths, weaknesses, opportunities, and threats appears below that. The primary means of interaction are listed in the middle row.

The focus should not be on a specific technique but rather on the broader concept of value alignment.

3. Experience Maps

Experience maps are relatively new. They illustrate experiences people have within a given domain. Figure 1-5 shows an example of an experience map created by Chris Risdon, also of Adaptive Path. This particular map shows the phases in a trip through Europe by train.

In the top portion, it describes the experience people have when traveling. At the bottom are opportunities for the business. The interactions between the two are embedded in the middle of the diagram.

4. Mental Model Diagrams

A mental model diagram is the broad exploration of human behaviors, feelings, and motivations. The approach was pioneered by Indi Young and detailed in her book *Mental Models*. These are typically very large diagrams that, when printed, can cover an entire wall. The example in Figure 1-6 shows a close-up of a mental model diagram for going to the movies.

A horizontal line in the middle divides the diagram into two parts. The top shows individual's tasks, feelings, and philosophies. These are grouped by topic into what are called towers, which are then sectioned off into goal spaces (e.g., "Choose Film" and "Learn More about a Film"). The boxes below the center line show support for achieving those goals from various products or services.

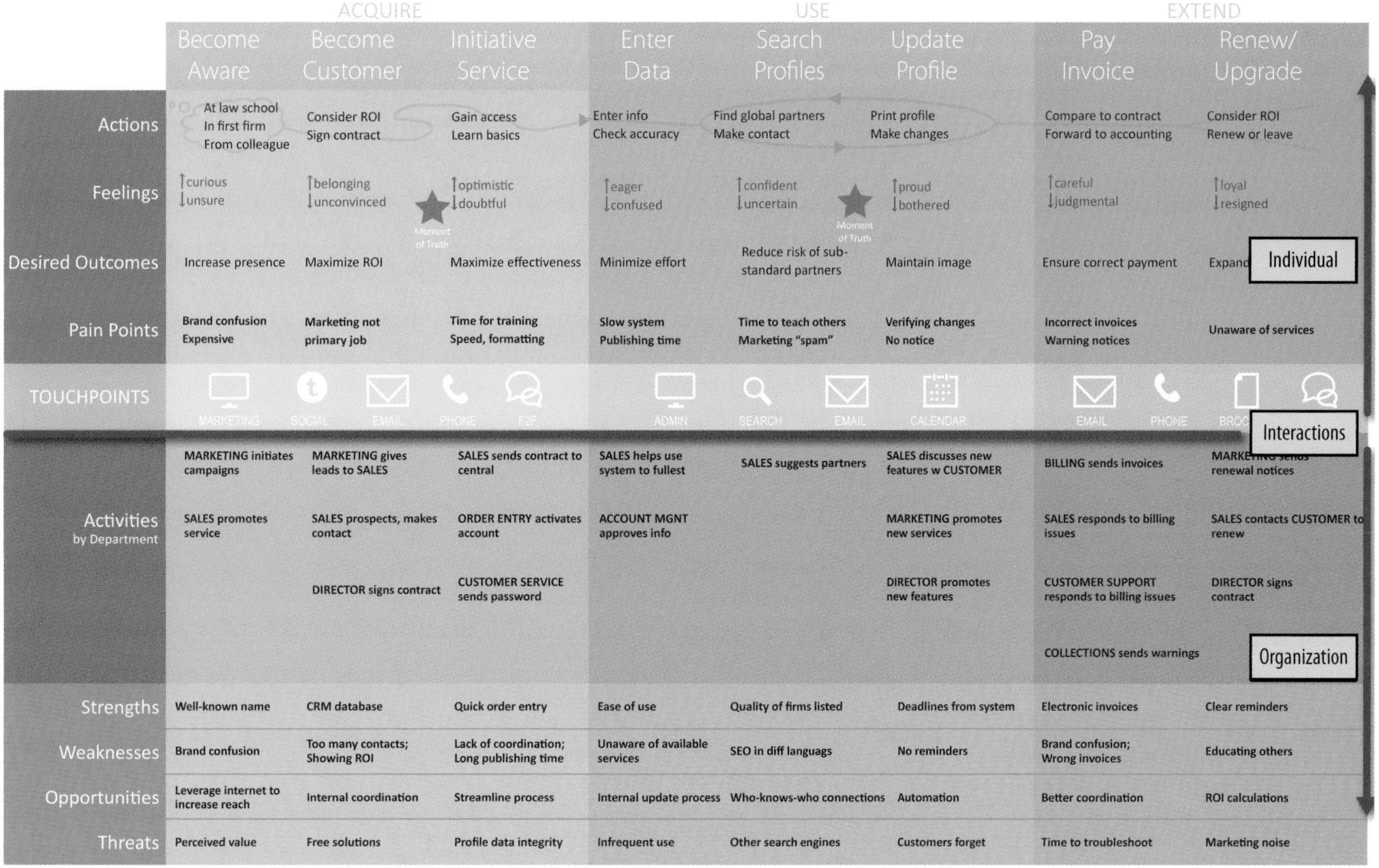

The journey map contains the following structured content:

Phases: ACQUIRE | USE | EXTEND

Stages: Become Aware | Become Customer | Initiative Service | Enter Data | Search Profiles | Update Profile | Pay Invoice | Renew/Upgrade

	Become Aware	Become Customer	Initiative Service	Enter Data	Search Profiles	Update Profile	Pay Invoice	Renew/Upgrade
Actions	At law school; In first firm; From colleague	Consider ROI; Sign contract	Gain access; Learn basics	Enter info; Check accuracy	Find global partners; Make contact	Print profile; Make changes	Compare to contract; Forward to accounting	Consider ROI; Renew or leave
Feelings	↑curious ↓unsure	↑belonging ↓unconvinced	↑optimistic ↓doubtful (Moment of Truth)	↑eager ↓confused	↑confident ↓uncertain	↑proud ↓bothered (Moment of Truth)	↑careful ↓judgmental	↑loyal ↓resigned
Desired Outcomes	Increase presence	Maximize ROI	Maximize effectiveness	Minimize effort	Reduce risk of sub-standard partners	Maintain image	Ensure correct payment	Expand
Pain Points	Brand confusion; Expensive	Marketing not primary job	Time for training; Speed, formatting	Slow system; Publishing time	Time to teach others; Marketing "spam"	Verifying changes; No notice	Incorrect invoices; Warning notices	Unaware of services
TOUCHPOINTS	MARKETING	SOCIAL; EMAIL; PHONE; F2F		ADMIN	SEARCH	EMAIL; CALENDAR	EMAIL; PHONE	BROC...

Individual | Interactions | Organization

Activities by Department	Become Aware	Become Customer	Initiative Service	Enter Data	Search Profiles	Update Profile	Pay Invoice	Renew/Upgrade
	MARKETING initiates campaigns	MARKETING gives leads to SALES	SALES sends contract to central	SALES helps use system to fullest	SALES suggests partners	SALES discusses new features w CUSTOMER	BILLING sends invoices	MARKETING sends renewal notices
	SALES promotes service	SALES prospects, makes contact	ORDER ENTRY activates account	ACCOUNT MGNT approves info		MARKETING promotes new services	SALES responds to billing issues	SALES contacts CUSTOMER to renew
		DIRECTOR signs contract	CUSTOMER SERVICE sends password			DIRECTOR promotes new features	CUSTOMER SUPPORT responds to billing issues	DIRECTOR signs contract
							COLLECTIONS sends warnings	

	Become Aware	Become Customer	Initiative Service	Enter Data	Search Profiles	Update Profile	Pay Invoice	Renew/Upgrade
Strengths	Well-known name	CRM database	Quick order entry	Ease of use	Quality of firms listed	Deadlines from system	Electronic invoices	Clear reminders
Weaknesses	Brand confusion	Too many contacts; Showing ROI	Lack of coordination; Long publishing time	Unaware of available services	SEO in diff languags	No reminders	Brand confusion; Wrong invoices	Educating others
Opportunities	Leverage internet to increase reach	Internal coordination	Streamline process	Internal update process	Who-knows-who connections	Automation	Better coordination	ROI calculations
Threats	Perceived value	Free solutions	Profile data integrity	Infrequent use	Other search engines	Customers forget	Time to troubleshoot	Marketing noise

FIGURE 1-4. A customer journey map for a service that helps customers find architects internationally.

Rail Europe Experience Map

Guiding Principles

| People choose rail travel because it is convenient, easy, and flexible. | Rail booking is only one part of people's larger travel process. | People build their travel plans over time. | People value service that is respectful, effective and personable. |

Customer Journey

STAGES	Research & Planning	Shopping	Booking	Post-Booking, Pre-Travel	Travel	Post Travel
RAIL EUROPE	Research destinations, routes and products	Enter trips / Review fares / Select Pass(es)	Confirm itinerary / Delivery options / Payment options / Review & Confirm	Wait for paper tickets to arrive	Activities, unexpected changes	Share experience / Follow-up on refunds for booking changes

DOING

Research & Planning: Destination pages, Look up time tables, raileurope.com, Plan with interactive map, Map itinerary (finding pass), Live chat for questions, Talk with friends, Blogs & Travel sites, Kayak, compare airfare, Google searches, Research hotels

Shopping / Booking: May call if difficulties occur, Print e-tickets at home, Paper tickets arrive in mail

Post-Booking: Change plans, Check ticket status, View maps, Look up timetables, web/apps, Plan/confirm activities, Arrange travel

Travel: E-ticket Print at Station, Get stamp for refund, Buy additional tickets

Post Travel: Share photos, Web, Share experience, Request refunds, Mail tickets for refund

Interactions

THINKING

• What is the easiest way to get around Europe? • Where do I want to go? • How much time should I/we spend in each place for site seeing and activities?	• I want to get the best price, but I'm willing to pay a little more for first class. • How much will my whole trip cost me? What are my trade-offs? • Are there other activities I can add to my plan?	• Do I have all the tickets, passes and reservations I need in this booking so I don't pay more shipping? • Rail Europe is not answering the phone. How else can I get my question answered?	• Do I have everything I need? • Rail Europe website was easy and friendly, but when an issue came up, I couldn't get help. • What will I do if my tickets don't arrive in time?	• I just figured we could grab a train but there are not more trains. What can we do now? • Am I on the right train? If not, what next? • I want to make more travel plans. How do I do that?	• Trying to return ticket I was not able to use. Not sure if I'll get a refund or not. • People are going to love these photos! • Next time, we will explore routes and availability more carefully.

FEELING

• I'm excited to go to Europe! • Will I be able to see everything I can? • What if I can't afford this? • I don't want to make the wrong choice.	• It's hard to trust Trip Advisor. Everyone is so negative. • Keeping track of all the different products is confusing. • Am I sure this is the trip I want to take?	• Website experience is easy and friendly! • Frustrated to not know sooner about which tickets are eTickets and which are paper tickets. Not sure my tickets will arrive in time.	• Stressed that I'm about to leave the country and Rail Europe won't answer the phone. • Frustrated that Rail Europe won't ship tickets to Europe. • Happy to receive my tickets in the mail.	• I am feeling vulnerable to be in an unknown place in the middle of the night. • Stressed that the train won't arrive on time for my connection. • Meeting people who want to show us around is fun, serendipitous, and special.	• Excited to share my vacation story with my friends. • A bit annoyed to be dealing with ticket refund issues when I just got home.

EXPERIENCE

Enjoyability	Enjoyability	Enjoyability	Enjoyability	Enjoyability	Enjoyability
Relevance of Rail Europe	Relevance of Rail Europe	Relevance of Rail Europe	Relevance of Rail Europe	Relevance of Rail Europe	Relevance of Rail Europe
Helpfulness of Rail Europe	Helpfulness of Rail Europe	Helpfulness of Rail Europe	Helpfulness of Rail Europe	Helpfulness of Rail Europe	Helpfulness of Rail Europe

Individual

Opportunities

GLOBAL

Communicate a clear value proposition. STAGE: Initial visit	Help people get the help they need. STAGES: Global	Support people in creating their own solutions. STAGES: Global
Make your customers into better, more savvy travelers. STAGES: Global	Engage in social media with explicit purposes. STAGES: Global	

PLANNING, SHOPPING, BOOKING

Enable people to plan over time. STAGES: Planning, Shopping	Visualize the trip for planning and booking. STAGES: Planning, Shopping	Arm customers with information for making decisions. STAGES: Shopping, Booking
Connect planning, shopping and booking on the web. STAGES: Planning, Shopping, Booking	Aggregate shipping with a reasonable timeline. STAGE: Booking	

POST-BOOK, TRAVEL, POST-TRAVEL

Improve the paper ticket experience. STAGES: Post-Booking, Travel, Post-Travel	Accommodate planning and booking in Europe too. STAGE: Traveling
Proactively help people deal with change. STAGES: Post-Booking, Traveling	Communicate status clearly, at all times. STAGES: Post...

Organization

| Information sources | Stakeholder interviews
Cognitive walkthroughs | Customer Experience Survey
Existing Rail Europe Documentation | Ongoing, non-linear | Linear process | Non-linear, but time based |

adaptive path

Experience Map for Rail Europe | August 2011

FIGURE 1-5. Experience map of Rail Europe created by Chris Risdon.

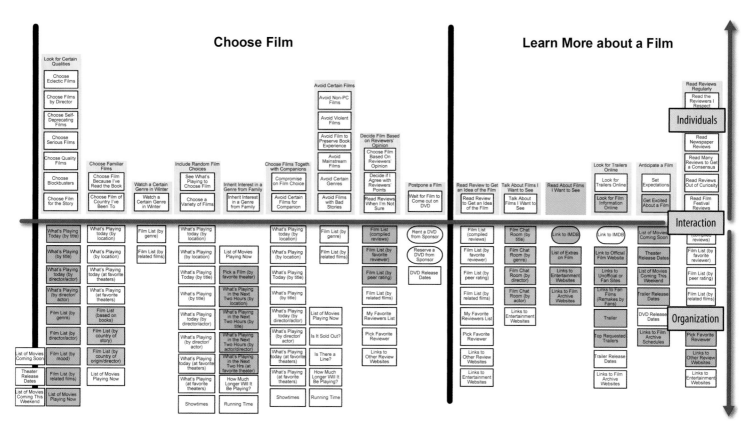

FIGURE 1-6. Mental model diagrams seek to hierarchically align customer behavior with business support, shown in two halves.

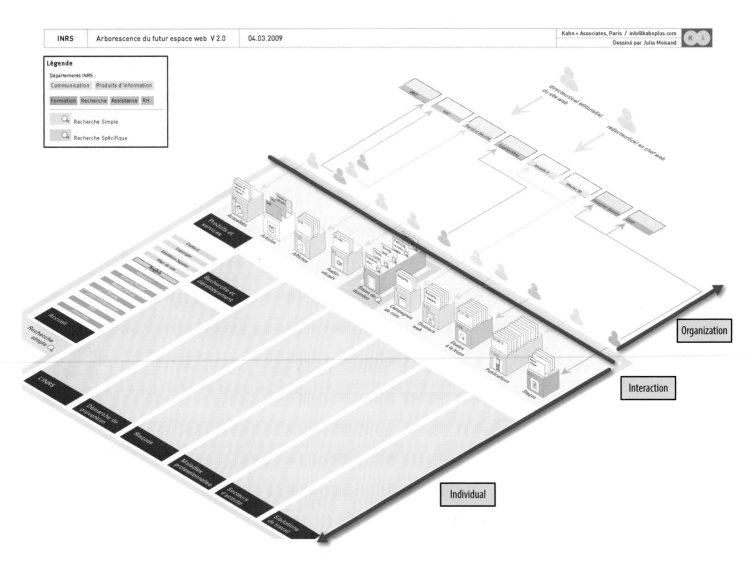

FIGURE 1-7. A spatial map created by Paul Kahn, Julia Moisand Egea, and Laurent Kling shows alignment of a content system to its users (in French).

Unlike customer journey maps, service blueprints, or experience maps, mental model diagrams have a hierarchical, rather than chronological, structure. Their two-part arrangement qualifies them as alignment diagrams nonetheless.

5. Spatial Maps

These diagrams map out aspects of an experience spatially. As the name implies, spatial maps are neither chronological nor hierarchical. The three-dimensional aspect of this example makes it unique from the previous examples.

Figure 1-7 shows an example of a spatial diagram called an isometric map. It was created by Paul Kahn, Julia Mois-and Egea, and Laurent Kling. On the left are rectangles, called "carpets." These reflect departments and divisions in a company. Individual "cards" shown in the middle represent different content types and artifacts used within the system

described. And on the right are users of this content, with touchpoints between the two parts.

Table 1-1 summarizes each of the previous diagram type examples through this lens. Each diagram types tells the story of value-centered design in a different way, with different conventions and representations.

Note that terminology is used inconsistently in practice. You may find that what one person calls a customer journey map, another calls an experience map or blueprint. The lines between these example are oftentimes blurred. Don't be overly concerned with the terminology; instead, focus on the results of your mapping effort. The notion of *alignment diagrams* finds common ground between these examples. As the fields of customer experience, user experience, and service design merge and overlap, it becomes increasingly important to have a range of approaches to solve unique problems.

DIAGRAM TYPE	STORY	INTERACTION	INDIVIDUAL	ORGANIZATION
Customer journey map	Chronological	Touchpoints	Actions, thoughts, feelings, pain points, etc.	Roles and departments involved in creating an experience
Experience map	Chronological	Touchpoints	Actions, thoughts, feelings, pain points	Physical and social artifacts in a system; opportunities
Service blueprints	Chronological	Line of interaction	Actions, physical evidence	Backstage actors and processes
Mental model diagrams	Hierarchical	Center line	Tasks, feelings, philosophies	Support—products and services available
Spatial maps	Spatial	Midpoint with arrows	Actions, needs, information flow	Data systems, departments

TABLE 1-1. Different ways to diagram aspects of value-centered design

Principles of Alignment

Understanding the common aspects of alignment diagrams opens up possibilities: you're not limited to one approach over another. Below are the principles of alignment.

Principle of Holism

Alignment diagrams focus on human behavior as part of a larger ecosystem. They are *not* about product research. As much as possible, look at what individuals do, think, and feel in a given context.

Principle of Multiplicity

Alignment diagrams illustrate multiple facets of information simultaneously. This is what the "alignment" part of the technique is really all about. Common aspects on the user side include actions, thoughts, feelings, states of mind, goals, and pain points. On the organization side, typical elements include processes, actions, objectives, and metrics, as well as actors or roles involved.

Principle of Interaction

Alignment diagrams expose touchpoints and the context of those touchpoints. The multiple layers of information come together to show an exchange of value. As a result, alignment diagrams prototype experiences. It's easy to walk through the touchpoints in slow motion, analyzing the broader circumstances around each interaction.

Principle of Visualization

Alignment diagrams show a composite view of experiences in a graphical overview. It's the immediacy of an all-at-once visualization that makes them powerful. A 10-page report or bulleted slides with the same information won't have the same impact. Visualizations make otherwise abstract and invisible concepts like "user experience" tangible.

Principle of Self Evidence

Alignment diagrams are compelling. They typically need little or no explanation. People can walk up to one and orient themselves relatively quickly. Keep in mind that a visual format itself does not guarantee simplicity: you'll still have to work hard to reduce information to just the most salient points.

Principle of Relevance

Alignment diagrams must be relevant to the organization. As the mapmaker, you must investigate and understand the goals, challenges, and future plans of the organization.

Principle of Validity

Alignment diagrams are grounded in investigation, not made up in isolation. They require some contact with the people in the real world through research and observation.

Benefits

Alignment diagrams are no panacea. They do not provide immediate answers outright. Instead, they are compelling visualizations that draw others into important conversations about creating value. Your ultimate goal is creating an inclusive dialog within the organization, not creating the diagram itself.

Mapping experiences has many potential benefits. These include building empathy, providing a common "big picture," breaking silos, reducing complexity, and finding opportunities. Alignment diagrams also generally enjoy a great deal of longevity.

Alignment diagrams help build empathy

It's often amazing how little organizations know about the actual experiences of the people they serve. Alignment diagrams shed light on real-world human conditions. In doing so they instill empathy into an organization.

Bruce Temkin, a leader in customer experience management, stresses the relevance and importance of such mapping activities. He writes in a blog post:

> Companies need to use tools and processes that reinforce an understanding of actual customer needs. One of the key tools in this area is something called a customer journey map… Used appropriately, these maps can shift a company's perspective from inside-out to outside-in.*

Looking back into the organization from the outside causes a change in perspective, one that is more sensitive to people's thoughts and feelings.

Alignment diagrams provide a common "big picture"

Diagrams serve as a shared reference, helping to build consensus. In this sense, alignment diagrams are strategic tools: they influence decision making at all levels and lead to consistency in actions.

For instance, Jon Kolko, VP of Consumer Design at Blackboard, believes diagrams help address what he calls "alignment attrition"—the tendency to get out of sync with one another. As he writes in his article "Dysfunctional Products Come from Dysfunctional Organizations," visualizations help.

> A visual model becomes one of the most effective tools for minimizing alignment attrition. A visual model captures and freezes a thought in time. By building a visual model together, alignment is offloaded to and "frozen in" the diagram. Your thoughts, opinions, and views will change, but the diagram won't, and so you've added a constraining boundary to the idea— and a tool for concretely visualizing how the product vision is changing.

What's more, diagrams also help retain a common big picture as organizations change personnel. Team members may come and go, and diagrams help maintain continuity. In this sense, they also play a knowledge management role.

---

* Bruce Tempkin. "It's All About Your Customer's Journey," *Customer Experience Matters* (2010).

Alignment diagrams break down silos

People experience a product or service in a holistic way. Ideal solutions can easily cross an organization's department lines. Illustrations of the customer experience typically reveal divisional joints in an organization. Discussion around them sparks cross-department collaboration.

Creating diagrams also aids in the design of cross-channel experiences. Consider the cross-channel blueprint (Figure 1-8) created by Tyler Tate, an entrepreneur and expert in search system design. While it doesn't include the richness of other types of alignment diagrams, it does align user behavior (along the top of the chart) with channels (vertically on the left) and support from the organization (the bottom row).

In this simple yet insightful example, a product taxonomy spans all channels. But in a typical organization, the print catalog department is likely different from the digital product team and from the physical store. In this case, the implementation of a cross-channel taxonomy requires these units to work directly with one another.

Alignment diagrams bring focus

In a study in 2011 by Booz and Company, a majority of the 1,800 executives surveyed indicated they were unable to focus on business strategy: they were being pulled in too many directions. As a result, many companies lack coherence.

Coherence in business strategy—or incoherence, as is often the case—is the subject of *The Essential Advantage* by Paul Leinwand and Cesare Mainardi. After years of research in corporate strategy, the authors conclude:

> *To unlock the benefits of coherence, you need to take deliberate steps—to reconsider your current strategy, overcome the conventional separation between your outward-facing and inward-facing activities, and bring your organization into focus.* [*]

Alignment diagrams represent such a deliberate step: they inherently match outward- and inward-facing endeavors. In doing so, they bring focus and coherency to organizations.

Alignment diagrams reveal opportunities

Visualizations offer an immediacy of comprehension, providing insight into previously unnoticed value-creation opportunities. Indi Young describes this potential in a common response to her mental model diagrams from stakeholders:

> *I have invited executives to presentations 15 minutes earlier than other folks, so they can stand in front of the diagram on the wall and walk from the left to right, asking me questions as they go. As I answer their questions, I explain how it will be used to direct product design. This kind of walkthrough is quick, to the point, and stays in the context of "missed" and "future" opportunities that executives usually focus on. Many executives have told me that they're never before seen all this information collected so succinctly in one place.* [†]

---

[*] Paul Leinwand and Cesare Mainardi. *The Essential Advantage* (Harvard Business Review Press, 2010).

[†] Indi Young. *Mental Models* (Rosenfeld Media, 2009).

Cross-Channel Blueprint

A tool for planning user tasks across multiple channels.

	Lookup	Explore	Compare	Organize	Purchase
Print Catalog	**Low priority** Table of contents Index	**High priority** Immersive photography	**Low priority** Flip pages back/forth	N/A Flip pages back/forth	**High priority** Order by phone Order by mail Order online
Website	**High priority** Search box	**High priority** Browse by category	**High priority** Table view of selected items	**High priority** Favorites Wish list / gift registry	**High priority** Standard checkout Expedited checkout Order by phone
Tablet App	**High priority** Search box Voice input	**High priority** Catalog-like browsing experience	**Medium priority** Table view of selected items	**Medium priority** Favorites Wish lists	**High priority** Expedited checkout Standard checkout
Mobile App	**High priority** Search box Voice input Barcode scanner	**Medium priority** Browse by category	N/A Impractical due to screen size	**Low priority** Add items to favorites and wish list, but limited ability to edit	**High priority** Expedited checkout
Physical Store	**High priority** Clear signage Store map Helpful staff	**High priority** Wander the aisles	**Medium priority** Compare side by side Ask staff	**Low priority** Gift registry / wish list	**High priority** Attendant-assisted Self-checkout Scan-as-you-go
Shared Assets	**Product taxonomy** All channels powered by a single set of categories		**Compare engine** Web & tablet powered by one component	**Universal Favs** Favorites list shared by web, tablet, mobile	**Checkout workflow** Universal checkout process for web, tablet, and mobile

by Tyler Tate licensed under a Creative Commons Attribution 3.0 Unported License

FIGURE 1-8. Cross-channel blueprint by Tyler Tate.

While the diagrams themselves don't give an immediate solution, their presentation to the team often has an *ah-ha* effect. They pinpoint areas for improvement in both operational efficiency and experience design, as well as expose opportunities for growth. Good diagrams are both compelling and engaging, providing an outside-in view of the organization.

Alignment diagrams enjoy longevity

Mapping an experience is a foundational activity. Because alignment diagrams uncover fundamental human needs and emotions, the data is not volatile. Once completed, diagrams tend not to change very quickly; they generally remain valid for years.

Summary

This chapter introduced the term *alignment diagrams*, a category of diagrams that visually align individuals' experiences with an organization. It is an umbrella term for various, contemporary approaches. Thus, alignment diagrams are not a specific technique or method but rather a reframing of existing practices.

Examples of alignment diagrams include service blueprints, customer journey maps, experience maps, mental model diagrams, and spatial maps.

By looking at the common principles of alignment found in this type of diagram, mapping takes on a more strategic function. There are many benefits to alignment diagrams:

- They build *empathy*, shifting an organization's view from inside-out to outside-in.
- Alignment diagrams give teams a *common big picture*.
- Mapping experiences help *break organization silos*.
- Visualizations *bring focus* to organizations.
- Alignment diagrams point to *opportunities* for improvement and innovation.

Alignment diagrams also enjoy substantial longevity. They are based on fundamental human needs and emotions. Once completed, they tend not to change quickly.

Alignment diagrams are foundational. They don't provide answers or solutions directly, but facilitate conversation and stimulate deeper reflection. As complexity in business increases, such approaches are no longer nice to have: they are imperative tools for an organization to learn about the experiences it creates and the relationships it forms.

Focusing on alignment opens up possibilities. To benefit from the range of options within the category of alignment diagrams requires making choices: which experiences to map, what areas to focus on, and what diagram might work best. Chapter 4 provides practical guidance on the selections you'll make when creating a diagram.

Further Reading

Jim Kalbach and Paul Kahn. "Locating Value with Alignment Diagrams," *Parsons Journal of Information Mapping* (April 2011); and Jim Kalbach, "Alignment Diagrams: Focusing the Business on Shared Value," *Boxes and Arrows* (Sept 2011)

> *These two articles by the author are the first concrete writings on alignment diagrams as defined in this book. They are based on a presentation given at the Euro Information Architecture conference in Paris in 2010. The first was coauthored with Paul Kahn, who greatly helped develop the concept of alignment diagrams.*

Harley Manning and Kerry Bodine. *Outside In: The Power of Putting Customers at the Center of Your Business* (New Harvest, 2012)

> *This is an excellent, full-length book on the value of customer experience design for businesses. "Customer experience is at the heart of everything you do—how you conduct your business, the way your people behave when they interact with customers and each other, the value you provide," the authors write. Mapping is a key activity to gain insight into the experience customers actually have with your organization.*

Jess McMullin. "Searching for the Center of Design," *Boxes and Arrows* (Sept 2003)

> *In this article, McMullin calls for us to think beyond user-centered design and embrace value-centered design. This principle underlies the basic notion of alignment diagrams.*

Andy Polaine, Lavrans Løvlie and Ben Reason. *Service Design* (Rosenfeld Media, 2013)

> *This book provides an excellent overview of the field of service design, with hands-on tools and tips for practitioners. Chapter 5 discusses service blueprints in some detail and positions them as a key activity in the service design process.*

Diagram and Image Credits

Figure 1-3: Brandon Schauer, "Service Blueprint for Seeing Tomorrow's Panel Services," retrieved from Flickr (CC Share-Alike 3.0).

Figure 1-4: Customer journey map created using Excel by Jim Kalbach, modified from its original form.

Figure 1-5: Experience map for Rail Europe taken from: Chris Risdon. "The Anatomy of an Experience Map" *Adaptive Path Blog* (2001), used with permission. *http://adaptivepath.org/ideas/the-anatomy-of-an-experience-map/*.

Figure 1-6: Section of a mental model diagram created by Indi Young and included in her book *Mental Models* (Rosenfeld Media, 2008), used with permission.

Figure 1-7: Isometric map created by Paul Kahn, Julia Moisand Egea, and Laurent Kling, originally appearing in: Paul Kahn and Julia Moisand. "Patterns That Connect: The Value of Mapping Complex Data Networks," *Information Design Journal* (2009).

Figure 1-8: Cross-channel blueprint by Tyler Tate, taken from "Cross-Channel Blueprints: A tool for modern IA." CC Share-Alike 3.0. *http://tylertate.com/blog/2012/02/21/cross-channel-ia-blueprint.html*.

"The purpose of visualization is insight, not pictures."

— Ben Shneiderman
Readings in Information Visualization

IN THIS CHAPTER

- Framing the mapping effort
- Touchpoints
- Moments of truth
- Value creation
- Case Study: Identifying Opportunities: Combining Mental Model Diagrams and Jobs to Be Done

CHAPTER 2

Fundamentals of Mapping Experiences

In my first book, *Designing Web Navigation*, I discuss the principle of *transitional volatility*. First described by David Danielson in 2003, transitional volatility is the degree of reorientation a person experiences when moving from page to page in a website. If there is too much volatility, they get lost in hyperspace.

Figure 2-1 shows this pattern of interaction. It's a sequence of becoming accustomed to one location (habituate), forming an expectation about the next point (predict), and then adjusting to a new position (reorient). The pattern then repeats.

We see the same thing happening on a larger scale when individuals interact with an organization. Instead of page to

page, they move from touchpoint to touchpoint. At each interaction there is a reorientation period, even if brief. If there is too much reorientation at each touchpoint, the experience feels disjointed.

A high degree of transitional volatility arises from an inconsistency in touchpoints. You've probably experienced this yourself. For instance, I once had an unpleasant incident with my credit card. The card issuer and the bank backing it seemed to disagree about who was responsible for my problem. Each blamed the other, and I got caught in the middle.

My experience spanned months and used various means of communication. For some things I used their website; for others I had to call. There were emails, regular mail, and even a fax. The degree of reorientation at each point was high. Apparently it was my job to figure it all out. Needless to say, they no longer have my business and I will not recommend them.

The advice is clear: don't force people to bridge gaps of your offering. That's your job. Mapping experiences allows you to locate transitional volatility within a broader system of interactions and find innovative solutions to address it.

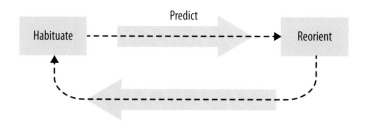

FIGURE 2-1. The pattern of transitional volatility across points of interaction.

This is not to say, however, that you must design every touch-point. That would be futile. Some aspects will be beyond your control. However, understanding multiple factors that make up an experience allows you to determine which parts to focus on as well as how to avoid negative experiences, even if beyond your control.

What's more, the aim isn't for uniformity across the board. Rather, strive for *coherency* in the conception and design of the overall system. Create a balanced perception of your organization, but still give people control to shape their own experiences.

Diagrams provide a systematic overview of the experiences you create. By fostering conversations across the organization, the process of mapping helps avoid negative transitional volatility and promote coherency. Regardless of the specific diagram type you create, there are overarching aspects to consider in mapping experience, covered in this chapter. These include:

1. Frame the effort clearly up front. Determine the point of view, scope, focus, and structure of the diagram, as well as how you intend to use it.

2. Identify the various *touchpoints* in the system, as well as critically charged points, called *moments of truth*.

3. Focus on creating value. Use the diagram to improve and to innovate your offering and your business.

By the end of this chapter, you should have a greater un-derstanding of the key decisions you'll have to make when mapping experiences.

Frame the Mapping Effort

The term *experience* defies precise definition. Still, we can point to some common aspects to better understand it:

Experiences are holistic.
> The notion of an experience is by its nature all-encompassing, including actions, thoughts, and feelings over time.

Experiences are personal.
> An experience is not an objective property of a product or service; it's the subjective perception of the individual.

Experiences are situational.
> I like rollercoasters, but not immediately after eating a large meal. In one case, the experience is exhilarating; in the other, it's a dreadful few minutes of nausea. The rollercoaster didn't change, the situation did. Experiences differ from situation to situation. Circumstance drives experience more than disposition.

How, then, do we approach mapping experiences? Put simply, it's a matter of selection. Maps are purposefully focused. As the mapmaker, it's up to you to decide which aspects to include and which to leave out.

Cartographic maps, for instance, are selective in what they show. Consider Harry Beck's famous map of the London Underground, first published in 1933 (Figure 2-2). It is sparing in what it includes: tube lines, stops, exchanges, and the River Thames—nothing more.

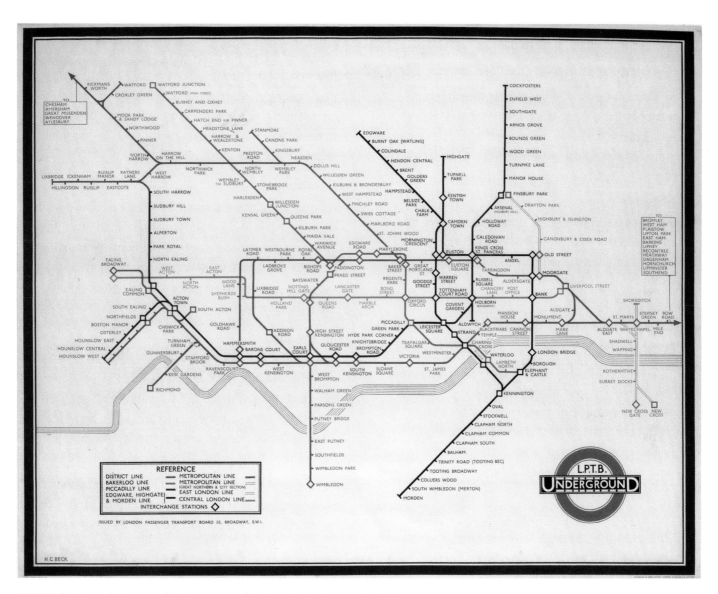

FIGURE 2-2. Harry Beck created his iconic map of the London Underground in 1933.

This map also distorts the train lines, relying only on horizontal, vertical, and 45-degree angled lines. Stops are spaced equidistantly as well, when in reality the distances vary greatly.

Beck's map has remained virtually intact for over 70 years with only minor updates. Its brilliance lies in what it *doesn't* show: streets, buildings, curves in lines, and actual distances between stops. The longevity of Beck's map is given by its appropriateness—it fulfills a specific need extremely well.

Likewise, mapping experiences requires choice: what to include and how to represent it. For now, it's important to understand the aspects that frame mapping efforts: point of view, scope, focus, structure, and how a diagram will be used.

Point of View

Mapping experiences requires a common thread or a "bouncing ball" to follow. The point of view of a diagram should answer the question, what is it about?

Point of view is given by two criteria: the people involved and the types of experiences focused on. For instance, a news magazine might serve two distinct audiences: readers and advertisers. The interactions each has with the publisher are very different. Whose experience you illustrate depends on the goals of the organization.

Once you've decided on the people to focus on—assume readers in this example—there are different experiences to choose from. Consider these three potential experiences for a news magazine reader:

Purchasing behavior

One point of view is to look at how readers *purchase* the news magazine: how they first hear of the magazine, why they bought it, if they make a repeat purchase, and so on. Mapping an experience from this point of view makes sense if there is a need to optimize sales. A customer journey map would be a good fit.

News consumption

Another point of view might be to look at how readers *consume news* in general. This would situate the magazine within a broader spectrum of human information behavior. This point of view could be beneficial if the magazine is looking to expand its offering. A mental model diagram could be useful in this case.

Day-in-the-life

You could also look at a *day-in-the-life* of typical readers: how does a news magazine fit into their daily actions? Where do they come in contact with the magazine? When? What else do they do to find and read news? An experience map may be appropriate for mapping this experience.

Each of these points of view has a different unit of analysis—purchasing, consuming news, or a daily routine. And each can be beneficial depending on the needs of the organization.

Typically, focus a given diagram on single point of view in a given diagram. A clear perspective generally strengthens the message of a diagram.

To compare different points of view, you could create several individual diagrams and display them together—for instance, by hanging them next to each other on a wall. But it's also entirely possible to include multiple people and multiple experiences within the same diagram. This provides an overview of the complete service ecosystem. If you do, just be clear about how different points of view come together. In the end, it's the mapmaker's job to determine which points of view to follow.

As the mapmaker, it's up to you to decide which aspects to include and which to leave out.

Scope

The equally spaced Tube stops on Beck's map of the London Underground allow the entire system to fit on one page. Actual spacing would have put the end stations far off the page. Given his scope—to show the entire system—this lack of fidelity is necessary.

Scope requires tradeoff in breadth versus depth. A map of an end-to-end experience reveals the big picture but leaves out detail. On the other hand, a detailed diagram may illustrate specific interactions, but cover less ground. Determine the boundaries of the experience and the granularity needed to tell a complete story.

For example, imagine you've been contracted by the tourist bureau of a city in the US to improve the experience of visiting tourists, with a specific goal of increasing the mobile services offered.

One approach could be to scope the entire visit starting from planning at home, to visiting the city, and all the way to follow-up actions afterwards. This would give you a broad picture across different touchpoint types across the entire service ecology for multiple stakeholders.

In another approach, you could limit the effort to only experiences in the city with mobile services. This journey might begin and end at the airport or train station, but would provide greater depth on mobile touchpoints for a particular user type.

Both approaches are valid depending on the needs of the organization, as well as their interests and gaps in knowledge. Are you focused on a discrete problem or do you need a view of the entire system? The point is to be explicit about the tradeoffs you're making upfront and set the right expectations.

Focus

The mapmaker also chooses which aspects come to the foreground. There are many types of elements to consider. The ones you choose depend on how you've framed the effort (see Chapter 4) and what aspects are most salient to the organization.

In describing the individual's experience you might include some of the following typical aspects:

- **Physical:** artifacts, tools, devices
- **Behavioral:** actions, activities, tasks
- **Cognitive:** thoughts, views, opinions
- **Emotional:** feelings, desires, state of mind
- **Needs:** goals, outcomes, jobs to be done
- **Challenges:** pain points, constraints, barriers
- **Context:** setting, environment, location
- **Culture:** beliefs, values, philosophy
- **Events:** triggers, moments of truth, points of failure

Elements that describe the organization can include:

- **Touchpoints:** mediums, devices, information
- **Offering:** products, services, features
- **Processes:** activities, workflow
- **Challenges:** problems, issues, breakdowns

- **Operations:** roles, departments, reporting structures
- **Metrics:** traffic, financials, statistics
- **Evaluation:** strengths, weaknesses, learnings
- **Opportunities:** gaps, weaknesses, redundancies
- **Goals:** revenue, savings, reputation
- **Strategy:** policy, design making, principles

The question of balance of the above elements comes into play as well. For instance, a customer journey map may focus primarily on an experience with only a minimal description of the organization. A service blueprint, on the other hand, may highlight the service provision process across channels at the expense of a detailed description of the user experience.

Structure

Alignment diagrams differ in structure. The most common scheme is chronological (Figure 2-3a), and many of the examples in this book have a chronological organization. However, other arrangements are possible, including hierarchical, spatial, and network structures (Figures 2-3b, 2-3c, 2-3d).

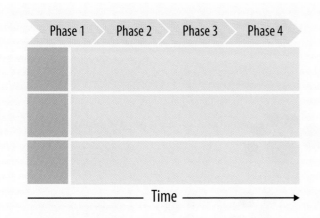

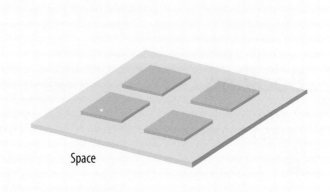

FIGURE 2-3a. CHRONOLOGICAL: Because experiences happen in real time, a chronological arrangement provides a natural sequence of human behavior. A timeline of some sort is the most prevalent way to structure alignment diagrams. See Chapters 9 to 11 on service blueprints, customer journey maps, and experience maps for more.

FIGURE 2-3c. SPATIAL: It's also possible to illustrate experiences spatially. This makes sense when interactions take place in a physical location—for example, in a face-to-face service encounter. But they can also be imposed on an experience in a metaphorical sense: spatial maps represent experiences as if they could exist in a 3D space even when they do not. Chapter 13 discusses spatial maps in greater detail.

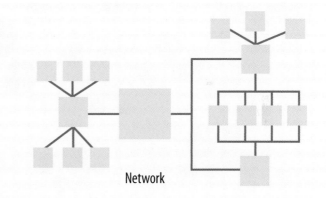

FIGURE 2-3b. HIERARCHICAL: Mapping experiences hierarchically removes the time dimension. This can have advantages when there are many aspects occurring simultaneously, which is difficult to show chronologically. Chapter 12 discusses mental model diagrams and other hierarchical arrangements.

FIGURE 2-3d. NETWORK STRUCTURE: A network structure shows a web of interrelationships between aspects of an experience that are neither chronological nor hierarchical.

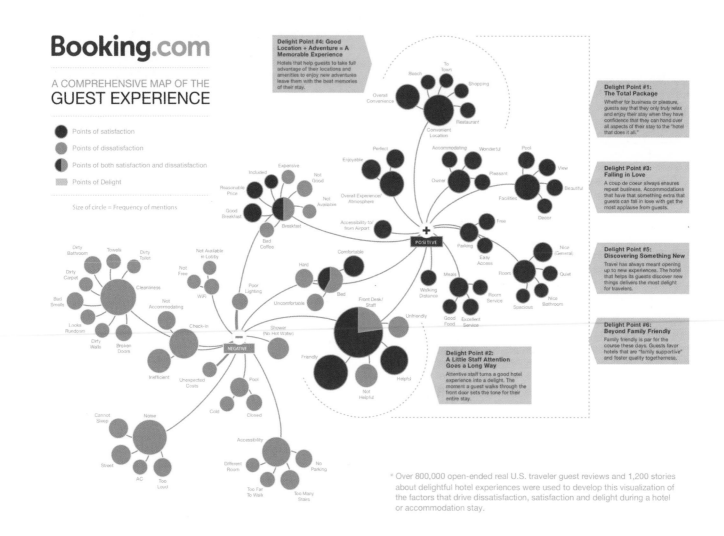

Booking.com

A COMPREHENSIVE MAP OF THE
GUEST EXPERIENCE

- ● Points of satisfaction
- ● Points of dissatisfaction
- ◐ Points of both satisfaction and dissatisfaction
- ▨ Points of Delight

Size of circle = Frequency of mentions

Delight Point #4: Good Location + Adventure = A Memorable Experience
Hotels that help guests to take full advantage of their locations and amenities to enjoy new adventures leave them with the best memories of their stay.

Delight Point #1: The Total Package
Whether for business or pleasure, guests say that they only truly relax and enjoy their stay when they have confidence that they can hand over all aspects of their stay to the "hotel that does it all."

Delight Point #3: Falling in Love
A coup de coeur always ensures repeat business. Accommodations that have that something extra that guests can fall in love with get the most applause from guests.

Delight Point #5: Discovering Something New
Travel has always meant opening up to new experiences. The hotel that helps its guests discover new things delivers the most delight for travelers.

Delight Point #6: Beyond Family Friendly
Family friendly is par for the course these days. Guests favor hotels that are "family supportive" and foster quality togetherness.

Delight Point #2: A Little Staff Attention Goes a Long Way
Attentive staff turns a good hotel experience into a delight. The moment a guest walks through the front door sets the tone for their entire stay.

* Over 800,000 open-ended real U.S. traveler guest reviews and 1,200 stories about delightful hotel experiences were used to develop this visualization of the factors that drive dissatisfaction, satisfaction and delight during a hotel or accommodation stay.

FIGURE 2-4. A network-like arrangement of actors and concepts shows positive and negative experiences with Booking.com.

Figure 2-4 is an example of the guest experience of the service Booking.com. It's an excellent example of illustrating an experience in network-like structure. The focus is on touchpoints that lead to positive or negative experiences.

Use

Keep the intended use of an alignment diagram in mind from the very beginning.

First, consider *who* will be consuming the information in your diagram. The London Underground map is read by everyday travelers on the Tube. They use it to determine how to travel between any two points on the network. But the engineers who maintain the switching signals in the London Underground would likely find Beck's map lacking in detail. They need specifications with a much higher degree of fidelity to accomplish their work. Beck's map is not intended for that audience.

Also consider *what* you'll use diagrams for. Frame the effort in a way that is appropriate for your team's needs. What questions does the organization have that a diagram can address? What gaps in knowledge does it fill? What problems will it help solve?

Finally, ask yourself *how* the diagram will be used. Will they be used to diagnose problems or improve the design of an existing system? Will they be used to create a strategy and plan for development? Or does your audience intend to use the alignment diagram to discover new opportunities for innovation and growth?

Keep in mind that the goal of a mapping effort isn't to complete an artifact, but to address the challenges the diagrams help discover and understand. Diagrams are compelling documents that invite engagement by others. Use this to your advantage to find ways of solving customer problems and creating value.

Identify Touchpoints

Framing the effort, as outlined above, provides a basis for illustrating the overall experience. Within that experience, you also need to consider the relationship between individuals and an organization. The concept of *touchpoints*, the means of value exchange, allows you to show the interaction between the two.

Typically, touchpoints include a range of things, such as:

- TV ads, print ads, brochures
- Marketing emails, newsletters
- Website, apps, software program
- Phone calls, service hotline, online chat
- Service counter, checkout register, consulting
- Physical objects, buildings, roads
- Packaging, shipping materials
- Bills, invoices, payment systems

Historically, there are three primary types of touchpoints:

Static

These touchpoints don't allow for users to interact with them. They include things such as an email newsletter or an advertisement.

Interactive

Websites and apps are interactive touchpoints, as are online chats.

Human

This type involves human-to-human interaction. Examples include a sales representative or a support agent on the phone.

Consider the inventory of touchpoints in Figure 2-5. This diagram was created by the Swiss-based marketing firm Accelerom, an international consultancy and research firm based in Zurich (*www.accelerom.com*), as part of their 360° touchpoint management process.* This shows a fairly comprehensive list of touchpoints a company has with its customers.

Notice that the touchpoints are grouped by channel in Figure 2-6—in this case, point of sale, one-to-one, indirect, and mass communication. A channel is not a touchpoint but rather a category of touchpoint given by the mode of delivery.

Diagrams are compelling documents that invite engagement by others.

Inventories such as the one in Figure 2-5 are necessary to get a comprehensive overview of touchpoints. But some people call for a broader perspective. Chris Risdon, for one, defines a touchpoint as the *context* around an interaction. In his article "Unsucking the Touchpoint" he writes:

A touchpoint is a point of interaction involving a specific human need in a specific time and place.

Jeanie Walters, a leading customer experience consultant, also advocates a broader definition. She is critical of touchpoint inventories, writing:

The challenge with viewing touchpoints this way is this approach often assumes the customer has a) been in a linear and direct relationship with the organization and b) reads and engages with these touchpoints in meaningful ways. In short, an examination of touchpoints is often entirely company-focused. (Sometimes, it is so company-focused the touchpoints are categorized by org chart: marketing; operations; billing, etc.).

---

* See Christoph Spengler, Werner Wirth, and Renzo Sigrist. "360° Touchpoint Management – How important is Twitter for our brand?" *Marketing Review St. Gallen* (Feb 2010).

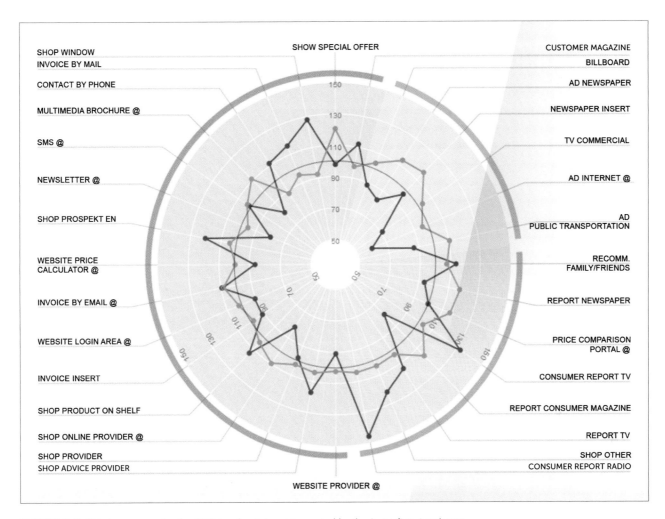

Labels around the figure (clockwise from top):

SHOW SPECIAL OFFER
CUSTOMER MAGAZINE
BILLBOARD
AD NEWSPAPER
NEWSPAPER INSERT
TV COMMERCIAL
AD INTERNET @
AD PUBLIC TRANSPORTATION
RECOMM. FAMILY/FRIENDS
REPORT NEWSPAPER
PRICE COMPARISON PORTAL @
CONSUMER REPORT TV
REPORT CONSUMER MAGAZINE
REPORT TV
SHOP OTHER
CONSUMER REPORT RADIO
WEBSITE PROVIDER @
SHOP ADVICE PROVIDER
SHOP PROVIDER
SHOP ONLINE PROVIDER @
SHOP PRODUCT ON SHELF
INVOICE INSERT
WEBSITE LOGIN AREA @
INVOICE BY EMAIL @
WEBSITE PRICE CALCULATOR @
SHOP PROSPEKT EN
NEWSLETTER @
SMS @
MULTIMEDIA BROCHURE @
CONTACT BY PHONE
INVOICE BY MAIL
SHOP WINDOW

Radial scale values: 50, 70, 90, 110, 130, 150

FIGURE 2-5. This is an example of a 360° touchpoint matrix created by the Swiss firm Accelerom.

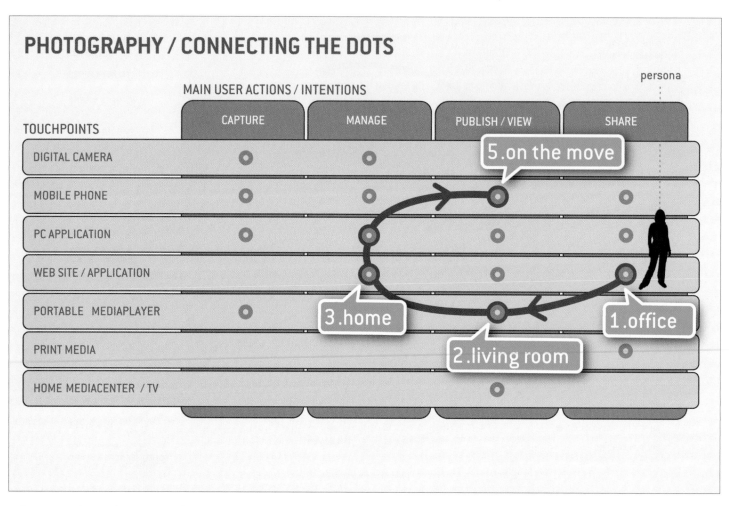

FIGURE 2-6. This touchpoint matrix for photography created by Gianluca Brugnoli shows a sequence of interactions.

In Gianluca Brugnoli's article "Connecting the Dots of User Experience," he offers the touchpoint matrix shown in Figure 2-6. This diagram illustrates various activities around photography. By providing a sequence and locations of interactions, Brugnoli provides context for touchpoints in a journey.

Brugnoli believes that the system is the experience. It's the sum of all touchpoints, as well as the connections between them. He writes:

> The challenge that logically follows is to design connections. In the system scenario, design should be mainly focused on finding the right connections within the network and its parts, rather than in creating closed and self-sufficient systems, tools and services.

Creating value in the 21st century will increasingly involve systems of experiences. Touchpoints are the basic building blocks that make up the system.

Organizations that take an ecological view on the experiences they provide have a competitive advantage. For businesses, this impacts the bottom line. One study from 2013 by Alex Rawson and colleagues found that optimization across touchpoints was a strong predictor of business health.* The researchers found a 20% to 30% correlation with improved outcomes, such as higher revenue, better retention, and positive word of mouth.

Alignment diagrams reinforce such an ecological view of the interaction with customers. They not only illustrate individual touchpoints but also provide an end-to-end picture of the experience.

Moments of Truth

Alignment diagrams are not just a collection of touchpoints. They also provide insight for identifying and understanding critical points in the experience. Called *moments of truth*, these key, emotional instances help focus attention on the aspects that matter most.

Moments of truth can be thought of as a special type of touchpoint. They are critical, emotionally charged interactions, and usually occur when someone has invested a high degree of energy in a desired outcome. Moments of truth either make or break the relationship.

The term *moments of truth* was popularized by Jan Carlzon, the then CEO of SAS Airlines, in his book of the same name. To illustrate his point, Carlzon starts his book with a story of a customer who arrived at the airport without his boarding pass. The SAS agents personally drove back to the hotel where he left it and delivered it to him at the airport. This left an indelible impression on the customer.

Or, consider something as simple as Twitter's infamous "fail whale." Now retired, the fail whale was an image of a whale (Figure 2-7) that appeared when Twitter servers were overloaded. Though disruptive at a critical moment—the point at which a person is posting a tweet—many people actually felt an emotional connection to the fail whale. Twitter turned a potentially negative moment of truth into something positive.

---

* See Alex Rawson, Ewan Duncan, and Conor Jones. "The Truth About Customer Experience" *Harvard Business Review* (Sep 2013).

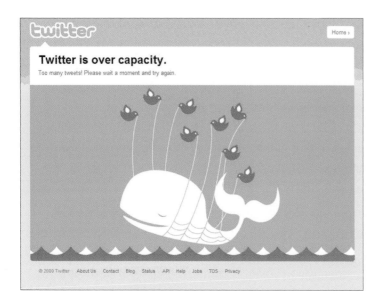

FIGURE 2-7. Twitter's now-retired fail whale turned a potentially negative moment of truth into a potentially delightful experience.

Moments of truth point to opportunities for innovation and growth. For instance, in their book *The Innovator's Method*, business scholars and consultants Nathan Furr and Jeff Dyer suggest creating what they call "journey lines," or a brief visualization of the steps customers take. They write:

> Create an in-depth visual portrait in which you identify pain points to understand how your customers do the job today and how they feel while doing it. Visually map out the steps customers take to achieve an outcome. It helps to assign a customer emotion to each step to identify how the customer is feeling.

Creating value in the 21ˢᵗ century will increasingly involve systems of experiences. Touchpoints are the basic building blocks that make up the system.

They go on to recommend looking for moments "that ignite their emotions"—in other words, moments of truth. Solutions that address these moments, they claim, are more likely to be monetizable: people are generally willing to pay for services that address critical needs. In this sense, moments of truth are points of opportunity for the organization.

The individual's perception of an organization is given by the sum of all moments of truth. These may be moments of delight—positive interaction after positive interaction. On the negative side, the relationship may suffer from a "death by a thousand cuts."

Focusing on moments of truth allows you to concentrate your energy on experiences that matter. The perceived coherency of your offering is given by how you handle moments of truth. Diagrams provide insight into these points across time, allowing organizations to design a more cohesive experience and reduce transitional volatility.

Zero Moment of Truth

Traditionally, there are three main touchpoint types in commerce situations.

- *Stimulus:* the very first time customers become aware of a given product or service.
- *First moment of truth:* the decision to buy a product or service.
- *Second moment of truth:* the first experience customers have using a product or service.

More and more, consumers read reviews by other consumers. They look at sites like Amazon to inform decisions. Or, they ask Twitter followers for opinions. And they look at who's behind a service as well, researching profiles on LinkedIn and even Facebook. Regardless of industry or sector, customers are far more informed today than just a decade ago.

In addition to the first and second moments of truth, market researchers at Google have identified a new critical touchpoint: the "Zero Moment of Truth," or ZMOT for short.* It falls between the stimulus and the decision to buy (Figure 2-8).

Content is critical at the ZMOT. But it can't come across as marketing fluff: information at the ZMOT touchpoint must be meaningful and valuable. Successful companies converse with their markets and engage in a dialog. They position themselves not as "buy me!" banners, but as trusted advisors.

Notice that product recommendations feeding into the ZMOT come after someone has already used a product. With this, the usage experience is now relevant before the purchase decision.

More importantly, people increasingly find meaning in the products and services they buy during the ZMOT. They want to know about the company and the people behind an offering. They want to know how it fits into their value system and how it will define them personally.

You may rightfully point out that people have always engaged in conversations with brands. Markets are conversations indeed. What's different now is a combination of the breadth of content available and the speed at which consumers can access it. Now, it's expected that a customer researches various aspects of your business before even coming in direct contact with you or your offerings.

In any event, the various parts of a product or service experience are now much more interrelated than they were just a decade ago. A holistic mindset is needed to connect moments of truth and design meaningful experiences for people.

---

* Jim Lecinski. *ZMOT: Winning the Zero Moment of Truth* (Google, 2011).

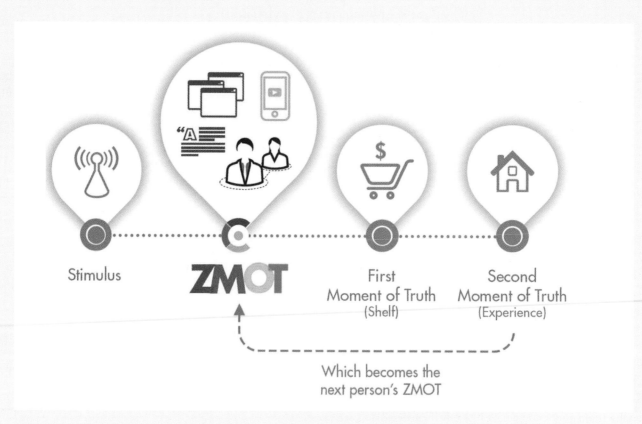

FIGURE 2-8. Zero Moment of Truth, a new phase in consumer behavior, was introduced by researchers at Google.

Focus on Creating Value

Business magnate Warren Buffet once said, "price is what you pay, value is what you get." In other words, from the individual's perspective value is a much richer, more dynamic concept than cost, involving human behavior and emotions. Value is a *perceived* benefit.

Existing frameworks help us understand the subjective nature of the concept. Sheth, Newman and Gross[*] identify five types of customer value:

- *Functional value* relates to the ability to perform a utilitarian purpose. Performance and reliability are key considerations with this type of value.

- *Social value* refers to the interaction among people, emphasizing lifestyle and social awareness. For instance, Skype in the Classroom is a program aimed at inspiring students with prominent speakers who lecture from remote locations.

- *Emotional value* emphasizes the feelings or affective responses a person has while interacting with an organization's offerings. For example, personal data security services tap into the fear of identity theft or data loss.

- *Epistemic value* is generated by a sense of curiosity or a desire to learn. This type of value emphasizes personal growth and the acquisition of knowledge. The Khan Academy, for instance, provides online courses for people to learn at their own pace.

- *Conditional value* is a benefit that depends on specific situations or contexts. For instance, the perceived value of pumpkins and monster costumes increases conditionally just before Halloween in the US each year.

Beyond these types, design strategist and educator Nathan Shedroff points to *meaning* as forms of what he calls "premium value."[†] This exceeds mere novelty and delight, and looks at the purpose products and services have in our lives. Products and services that provide meaningful experiences help us make sense of the world and give us personal identity.

Together with coauthors Steve Diller and Darrel Rheas Shedroff identifies 15 types of premium value in the book *Making Meaning*:

1. *Accomplishment.* The sense of pride in achieving goals

2. *Beauty.* The appreciation of aesthetic qualities that give pleasure to the senses

3. *Community.* A sense of connectedness with others around us

---

[*] Jagdish Sheth, Bruce Newman, and Barbara Gross. *Consumption Values and Market Choices* (South-Western Publishing, 1991).

[†] See Nathan Shedroff's talk at Interaction South America on the topic of design and value creation: "Bridging Strategy with Design: How Designers Create Value for Businesses" (Nov 2014), *http://bit.ly/1WM0410.*

4. *Creation.* The satisfaction of having produced something

5. *Duty.* The satisfaction of having fulfilled a responsibility

6. *Enlightenment.* The gratification of learning about a subject

7. *Freedom.* A sense of living without constraints

8. *Harmony.* The pleasure of balance between parts of a whole

9. *Justice.* The assurance of just and fair treatment

10. *Oneness.* A sense of unity with people and things that surround us.

11. *Redemption.* Deliverance from past failure

12. *Security.* A freedom from worry about loss

13. *Truth.* A commitment to honesty and integrity

14. *Validation.* External recognition of one's worth

15. *Wonder.* Experiencing something beyond comprehension

Diagrams illuminate the human dynamics of value creation at all levels. They embrace the subjective nature of value and provide organizations an outside-in view to the value they actually create.

As a class of documents, alignment diagrams foster value-centered design. They allow you to visualize and locate value within your offering ecosystem. From this you can ask, what is your value proposition at each point in the experience? Or, how is the organization meaningfully unique from the customer's perspective? And, what meaning can you create for customers?

Jobs to Be Done

The concept of *jobs to be done* provides a lens through which to understand value creation. The framework looks at customer motivations in business settings. When we map experiences, we are effectively mapping jobs to be done.

The term was made popular by business leader Clayton Christensen in his book *The Innovator's Solution*, the follow-up to his landmark work *The Innovator's Dilemma*. It's a straightforward principle: people "hire" products and services to get a job done.

For instance, you might hire a new suit to make you look good at a job interview. Or, you hire Facebook to stay in touch with friends on a daily basis. You could also hire a chocolate bar to relieve stress. These are all jobs to be done. For each job, there are three dimensions to consider:

Functional job
> The practical task at hand to meet a person's requirements.

Emotional job
> The feelings a person desires while completing a job.

Social job
> How a person believes he or she will be perceived socially while using the solution.

Typically, a job to be done is expressed in terms of its functional jobs. As a result, many people assume the technique is nothing more than task analysis or a list of use cases. This is a fallacy. Jobs to be done are ultimately about an underlying need and desired outcomes.

Value is a much richer, more dynamic concept than cost involving human behavior and emotions. Value is a perceived benefit.

For instance, a homeowner may buy a digital keyless lock for their front door. The desired outcome is to reduce the chance that an intruder can enter their home. But there's also an emotional job: to increase the homeowner's sense of safety and security. Socially, the digital lock also fulfills the jobs of letting invited guests in and out as desired.

Viewing value creation in this way shifts focus from the psycho-demographic aspects of individuals to their goals and motivations. It's not about the user but about usage.

Finally, the context of the job is critical to understand. Christensen writes:

> Companies that target their products at the *circumstances* in which customers find themselves, rather than at the *customers* themselves, are those that can launch predictably successful products. Put another way, the critical unit of analysis is the *circumstance and not the customer.*

Alignment diagrams describe those circumstances—the broader context of goals, desired outcomes, and emotions, as well as constraints and pain points. Mapping experiences illustrates conditions of jobs to be done in an holistic way for everyone in an organization to learn from.

Summary

The concept of *transitional volatility* in web navigation serves as an analogy for the experiences people have when moving from touchpoint to touchpoint of a provider. If individuals have to constantly reorient themselves, the experience feels incoherent. Coherency in experience is a common goal for most organizations, and has been shown to increase profits.

But experiences are frustratingly intangible and overwhelmingly broad. As the mapmaker, it's your job to frame the diagram and experiences you'll be mapping. This includes decisions about the perspective, scope, focus, structure, and use. Chapter 4 discusses the process of selection in more detail.

Touchpoints are the means by which an interaction between individuals and an organization can take place. Typically, these are seen in terms of interaction with an advertisement, applications, websites, a service encounter, and a phone call.

A broader definition of touchpoints, however, sees them as the context in which they occur. The interaction between an individual and an organization happens at a given time and within a given environment. Organizations that design for and manage coherency across touchpoints see enormous benefits: greater satisfaction, stronger loyalty, and larger returns.

Moments of truth are critical, emotionally intense moments. They are those instances that make or break a relationship. Looking for the moments of truth gives points to potential opportunities for innovation.

From the individual's perspective, value is subjective and complex. There are many types of value they may consider: functional, emotional, social, epistemic, and circumstantial. Premium value goes beyond these types to include meaning and identity.

Jobs to be done is an existing framework that helps view value from an individual's standpoint. Popularized by Clayton Christensen, the practice looks at why people "hire" products and services to reach a desired outcome.

Further Reading

"Adaptive Path's Guide to Experience Mapping" (2013) *http:// mappingexperiences.com*

> *This is a free guide to experience mapping from the good folks at Adaptive Path. In less than 30 pages they are able to describe the mapping process with clarity. This includes an excellent discussion of the advantages of experience mapping in general.*

Gianluca Brugnoli, "Connecting the Dots of User Experience," *The Journal of IA* (Spring, 2009)

> *This is a well-referenced article on cross-channel design. Gianluca provides some practical tips on how to map systems. The highlight of the article is his customer journey matrix. He observes: "The user experience takes shape on many interconnected devices and through various interfaces and networks used in many different context and situations."*

Harvey Golub et al. "Delivering value to customers," *McKinsey Quarterly* (Jun 2000)

> *This is an excellent summary of articles from the prior three decades on the creation and delivery of customer value. It highlights the work of McKinsey employees with references to their respective full articles on the subject.*

Marc Stickdorn and Jakob Schneider. *This Is Service Design Thinking: Basics-Tools-Cases* (BIS Publishers, 2012)

> *This is a collection of chapters by leaders in the service design field. It includes many diagrams and descriptions of tools, many of which are mapping exercises. This is a comprehensive book on service design that belongs on every designer's desk.*

Identifying Opportunities: Combining Mental Model Diagrams and Jobs to Be Done

by Jim Kalbach, with Jen Padilla, Elizabeth Thapliyal, and Ryan Kasper

A key challenge in product development is selecting areas of improvements and innovation to focus on. A solid theory is needed to connect user insights to development decisions.

To that end, the GoToMeeting user experience design team at Citrix embarked on efforts to provide actionable needs-based insight for product development. The approach combined mapping out user behaviors and motivations through a mental model diagram and prioritizing the users' needs using the "jobs to be done" theory. This provided a visual map of the landscape as well as directions on how to create value to their customers.

The overall process had six steps:

1. Conduct primary research.

   We started with contextual inquiry. Broadly looking at the domain of work collaboration and communication, we conducted over 40 on-site interviews. Stakeholders and team members were included in the interviewing process.

   Data collection included field notes, photos, audio recordings, and video. A third-party vendor transcribed all of the over 68 hours of audio recordings. This resulted in nearly 1,500 pages of text.

1. Create a mental model diagram.

   Following Indi Young's approach closely, we analyzed the transcriptions for the jobs people were trying to get done. Through an iterative process of grouping, we created the mental model diagram. This is a bottom-up approach that entails clustering individual findings into themes, which are in turn grouped into categories.

   Fundamental goals and needs began to emerge. The result was illustration of "work collaboration" based directly on field research.

   The process also included the mapping of current products and features that support customer goals and needs. This allowed the team to see how our current offerings fit into a customer's mental model.

2. Hold a workshop.

   In a workshop with approximately 12 stakeholders from various departments, we read through the diagram in breakout groups. Each group got about a third of the overall mental model to work with. The goal was to have stakeholders first empathize with the current user experience (Figure 2-9).

FIGURE 2-9. Using a mental model diagram in a workshop with stakeholders. (The author is pictured with expert UX researcher Amber Brown.)

We then brainstormed concepts using scenarios around the "future of work." To do this, we presented each group with key trends about the future of work taken from industry reports. At each section of the diagram, we posed the question to the group, "If each trend came true, what must we do to support customers and ultimately to evolve as a company?"

To help socialize the outcomes of the workshop, we created an infographic summarizing the main conclusions. We printed this graphic on a single sheet of paper, had it laminated, and sent it by regular mail to workshop participants. A year or more later, it was still possible to see this infographic on teammates' desks.

2. Map concepts to diagram.

After the workshop, we updated the diagram with comments and input from stakeholders. We then mapped various concepts back to the diagram below the support towers. This resulted in an extended map and composite picture: the user's experience on the top, the support we currently offer in the middle, and future enhancements and innovations at the bottom (Figure 2-12).

But which gaps in people's ability to collaborate should we aim to solve first? Jobs to be done (described above) then helped us focus on the concepts with the most potential.

3. Prioritize jobs to be done.

We prioritized the jobs represented in the diagram by two factors:

— The level of importance associated with getting the job done

— The level of satisfaction associated with getting the job done

Graphed on a chart, the jobs that are highly important but least satisfied have the highest chance of customer adoption (Figure 2-10). They fulfill an unmet need.

To find this sweet spot, we employed a specific technique developed by Tony Ulwick. For more on this method, see Ulwick's writings, listed in the "Further Reading" section.

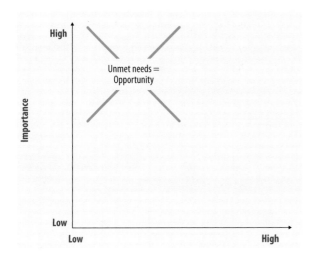

FIGURE 2-10. Solutions that meet unmet needs—or jobs that are important but unsatisfied—have a higher chance of succeeding.

The technique starts with generating so-called desired outcome statements, or the success measures for completing a job successfully. These were based directly on the mental model diagram.

Next, we launched a quantitative survey with the complete set of about 30 desired outcome statements. Respondents were asked to rate each desired outcome statement for both importance and satisfaction.

We then calculated the opportunity score for each statement. We determined this by taking the score for importance and adding the satisfaction gap, which is importance minus satisfaction. For instance, if for a given statement respondents rated importance 9 and satisfaction 3, the result is 15 for the opportunity score ($15 = 9 + (9 - 3)$). See Figure 2-11.

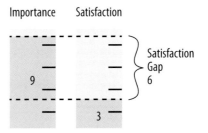

Importance + Satisfaction Gap = **Opportunity Score**

$$9 \quad + \quad 6 \quad = \quad 15$$

FIGURE 2-11. Opportunity scores for finding unmet jobs to be done.

Note that this score intentionally focuses on customer opportunity, not financial opportunity or market size opportunity. In other words, we were looking to solve for customer needs that would bring the chance of adoption by customers.

3. Focus innovation efforts.

The tasks in the mental model diagram, the opportunity scores, and proposed concepts were visually aligned, providing a clear picture of the opportunity space (Figure 2-12).

Efforts were prioritized against this information. This gave the team confidence that we were moving in the right direction—one that was firmly grounded in primary insights.

Product managers, marketing managers, and engineers found the information useful to their work. The prioritized list of people's needs turned out to be a highly consumable format for teams to engage with the research. One product owner said: "It's great to have this data to help make informed decisions. I'm looking forward to incorporating it more and more."

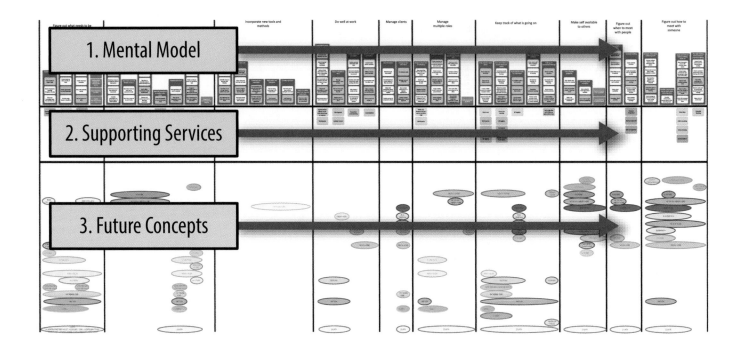

FIGURE 2-12. A portion of the extended mental mode diagram showing the highest areas of opportunity. Note that the resolution on this diagram is intentionally low to protect confidential information from being read. The point is to understand the alignment of four layers of information:
1. The individual's experience represented as a mental model diagram
2. Services that currently support their experience
3. Future concepts developed by the team
4. The areas of unmet needs reflecting the highest opportunity, determined by the jobs to be done research

Through these efforts multiple concepts have been prototyped and two innovations are being launched in the Apple Store, along with several patent submissions. Overall, the approach gave a rich, user-centered theory for service development. The combination of the mental model and jobs to be done methods has served as a centerpiece in the process, fostering many conversations and gathering consensus.

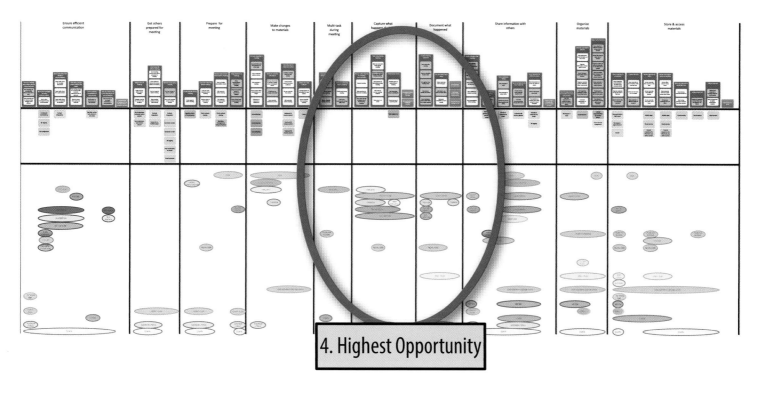

4. Highest Opportunity

Further Reading

Anthony Ulwick. *What Customers Want* (McGraw Hill, 2005).

Anthony Ulwick. "Turn Customer Input into Innovation," *Harvard Business Review* (2003).

About the Coauthors

Jen Padilla is an expert user researcher who has worked at software companies in the San Francisco area, including Microsoft, Citrix, and Cisco.

Elizabeth Thapliyal is a lead UX designer coleading needs-based innovation projects at Citrix with an MBA in Strategic Design from the California College of the Arts.

Ryan Kasper is a UX researcher, currently at Facebook, and holds a PhD in Cognitive Psychology from the University of California, Santa Barbara.

Diagram and Image Credits

Figure 2-2: Harry Beck's London Underground map, licensed from © TfL from the London Transport Museum collection.

Figure 2-4. Image of Booking.com, used with permission. See: Andre Manning. "The Booking Truth: Delighting Guests Takes More Than a Well-Priced Bed" (Jun 2013). *http://news.booking.com/the-booking-truth-delighting-guests-takes-more-than-a-well-priced-bed-us*.

Figure 2-5: 360° Touchpoint matrix Accelerom AG, international consultancy and research firm based in Zurich (*www.accelerom.com*), used with permission. Accelerom has been combining management practice, cross-media marketing research, and cutting-edge analysis and visualization technologies for over a decade. For more, see: *http://bit.ly/1WM1QyU*.

Figure 2-6: Touchpoint matrix created by Gianluca Brugnoli, used with permission, originally appearing in: Gianluca Brugnoli. "Connecting the Dots of User Experience," *Journal of Information Architecture* (2009). *http://journalofia.org/volume1/issue1/02-brugnoli/jofia-0101-02-brugnoli.pdf*.

Figure 2-8: Zero Moment of Truth from: Jim Lecinski. *ZMOT: Winning the Zero Moment of Truth* (Google, 2011). *https://ssl.gstatic.com/think/docs/2011-winning-zmot-ebook_research-studies.pdf*.

Figure 2-9: Original photo by Elizabeth Thapliyal, used with permission.

Figure 2-12: Extended mental model diagram created by Amber Brown, Elizabeth Thapliyal, and Ryan Kasper, used with permission.

*"You've got to start with the customer experience
and work back towards the technology."*

— Steve Jobs

IN THIS CHAPTER

- A new way of seeing
- Reframing competition, creating shared value
- Reimagining value delivery, organizing for innovation
- Visualizing strategy

CHAPTER 3

Visualizing Strategic Insight

A number of years ago, I facilitated a multiday strategy workshop at the company I was working for. During dinner the director of sales explained his perspective on the workshop's purpose: "We have to figure out how to get customers for all they are worth." He gestured as if wringing a towel. "If the towels gets dry, you have to squeeze harder. A good leader knows how to do that, and a good strategy makes it easier."

He was serious. I was horrified. Our markets are not people "out there" we shake down for loose change. Customers are our most valuable assets, I thought. We should strive to learn from them so that we can provide better products and services.

The director's perspective was shortsighted. He believed the business of our business was more sales. That may be fine in the short term, but ultimately this narrow perspective leads to failure. Organizations looking for sustained success need to break this mold.

Companies frequently don't realize that as the business grows, it must also widen its strategic field of vision. I call this misstep *strategy myopia*. It happens time and time again: organizations ultimately don't know what business they are really in.

Take Kodak. The film giant dominated the film market for over a century, but filed for bankruptcy in 2012. Many people believe that Kodak failed because it missed digital camera technology. This is not true. In fact, Kodak invented the first digital camera in 1975.

Kodak failed because it had the myopic view that it was in the *film* business instead of the *storytelling* business. Leaders feared digital technology would cannibalize profits. They believed they could protect their existing business through marketing and sales. It was a nearsightedness in strategy, not technology, that led to Kodak's downfall.

Successful organizations continually innovate and expand their horizons. Incremental improvements are not enough. Technical R&D is not enough. Instead, they must grow by questioning the type and scope of value they create.

Diagrams of experiences offer a type of insight that is often overlooked in strategy creation: a view from the individual's perspective. This chapter shows how mapping experiences can contribute missing strategic insight and ultimately serve as a corrective lens for strategy myopia.

The chapter concludes with a review of some complementary techniques that extend experience mapping in order to better visualize strategy. By the end of the chapter you should get a sense of how diagrams broaden your field of vision.

A New Way of Seeing

The context of business has changed over the last few decades. Consumers have real power: they have access to prices, product information, and alternative providers around the world. Traditional approaches to sales—wringing a market for what it's worth—do not work anymore for sustained growth.

Instead, organizations need to reverse their thinking. Renowned business leader Ram Charan, for one, urges companies to invert the traditional sales perspective. In his book *What the Customer Wants You to Know*, he illustrates a flow of value insight opposite to traditional approaches (Figure 3-1).

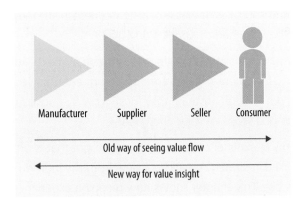

FIGURE 3-1. Understanding value from the consumer's perspective reverses the flow of insight.

Insight about users is not a nuisance, it's a strategic opportunity. The objective is not a *push*, it's a *pull*. You don't sell products, you buy customers.

This idea runs contrary to typical strategic decision-making, but it is not new. As early as 1960, renowned Harvard business professor Theodore Levitt discussed the importance of focusing on human needs first. In his influential article, "Marking Myopia,"* Levitt writes:

> *An industry begins with the customer and his needs, not with a patent, a raw material, or a selling skill. Given the customer's needs, the industry develops backwards, first concerning itself with the physical delivery of customer satisfaction. Then it moves back further to creating the things by which these satisfactions are in part achieved.*

Consider the failure of the railroad industry in the US, a favorite example of Levitt. During their heyday at the beginning of the 20th century, railroads were extremely profitable and attractive to Wall Street investors. No one in that business could imagine its demise just a few decades later.

But railroads didn't stop growing in the middle of the century because of competition from the technology of cars, trucks, planes, and even telephones. They stopped growing because they let rivals take customers. Their intense focus on their own

---

* Many of the themes and ideas in this chapter were directly derived from Levitt's landmark article, including the term *strategy myopia*. This article is still relevant and highly recommended. See Theodore Levitt. "Marketing Myopia," *Harvard Business Review* (1960).

products led to strategy myopia: they saw themselves in the *railroad* business rather than the *transportation* business.

Though no panacea, mapping experiences provides insight that helps expand the strategic aperture. For example, Tim Brown, CEO of IDEO, describes his company's work with Amtrak in his book *Change by Design*. His firm was brought in to redesign the seats of the Acela trains. The goal was to make the travel experience more pleasurable.

> *Successful organizations continually innovate and expand their horizons. They must grow by questioning the type and scope of value they create.*

Rather than diving into the seat redesign, however, they first mapped an end-to-end journey around train travel in general. They identified about 12 unique stages in the experience. This led to different conclusions about their focus and how to improve the travel experience. Brown writes:

> The insight that proved most striking was that passengers did not take their seats on the train until stage eight—most of the experience of train travel, in other words, did not involve the train at all. The team reasoned that every one of the prior steps was an opportunity to create a positive interaction, opportunities that would have been overlooked if they had focused only on the design of the seats.

Alignment diagrams are a type of tool that points to such new opportunities. They visually align a description of the individual's experience with the offerings of an organization. They start with the customer's experience and work back toward the technology, as Steve Jobs advised in the quote opening this chapter.

Consider the *opportunities* highlighted at the bottom of the Rail Europe diagram created by Chris Risdon in Chapter 1 (see Figure 1-5). These suggest tactical solutions, but go beyond that to point to larger, strategic questions. Should they become a provider of travel information? Should they integrate with retailers and ecommerce partners? How can they reinvent support or the ticketing experience? This strategic insight is directly tied to the actual experience of train travel and shown in context in the diagram.

In this sense, diagrams offer a *new way of seeing* your markets, your organization, and your strategy—from the outside-in rather from the inside-out. Logically, they are most effective at initial stages of providing a service (Figure 3-2).

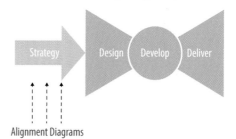

FIGURE 3-2. Alignment diagrams provide insight from the outside-in and are best created up front to inform strategic decisionmaking.

I believe the process of mapping helps correct strategy myopia. In my experience, the resulting diagrams invariably show a much broader picture of customer needs than a business currently addresses.

But expanding your strategic field of vision requires change. The organization as a whole must adapt to a new mindset. In particular, there are four key aspects involved:

- Reframing competition
- Creating shared value
- Reimagining value delivery
- Organizing to innovate

The next sections describe these aspects and how mapping experiences can play a role in each.

1. Reframe Competition

Traditionally, firms categorize customers by demographic or psychographic attributes (age, income, race, marital status, etc.), or they look at purchasing behavior or company size.

In doing so, managers create categories that don't match their actual customer needs and motivations. No one ever bought a product *because* of their age or income. The typical one-size-fits-all approach inevitably fails, causing managers to reshuffle their demographic categories arbitrarily.

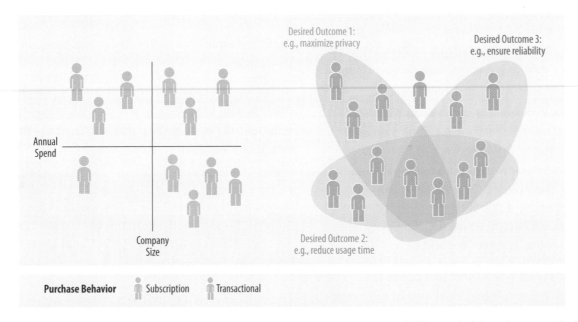

FIGURE 3-3. Typical segmentation focuses demographic and behavioral dimensions (left) instead of desired outcomes (right).

An alternative model sees the market from the customer's perspective. Put simply, people buy products to get a job done. The outcomes people seek, not the customers themselves, are the primary dimension for meaningful segmentation (Figure 3-3).

Recalling Levitt, Clayton Christensen and coauthors Scott Cook and Taddy Hall point to the failure of traditional segmentation practices. In their article "Marketing Malpractice," they write:

> The prevailing methods of segmentation that budding managers learn in business schools and then practice in the marketing departments of good companies are actually a key reason that new product innovation has become a gamble in which the odds of winning are horrifyingly low.

> There is a better way to think about market segmentation and new product innovation. The structure of a market, seen from the customers' point of view, is very simple: They just need to get things done, as Ted Levitt said. When people find themselves needing to get a job done, they essentially hire products to do that job for them.

Insight about users is not a nuisance, it's a strategic opportunity.

Shifting your perspective on segmentation reframes the competition. The job, not the industry or category as defined by analysts, determines competition in the mind of the user. You don't compete against products and services in your category: you compete against anything that gets the job done from the user's point of view.

For instance, Scott Cook, founder of the tax software giant Intuit, once said:

> The greatest competitor [in tax software] … was not in the industry. It was the pencil. The pencil is a tough and resilient substitute. Yet the entire industry had overlooked it.*

Think about it: when you're preparing taxes, making a quick calculation on a pad of paper is natural and hard to improve on. Cook knew his software needed to not only outperform other tax software packages, it also needed to be more effective and simple to use as a pencil. Seen this way, tax software competes with pencils and anything else that gets the job done.

Diagrams can be used to track alternative means of getting a job done. For example, Figure 3-4 is an excerpt from a diagram detailing the workflow of barristers in Australia. It was part of a research effort I led while at LexisNexis, a leading provider of legal information.† The bottom row shows how we mapped different ways of getting work done (in grey) to the steps in the workflow.

---

* Quoted in Scott Berkun's book *The Myths of Innovation* (O'Reilly, 2007).

† See the case study included in Chapter 11 for more details on this project.

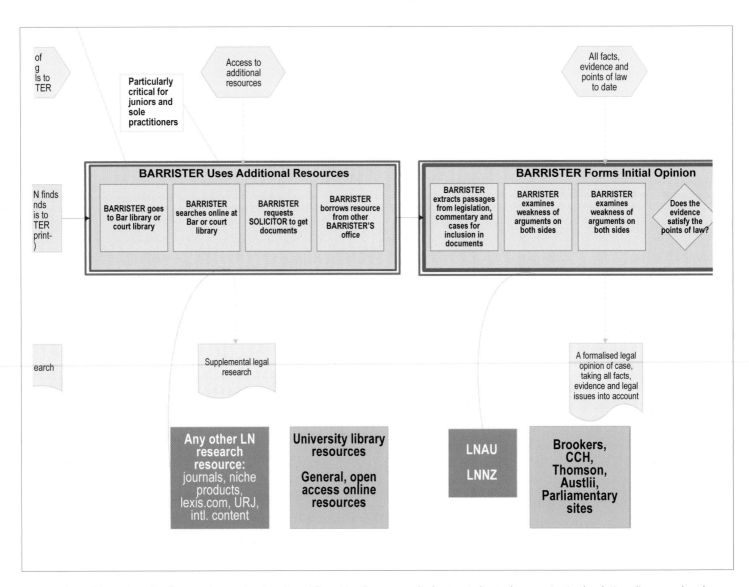

FIGURE 3-4. This section of a diagram shows a barrister's workflow. The elements at the bottom indicate the organization's solutions (in orange) and competing solutions (in grey).

After visualizing competing solutions across the entire experience, I found barristers are as likely to do legal research at libraries or with free online resources as with our flagship database. This was eye-opening for stakeholders. The diagrams clearly illustrated how and where they contend with different services. Business leader Rita Gunther McGrath believes markets should be seen in terms of what she calls *arenas*. Arenas are characterized by the experiences people have and their connection to a provider. She writes in her bestselling book *The End of Competitive Advantage*:

The driver of categorization will in all likelihood be the outcomes that particular customers seek ("jobs to be done") and the alternative ways those outcomes might be met. This is vital because the most substantial threats to a given advantage are likely to arise from a peripheral or nonobvious location.

Diagrams of experiences challenge assumptions of who your competition really is. They reflect the needs of individuals and illustrate the broader experience in which they are relevant. This in turn enables you to see the market from the perspective of the customer, not by synthetic segmentation and traditional industry categorization.

2. Create Shared Value

After World War II, US corporations assumed a general *retain-and-reinvest* approach to strategy. They put earnings back into the company, benefiting employees and making the firm more competitive.

This gave way to a *downsize-and-distribute* posture in the 1970s. Reducing costs and maximizing financial returns, particularly for shareholders, became a priority. The widely held economic policy belief was that profit is good for society: the more companies can earn, the better off we all are.

This policy has not made America more prosperous.[*] As a whole, we are not better off. Since the 70s, American workers have been working more and making less. At the same time, shareholder value in the form of dividends and CEO wages has experienced a massive upturn. As a result, trust in corporations is at an all-time low. Businesses are increasingly blamed for many social, environmental, and economic problems in general.

The good news is that the balance is shifting. There's a move from *shareholder* value to *shared value*. In his landmark article, "Creating Shared Value," strategy expert Michael Porter recognizes a tipping point in business: no longer can companies operate at the expense of the markets they serve. He writes:

> A big part of the problem lies with companies themselves, which remain trapped in an outdated approach to value creation that has emerged over the past few decades. They continue to view value creation narrowly, optimizing short-term financial performance in a bubble while missing the most important customer needs and ignoring the broader influences that determine their longer-term success.

---

[*] For more on the adverse effects of maximizing shareholder value on society, see William Lazonick's critical article "Profits Without Prosperity," *Harvard Business Review* (Sep 2014).

This position is contrary to the well-articulated belief that businesses have no agenda beyond making profit. Shared value instead links revenue to creating social benefit. This, in turn, provides a competitive advantage back to the organization. It's a win-win approach.

Shared value goes beyond social responsibility. It touches the heart of an organization's strategy. Every time a customer interacts with a company it creates value for society. There are three ways of thinking about shared value strategically.

Reconceive your offering.

For example, Skype launched a program called "Skype in the Classroom." With this, teachers can collaborate with other instructors around the world and design different learning experiences for their students. In other words, *Skype is not only in the* videoconferencing *business, they provide* educational collaboration *opportunities for customers.*

Innovate how products and services are produced.

For example, Intercontinental Hotels Group (IHG) introduced its GreenEngage program in 2009 to address its environmental footprint. To date, they've achieved energy savings of about 25%, and IHG differentiates itself with this program to customers. In other words, *IHG is not just a provider of* hotel rooms, *they are in the business of creating* environmentally conscious communities.

Collaborate with partners in new ways.

Nestlé, for example, worked closely with dairy farmers in India, investing in technology to build competitive milk supply systems. These simultaneously generated social benefits through improved health care. In other words, *Nestle doesn't just produce* food products, *they are in the* nutrition *business.*

The notion of shared value means that organizations need to conceive their value proposition in a way that takes many perspectives into account. Chief among these is a deep understanding of human needs. For instance, in a video interview Porter advises:

> *Figure out what your product is and what your value chain is. Understand where those things touch important social needs and problems. If you're in financial services, let's think about 'saving' or 'buying a home'— but in a way that actually works for the consumer.*

Now consider Figure 3-5, a diagram of buying a home created by Sofia Hussain, a leading digital strategist in Norway. It shows the services of a fictitious home-listings company in the inner circle, labeled *inside activities*. The activities of the user—the *outside activities*—are listed in the bigger circle. Also included are touchpoint types, illustrated with small icons. In her article, "Designing Digital Strategies, Part 2," Hussain suggests a strategic scenario for the company: they want to expand their business with services that address more customer needs in this domain. The intent is to move from a business for simply *buying a home and moving* to one that

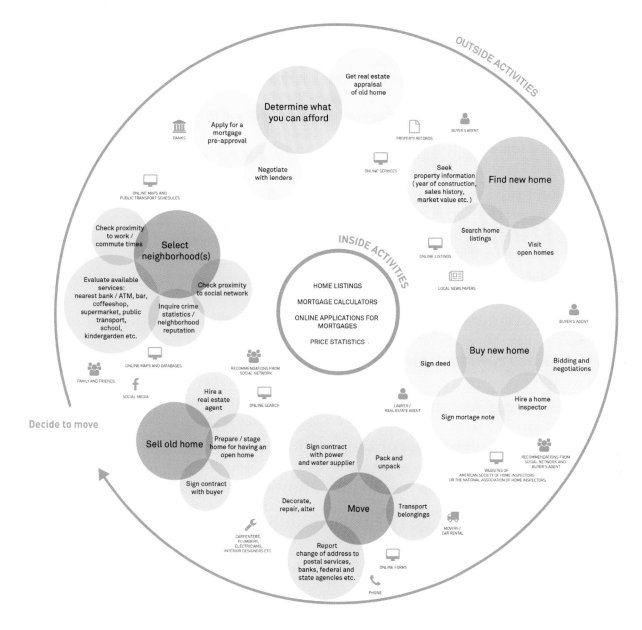

FIGURE 3-5. This map created by Sofia Hussain illustrates the experience of "buying a home."

helps people settle into a new home. This diagram can be used to illustrate how that expansion fits into the overall experience from the customer's perspective.

Shared value goes one step further by increasing services or moving into a playing field. It requires the company to ask how it might also create social benefit.

For example, the company might promote healthier lifestyles by coordinating home listings with information about neighborhood *walkability*. In the map in Figure 3-5, services around *selecting a neighborhood* and *finding a new home* are points of interaction where presenting walkability information makes sense.

But potential saved costs of walking could also be included in *determining what you can afford*. Perhaps the system could show how much money is saved by reducing gas expenses or getting rid of a car altogether.

With shared value in mind, the strategic aspiration of the company becomes even broader: it's about more than just buying a home or even settling into a home: it's about *creating a healthier, environmentally friendly lifestyle when buying a new home.*

Diagrams help us think through the interactions and customer needs in a holistic way. To recall Porter, they look at an offering in a way that actually works for the consumer. Finding shared business value relies on such examinations of the overall experience.

3. Reimagine Value Delivery

As the size of computer chips gets smaller and smaller, it becomes increasingly more feasible to embed processing power into common objects. Once fitted with a microcontroller, physical products can connect to the Internet. Dubbed the Internet of Things (IoT), smart, connected devices expand possibilities about how you deliver value.

The Belkin Crock-Pot (Figure 3-6), for example, takes a regular kitchen appliance and connects it to the Internet. With an accompanying app, cooks can now control the device remotely. The Crock-Pot can also be linked to other devices inside and outside the home.

FIGURE 3-6. The Belkin WeMo Crock-Pot Slow Cooker is connected to the Internet.

When everything from computers to cookware has a digital component, the design of the overall experience becomes more challenging. Success is determined by how well their services fit with each other and, more importantly, how well they fit into people's lives. Part of the value that organizations deliver, then, is how their offerings integrate into a larger ecosystem (Figure 3-7).

Diagrams visualize the components of the ecosystem. For example, Claro Partners, a leading European design consultancy based in Barcelona, developed a straightforward approach for mapping the various elements in an IoT system. They created a series of cards for the different aspects typically involved. Teams fill out cards and then arrange them into a diagram of the ecosystem.

Figure 3-8 shows an example of a resulting map, in this case for the Nike FuelBand. It reveals important interdependencies in the experience, such as a relationship between FuelBand users, as well as a connection between physical devices, software, and data services.

IoT doesn't just make it harder to conceive and design new products. It fundamentally changes strategy. Your service will inevitably be part of a system of services. Creating and delivering value into that system cannot be ignored. Diagrams help you understand the complexities and interrelationships involved.

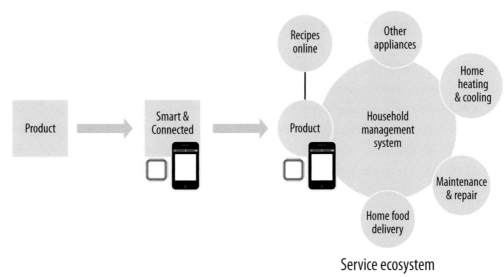

Service ecosystem

FIGURE 3-7. As products become smart and connected, they fit into an ecosystem of services.

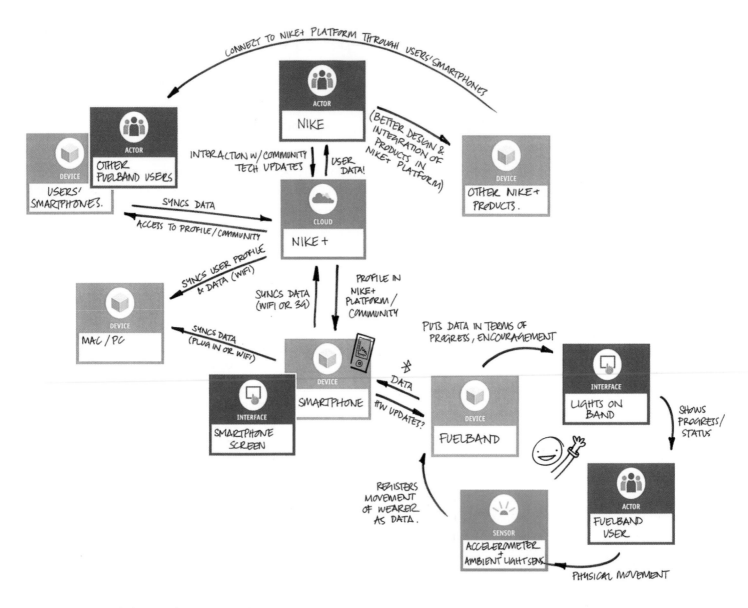

FIGURE 3-8. A simple diagram of an ecosystem shows connected services created by Claro Partners.

4. Organize for Innovation

Some leaders have a Darwinian view of innovation: they believe that the best new concepts will rise to the surface on their merit alone. This perspective fails to take into account corporate antibodies motivated to protect existing revenue that can squash fledgling ideas summarily.

How the organization is structured is part of the problem. The best ideas will fail if they are fed into an organization that is not set up to accept them. The first step is to overcome motivations and incentives that seek to optimize short-term financial returns.

Charles O'Reilly and Michael Tushman recommend establishing an *ambidextrous* organization. To do this, set up divisions within the organization that have separate goals and expectations (Figure 3-9). This is particularly important for emerging businesses, where new ideas need a chance to take hold.

Beyond becoming ambidextrous, you also need to organize around the customer experience. For instance, a client at an ecommerce provider once introduced himself as a member of the *Discovery* group. He explained their job was to help people find the products they offered, regardless of channel or medium. They also had teams for *Purchasing* and *Success*. In other words, their organization mirrored the customer journey, not functional lines or technology types (Figure 3-10).

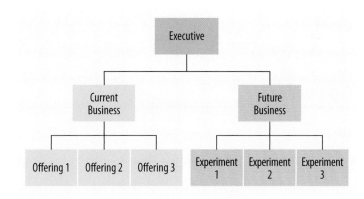

FIGURE 3-9. The ambidextrous organization separates effort types structurally.

Some functions spanned these experience-centric teams. But people in those roles were compelled to align to the customer-oriented teams in conversations and in decision making. The effect was a new type of creative problem solving within the organization. Solutions better matched customer needs.

Alignment diagrams provide the basis for this type of organization. They reveal a model to follow that mirrors the individual's experience. This leads to a new way of seeing your offerings, which in turn fosters innovation.

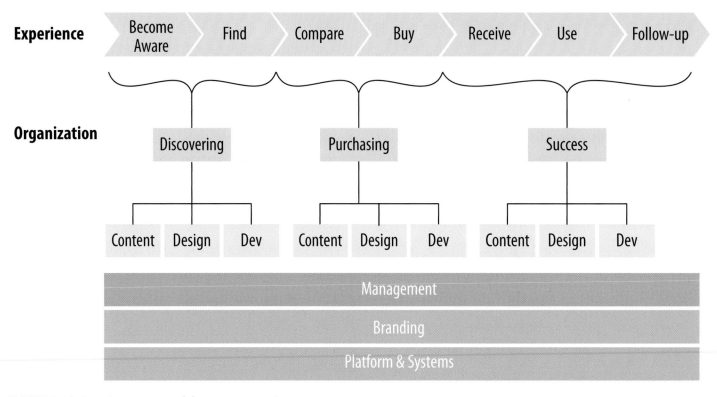

FIGURE 3-10. Organize teams around the customer experience.

Mapping Strategy

Strategy is typically created behind closed doors at the top levels of an organization. Leaders then reveal the strategy to the rest of the organization—usually as a PowerPoint presentation. Employees are then expected to "get it" and somehow be able to magically align their work to the strategy.

But when things go wrong later on, these same leaders blame failure on poor execution. They overlook the fact that strategy and its execution are related: a brilliant strategy that can't be implemented isn't brilliant.

Poor communication is only part of the problem. *How* strategy gets created also matters. The process must overcome gaps in understanding across the entire organization. Otherwise, the realization of strategic intent has no chance.

Business consultant and author Nilofer Merchant has observed a disconnect between the top and bottom layers in many organizations. She describes it as an *Air Sandwich* in her book *The New How* (O'Reilly, 2009). Merchant explains:

> *An Air Sandwich is, in effect, a strategy that has a clear vision and future direction on the top layer, day-to-day action on the bottom, and virtually nothing in the middle—no meaty key decisions that connect the two layers, no rich chewy center filling to align the new direction with the new actions within the company.*

To address the Air Sandwich, companies should view strategy creation as an inclusive endeavor. But the traditional tools of strategy creation only confound the situation. Words are abstract and open to interpretation. Documents bewilder and confuse. Emails and communications are unintelligible by those who must implement a strategy.

Diagrams are an antidote. They open up strategy for broader involvement across an organization and increase general comprehension.

The next sections describe several tools that *complement* alignment diagrams. They all seek to visualize strategy or parts of it. These include strategy maps, the strategy canvas, the strategy blueprint, and the business model canvas and value proposition canvas. Diagrams of experiences plug in to these techniques, informing customer-related aspects.

A brilliant strategy that can't be implemented isn't brilliant.

Strategy Map

A *strategy map* represents an organization's entire strategy on a single sheet of paper. The technique was made popular by veteran business consultants Robert Kaplan and David Norton in their book *Strategy Maps*. This approach emerged from research and years of experience consulting with client companies and is part of their earlier framework called *the balanced scorecard*.

Figure 3-11 shows an example of a generic strategy map. Each row represents objectives from one of four strategic perspectives.

Learning and growth of employees

> This perspective outlines the knowledge, skills, and systems that the organization needs in order to deliver the intended value.

Internal processes

> Goals at this level reflect the capabilities and efficiencies of the organization as a whole.

Customers

> This perspective represents the value proposition. Here, alignment diagrams reveal what customers actually perceive as valuable.

Financials

> These are the top-level objectives centered on the value captured by the organization in terms of financial gains.

The resulting map is more than just a list of goals. The map connects the objectives to show causality. From this standpoint, strategy is a series of IF-THEN statements, as Kaplan and Norton point out.

Consider a simple example strategy map for Patagonia (in Figure 3-12), created by Michael Ensley, a business consultant with PureStone Partners. Environmental goodwill is a key strategic objective prominent in the diagram. Anchoring it here makes it visible to everyone else in the organization.

The center of this example shows how Patagonia intends to create customer value. A key internal process is indicated as *solve their [i.e., customer] problems*, which is linked to two aspects: *provide extreme gear* and *protect our clients*. Alignment diagrams foster the type of conversations needed to arrive at these problems to solve.

Strategy maps provide a balanced view of the interlocking set of strategic choices an organization makes. They illustrate the relationships in objectives and allow others to see how their activities fit into the strategic whole.

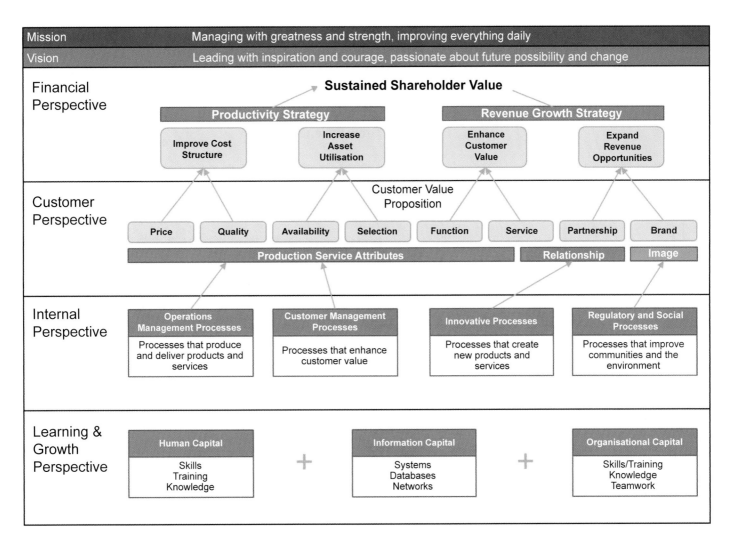

| Mission | Managing with greatness and strength, improving everything daily |
| Vision | Leading with inspiration and courage, passionate about future possibility and change |

Financial Perspective

Sustained Shareholder Value

Productivity Strategy

| Improve Cost Structure | Increase Asset Utilisation |

Revenue Growth Strategy

| Enhance Customer Value | Expand Revenue Opportunities |

Customer Perspective

Customer Value Proposition

| Price | Quality | Availability | Selection | Function | Service | Partnership | Brand |

Production Service Attributes | **Relationship** | **Image**

Internal Perspective

| Operations Management Processes | Customer Management Processes | Innovative Processes | Regulatory and Social Processes |
| Processes that produce and deliver products and services | Processes that enhance customer value | Processes that create new products and services | Processes that improve communities and the environment |

Learning & Growth Perspective

| Human Capital | Information Capital | Organisational Capital |
| Skills Training Knowledge | Systems Databases Networks | Skills/Training Knowledge Teamwork |

FIGURE 3-11. A generic strategy map shows the hierarchy of relationships between objectives.

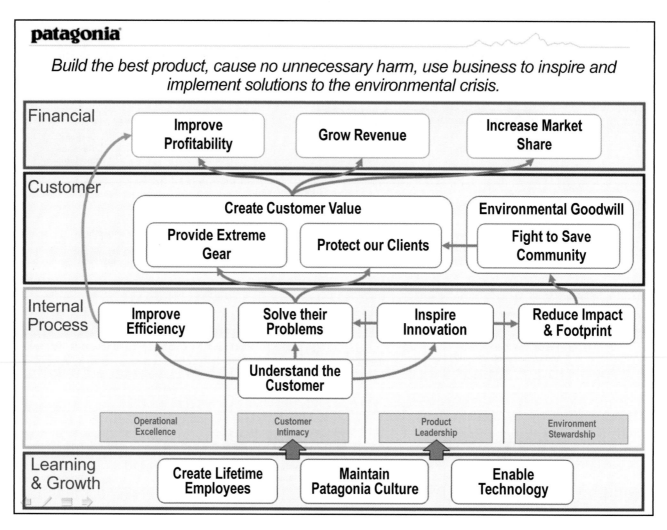

patagonia

Build the best product, cause no unnecessary harm, use business to inspire and implement solutions to the environmental crisis.

Financial
- Improve Profitability
- Grow Revenue
- Increase Market Share

Customer
- Create Customer Value
  - Provide Extreme Gear
  - Protect our Clients
- Environmental Goodwill
  - Fight to Save Community

Internal Process
- Improve Efficiency
- Solve their Problems
- Inspire Innovation
- Reduce Impact & Footprint
- Understand the Customer

Operational Excellence | Customer Intimacy | Product Leadership | Environment Stewardship

Learning & Growth
- Create Lifetime Employees
- Maintain Patagonia Culture
- Enable Technology

FIGURE 3-12. An example of a strategy canvas for the sporting goods company Patagonia shows their focus on environmental goodwill.

Strategy Canvas

The *strategy canvas* is a visual tool to both diagnose existing strategies and build alternative ones. It was developed by W. Chan Kim and Renée Mauborgne around 2000 and featured in their groundbreaking book *Blue Ocean Strategy*. Figure 3-13 shows an example strategy canvas for Southwest Airlines.

Across the bottom are the primary factors of competition. These are aspects that create value for customers and the dimensions along which firms compete. The vertical axis indicates relative performance for each factor from low to high.

This arrangement reveals a picture of how several organizations create value compared to each other.

A strategy canvas reflects the key dynamic in the *blue ocean strategy* approach. Red oceans, Kim and Mauborgne explain, represent fierce competition among existing industries in a given domain. As the space gets crowded, market share for each organization dwindles, and the waters become bloody.

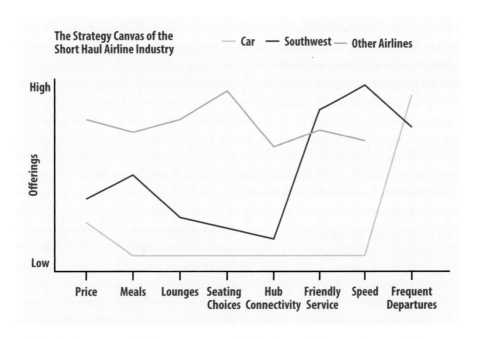

FIGURE 3-13. An example of a strategy canvas for Southwest Airlines reveals competitive differentiators.

Blue oceans represent uncontested market space. Demand is *created* rather than fought over. Their advice is clear: don't directly compete with rivals. Instead, make them irrelevant.

To do this you must make hard tradeoffs. Southwest chooses *not* to compete along the traditional factors of airline service. Instead, they focus on frequent departures from smaller airports. In doing so, Southwest competes with car travel: customers who may have driven between two cities might now consider flying with Southwest instead.

The process for creating a strategy canvas takes the following steps.

1. Determine factors of value creation. It may be easy to come up with dozens of potential factors. The key is to focus on the most important ones. This is where alignment diagrams come in: they help identify these factors. They show what problems the organizations have and how value is perceived from their perspective.

2. Determine competitor types. The trick is to select a limited set of representative competitors. Three is ideal. Including more than four competitors reduces the impact of the resulting diagram greatly.

3. Rate performance for each factor. Typically this is estimated on a relative scale of low to high. It's also possible to get empirical evidence for each rating, such as through a survey.

An alternative approach to determining the factors of value creation is to focus on *types of experiences* individuals have. For instance, from a customer journey map you may have identified half a dozen or so phases of interaction (e.g., becoming aware, purchasing, initiating the service, using the service, extending and renewing, and getting support). For each you can compare how competing services perform (see Figure 3-14).

This approach may not help you find a blue ocean per se, but provides valuable insight and an experience-based view of the strategic landscape.

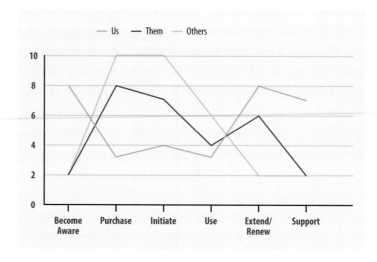

FIGURE 3-14. An example of an experience-based strategy canvas comparing types of experiences.

Strategy Blueprint

Strategy is difficult to define precisely. On the one hand, it gets confused with *analysis*. This includes everything from market size to technical assessments to financial prognosis. The result is often reports that fill up dozens of pages.

On the other hand, strategy gets conflated with *planning*. You've probably witnessed annual strategy retreats in your organization, where leaders spend several days forging plans for the upcoming year. They then emerge from seclusion with detailed roadmaps and financial plans that become quickly obsolete.

Analysis and planning, while necessary inputs and outputs in the strategy creation process, are not the core of strategy. You can't analyze your way to strategy: the answers don't magically emerge from data. And detailed roadmaps don't provide the rationale for the activity they organize. Strategy does (see Figure 3-15).

Strategy is about devising a way you believe you'll best overcome challenges to reach a desired position. It is a creative endeavor, not based on analysis and planning alone. Strategy represents the logic that connects analysis and planning. Ultimately, it's how your organization makes sense of its actions and decisions over time.

I developed the *strategy blueprint* as a tool to visualize this central strategic rationale.* It uses a canvas format to help visualize the relationships between elements of the strategy.

Figure 3-16 shows an example of a completed strategy blueprint. In this case, it reflects the strategy of a fictitious company, Einstein Media Company, a publisher of scientific journals, books, and information. The company has led the industry for nearly 100 years, and scientists around the world trust their brand name.

The elements in the strategy blueprint are based on research in the field. First, it borrows from Henry Mintzberg's five Ps of strategy from his book *Strategy Safari*. These are combined with Roger Martin and A.G. Lafley's five questions of strategy in their recent book *Playing to Win*. (Both books are highly recommended.)

FIGURE 3-15. Strategy provides logic between analysis and planning.

---

* You can download a PDF of the strategy blueprint from my blog: *https://experiencinginformation.wordpress.com/2015/10/12/strategy-blueprint/*.

Strategy Blueprint

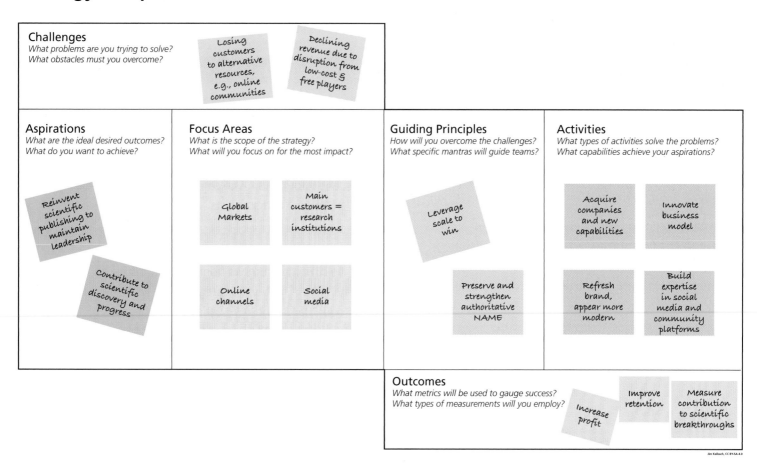

Challenges
What problems are you trying to solve?
What obstacles must you overcome?

Losing customers to alternative resources, e.g., online communities

Declining revenue due to disruption from low-cost & free players

Aspirations
What are the ideal desired outcomes?
What do you want to achieve?

Reinvent scientific publishing to maintain leadership

Contribute to scientific discovery and progress

Focus Areas
What is the scope of the strategy?
What will you focus on for the most impact?

Global Markets

Main customers = research institutions

Online channels

Social media

Guiding Principles
How will you overcome the challenges?
What specific mantras will guide teams?

Leverage scale to win

Preserve and strengthen authoritative NAME

Activities
What types of activities solve the problems?
What capabilities achieve your aspirations?

Acquire companies and new capabilities

Innovate business model

Refresh brand, appear more modern

Build expertise in social media and community platforms

Outcomes
What metrics will be used to gauge success?
What types of measurements will you employ?

Increase profit

Improve retention

Measure contribution to scientific breakthroughs

Jim Kalbach, CC BY-SA 4.0

FIGURE 3-16. The strategy blueprint reveals the key logic of strategy, in this case for the fictitious Einstein Media Company.

Table 3-1 summarizes and aligns these two existing frameworks. The last column reveals their thematic intersection, yielding six common elements of strategy. Each element is given a box in the blueprint.

- *Challenges.* Strategy implies the need for change, a desire to move from point A to point B. What are the hurdles to doing so? What opposing forces must you overcome to be able to reach your goals?

- *Aspirations.* What kind of organization do you aspire to be? What do you aspire for customers and for society?

- *Focus areas.* Setting a scope to your strategy helps you concentrate effort on the things that matter most. Who will you serve? What regions will you play in? Which jobs to be done will you target?

- *Guiding principles.* These are the pillars of the strategy you believe will overcome the challenges you face. What mantras will unite teams and unify decision making?

- *Activities.* What types of activities are needed to implement the strategy and achieve your aspirations? Note that this is not about making a roadmap or plans but rather looking at the skills and capabilities you'll ultimately need.

- *Outcomes.* How will you know your strategy is on track? How can you show progress and success?

Building strategy is a creative endeavor. The strategy blueprint allows you to explore options with no initial risk. Try alternatives, cross items off, rework ideas, and start over again. The blueprint helps you design strategy. Use it in briefings, in workshops, or as a reference document.

There is no prescribed order to completing the blueprint. Typically, it's best to start with the challenges and aspirations. After that you may find yourself moving freely between the boxes. The blueprint helps you see all the moving parts of strategy at once, making it tangible and inclusive to others.

Lafley and Martin	Mintzberg	Elements of strategy
	Pattern	What challenges motivate you?
What is your winning aspiration?	Position	What are your aspirations?
Where will you play?	Perspective	What will you focus on?
How will you win?	Ploy	What are your guiding principles?
What capabilities are needed?	Plan	What types of activities are needed?
How will you manage strategy?		How will you measure success?

TABLE 3-1. The intersection of existing frameworks gives rise to the six elements of the strategy blueprint.

Business Model Canvas

The *business model canvas* is a strategic management tool that helps business owners and stakeholders discover different business models. Alexander Osterwalder first introduced it in his book *Business Model Generation* (Wiley, 2010). It has become very popular since them.

The nine boxes of the canvas represent the key components of a business model (Figure 3-17). There is logic to their arrangement. The boxes on the right represent market-facing aspects, called the *front stage*. On the left are the *back stage* elements of a business model—the internal business processes. The visual format of a canvas promotes exploration. You can quickly try out alternative models and evaluate them before making a commitment in any one direction. It allows you to apply creativity to business decisions.

Figure 3-18 shows a visualization of the business model for the silicon provider

Xiameter compared to its parent company, Dow Corning. It is based on the article "Dow Corning's Big Pricing Gamble," by Loren Gary. The green notes represent Dow Corning's core business. The orange notes show the Xiameter model. Interestingly, Xiameter seems to have had an effect back on the core business model, according to the article. These aspects are shown in blue notes.

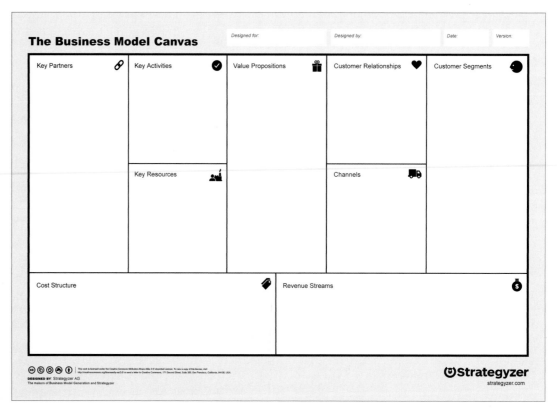

FIGURE 3-17. The business model canvas is a popular management tool, created by Alexander Osterwalder.

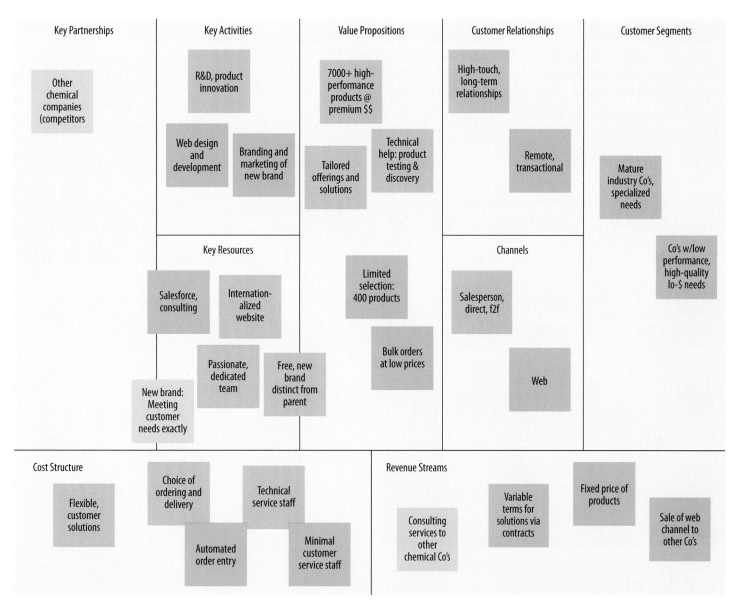

Key Partnerships

Other chemical companies (competitors

Key Activities

R&D, product innovation

Web design and development

Branding and marketing of new brand

Value Propositions

7000+ high-performance products @ premium $$

Tailored offerings and solutions

Technical help: product testing & discovery

Customer Relationships

High-touch, long-term relationships

Remote, transactional

Customer Segments

Mature industry Co's, specialized needs

Co's w/low performance, high-quality lo-$ needs

Key Resources

Salesforce, consulting

Internation-alized website

Passionate, dedicated team

Free, new brand distinct from parent

New brand: Meeting customer needs exactly

Limited selection: 400 products

Bulk orders at low prices

Channels

Salesperson, direct, f2f

Web

Cost Structure

Flexible, customer solutions

Choice of ordering and delivery

Automated order entry

Technical service staff

Minimal customer service staff

Revenue Streams

Consulting services to other chemical Co's

Variable terms for solutions via contracts

Fixed price of products

Sale of web channel to other Co's

FIGURE 3-18. This example of the business model canvas compares the business models of Xiameter, a provider of silicon, to its parent, Dow Corning.

Figure 3-19 shows a photo of a canvas I completed with stake-holders after an ideation session. Using sticky notes, we were able to move information around as needed and consider any possible alternatives. This allowed us to test assumptions of a new concept from a standpoint of business viability.

Working with the business model canvas takes some practice. You have to be able to recognize different types of information quickly and sort them into their respective boxes. Once you get the hang of it, use the canvas to quickly discover alternatives. There are many resources online to learn more about the business model canvas.

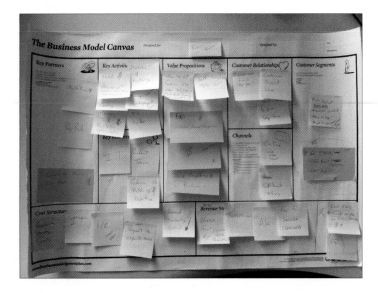

FIGURE 3-19. The business model canvas is well suited for using sticky notes to explore options.

Value Proposition Canvas

The basic grid structure of the business model canvas inspired the development of similar tools. One such example is the *value proposition canvas* (see Figure 3-20), also created by Alexander Osterwalder. It is directly related to the business model canvas and plugs into two business model elements: the *customer segments* you wish to create value for and the *value proposition* you believe will attract customers.

The value proposition canvas allows you to design and test the fit between what you offer and what customers want.

There are two parts. On the right is the customer profile with three components:

- *Jobs to be done.* These are the important issues people want solved and the needs they are trying to satisfy.

- *Pains.* These are the barriers, hurdles, and annoyances people have in trying to get a job done. This includes negative emotions and risks they may encounter.

- *Gains.* These are positive outcomes or benefits the individual desires.

The other half of the canvas on the left side details the three features of your value proposition.

Products and services

These represent your offering, including the features and support you provide.

Pain relievers

This is a description of how your offering will alleviate the customer's pains. These show which problems you're addressing.

Gain creators

These make explicit how your products and services benefit customers.

By mapping the left side to the right side, you can make explicit how you are creating value for your customers. When the pain relievers and gain creators correlate to the pains and gains of customers, you have a potential strong fit. Validate your assumptions with your markets once you have formed a clear position.

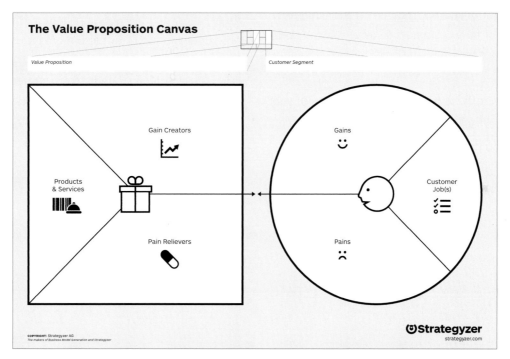

FIGURE 3-20. The value proposition canvas, created by Alexander Osterwalder and his company, Strategizer, complements the business model canvas.

Summary

As organizations mature, they develop *strategy myopia*—a failure to see the broader landscape of their business and how they can continue to create meaningful value. Successful enterprises start with insights about customer needs and work backward to their strategy. This reverses many existing practices in business that seek to push products and service through traditional sales channels.

To change, organizations need to consider additional sources of insight often left out of strategy creation. This includes a deep understanding of how customers perceive value. Visualizations of various kinds broaden your field of vision and offer a new way of seeing.

First, consider how to *reframe competition*. In the eyes of your customer, anything that gets the job done is your rival.

Also consider how you contribute back to society and *create shared value*. Shared value is about creating societal benefits with every customer interaction, going far beyond corporate social responsibility.

The Internet of Things forces us to *reimagine value delivery*. Connected, smart products inevitably become part of a larger ecosystem. The value you create is delivered and experienced as part of that context.

Finally, *organize to innovate*. First, separate protecting existing value from creating new value by setting up different divisions in the organization. Then, organize teams to align with the customer experience.

Visualizations tend to open up strategy, making it not only more understandable but also more inclusive across the organization. Several techniques help illustrate strategy graphically. These include strategy maps, strategy canvases, the strategy blueprint, and the business model canvas and value proposition canvas. They complement and extend alignment diagrams.

Further Reading

A.G. Lafley and Roger Martin. *Playing to Win: How Strategy Really Works* (2013)

> This book offers a clear framework for understanding strategy in general, based on five key questions. It is one of the most lucid and useful approaches to strategy available today. The authors provide case studies and examples from their decades of experience. This is essential reading for anyone looking to understand strategy.

W. Chan Kim and Renee Mauborgne. *Blue Ocean Strategy* (Harvard Business Review Press, 2005)

> This landmark book from the pioneers of blue ocean strategy explains the approach in detail. The key isn't to compete with rivals directly, the authors urge but rather to make them irrelevant. To do this, organizations need to find new attributes of value creation. Visualizing the landscape in a strategy canvas is a key way to identify opportunities of this kind. Many of the blue ocean strategy tools and resources are available on the Internet—for example, at *www.blueoceanstrategy.com*.

Rita McGrath. *The End of Competitive Advantage* (Harvard Business Review Press, 2013)

> Strategy is stuck, declares McGrath in this compelling book. Existing frameworks view strategy as achieving a sustainable competitive advantage. Instead, organizations need to develop a new set of practices based on transient competitive advantage. This entails not only constantly finding new value, but also ramping down existing offerings as they become exhausted. This is an eye-opening book that is accessible to non-business readers.

Alexander Osterwalder. *Business Model Generation* (Wiley, 2011)

> After researching business models for his thesis work, Osterwalder wrote this practical, inspiring book to accompany his business model canvas. This is a colorful, fully illustrated book that is accessible to anyone and a pleasure to read. Osterwalder highlights the importance of artifacts like personas and advocates design thinking throughout the book.

Michael Porter "What Is Strategy," *Harvard Business Review* (1996)

> This is one of the most cited articles on strategy. Though dense at times, strategy guru Michael Porter lays out a clear perspective on strategy. The crux of strategy, he explains, is making tradeoffs that differentiate one firm's offerings from another.

Diagram and Image Credits

Figure 3-1: Diagram re-created and adapted from a figure appearing in Ram Charan's book *What the Customer Wants You to Know*.

Figure 3-4: Excerpt of a diagram created by Jim Kalbach for LexisNexis.

Figure 3-5: Ecosystem map created by Sofia Hussain, appearing in her article. "Designing Digital Strategies, Part 2: Connected User Experiences," UX Booth (Jan 2015), used with permission. *http://www.uxbooth.com/articles/designing-digital-strategies-part-2-connected-user-experiences/*

Figure 3-8: Ecosystem map for Nike FuelBand created by Claro Partners (*www.claropartners.com*) from their free resource "A guide to succeeding in the Internet of Things" (*http://www.claropartners.com/IoTGuide/Guide-to-succeeding-in-the-IoT_Claro%20Partners.pdf*), used with permission.

Figure 3-11: Strategy map example created by Intrafocus Limited, UK (*www.intrafocus.com*), used with permission thanks to Clive Keyte.

Figure 3-12: Patagonia strategy map created by Michael Ensley of PureStone Partners, originally appearing on his blog post "Going Green": *http://purestonepartners.com/2009/06/17/going-green/*, used with permission.

Figure 3-13: Strategy canvas for Southwest Airlines, redrawn and adapted from Kim and Mauborgne.

Figure 3-16: Strategy blueprint created by Jim Kalbach.

Figure 3-17: Business model canvas, by Alexander Osterwalder, downloaded from *http://www.businessmodelgeneration.com/canvas/bmc*, Creative Commons share alike 3.0.

Figure 3-18: Example of a completed business model canvas comparing Xiameter to Dow Corning, created by Jim Kalbach. For more on this case study, see "Business Model Design: Disruption Case Study" (Sep 2011). *https://experiencinginformation.wordpress.com/tag/business-model-canvas/*

Figure 3-19: Photo of a business model canvas used in a workshop, by Jim Kalbach.

Figure 3-20: The value proposition canvas, created by Alexander Osterwalder and Strategizer, downloaded from *http://www.businessmodelgeneration.com/canvas/vpc*, used with permission.

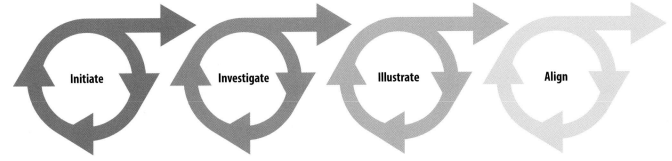

Initiate   Investigate   Illustrate   Align

ENVISION

PART 2
A General Process for Mapping

A general process for experience mapping consists of four iterative modes of activity:

Initiate: Chapter 4 deals with the details of setting up a mapping initiative.

Investigate: Alignment diagrams must be grounded in evidence. Techniques for research are detailed in Chapter 5.

Illustrate: Visually representing the value creation process between an individual and an organization is a core aspect of alignment mapping. Chapter 6 covers aspects of illustrating a diagram.

Align: Chapter 7 shows ways to use diagrams in an alignment workshop, as well as planning subsequent experiments.

The above process results in *current state maps*: depictions of experiences as you observe them today. The logical next step is to *envision future experiences*, outlined in Chapter 8. This chapter offers a collection of complementary techniques.

Note that this approach does not describe a process for design but rather the process of creating and using diagrams. It can apply to many existing fields of practice—service design, user experience design, and design thinking approaches alike.

Additionally, the duration of a formal effort might last for weeks or even months. But it may also only take days: mapping experiences can be lean, too. In either case, the aforementioned modes of working still apply.

Finally, be sure to involve stakeholders and team members *throughout* the process. Get their feedback on your initial proposal, include them in the investigation, co-create the diagram together, and come together for a workshop at the end of the effort. Don't make mapping a solitary effort.

Remember: diagrams won't provide solutions for you, but they foster conversations that do.

"The secret of getting ahead is getting started. The secret of getting started is breaking your complex overwhelming tasks into small manageable tasks, and starting on the first one."

— Mark Twain

IN THIS CHAPTER

- Identifying the need
- Convincing decision makers
- Determining the direction
- Creating a proposal

CHAPTER 4

Initiate: Starting a Mapping Project

One of the most common questions I get in my workshops on mapping is, "How do I begin?" Aspiring mapmakers may see the immediate value in these techniques, yet they have barriers getting started.

Getting stakeholder buy-in is a common challenge. I've been fortunate to have had opportunities to create diagrams of all kinds and have found that stakeholders see the value in mapping only after the process is complete. As a result, initiating an effort requires convincing them up front.

What's more, a mismatch of expectations early on can lead to problems later on. It's therefore crucial to frame your intent clearly from the outset, particularly when multiple stakeholders are involved. With the range of possibilities, it's up to you to define your mapping effort appropriately. Some key points to remember are:

Include others in the process

The mapmaker has different roles throughout the effort: researcher, interpreter, and facilitator. It's critical to get participation from others at all points in the process.

Remember: the objective is not just to create a diagram, but to engage others in conversations and develop solutions together as a team.

Consider both current and future states

This book focuses on creating what can be described as *current state* diagrams: visualizations of existing experiences. Envisioned future products, services, and solutions are generally seen as an added layer to these diagrams. I believe it is important to see both at once: cause and cure are visible simultaneously. Complementary techniques, however, help flesh out envisioned future experiences, some of which are discussed in Chapter 8.

Realize you can't control everything

Strive for coherency across the entire experience, but also understand that you won't be able to design every touchpoint. There may be interactions you can't or choose not to control. Still, an awareness of the interdependencies across actors and touchpoints informs your strategic decisions.

Start a mapping project as you would any other effort: determine your goals, scope, costs, and time frame, and make them explicit. This need not be lengthy or time consuming—it may only take a single meeting. But getting off on the right foot increases your chances of success.

This chapter details some of the pitfalls and lessons I've learned when initiating a mapping project. By the end of this chapter, you'll know what key questions to ask up front and how to get a mapping effort off the ground.

Start a New Project

With increasing frequency, managers and clients are directly requesting artifacts such as customer journey maps or experience maps by name. This makes getting started easier.

Without an educated audience, however, starting a mapping effort can prove difficult. Stakeholders may not be immediately aware of the benefits of mapping. It provides a type of insight that organizations need to know, but they don't realize they need to know it until they go through the process.

Before embarking on a project, first determine the level of formality, then convince the decision makers to get started.

Determine the Level of Formality

⚡ Every team can benefit from mapping in some form— from sketching by hand or working with detailed diagrams. The scope of the effort can vary greatly. Determine the level of formality that's most appropriate before beginning.

This book describes a *formal* approach to mapping. In some cases, such as an external consultant working with a large organization, a rigorous approach makes sense. In other situations, a full-blown process may be inappropriate. For instance, when you're working in a startup an *informal* approach is fine.

The formality of a mapping effort can be seen along three dimensions, shown in Figure 4-1.* The horizontal axis ranges from producing a single product to providing service ecosystems. The vertical axis indicates movement from the design of

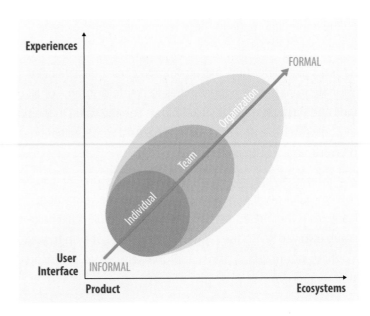

FIGURE 4-1. The need for models increases when entire organizations design experiences for ecosystems.

---

* This diagram is adapted from a talk by Hugh Dubberly: "A System Perspective on Design Practice," video talk at Carnegie Mellon (2012).

Remember: the objective is not just to create a diagram, but to engage others in conversations and develop solutions together as a team.

a discrete interface to the design of holistic experiences. The third dimension, in the middle of the graph, shows an increase in the group size.

Efforts tend to become more formal as you move up and to the right in this chart. For instance, a designer working alone on a single product may not need a formal diagram. But a large team dealing with an entire service ecosystem likely would. Consider where your organization falls on this chart.

Finally, the nature of the engagement also affects the level of formality. External consultants will be motivated to assume a more official approach. Teammates in a small startup, on the other hand, may map experiences more casually.

The point is to consider the appropriate level of formality before beginning. This will determine how much effort you put into each of the phases outlined in this book. Only do as much work as needed.

Convince Decision Makers

Once you determine the level of formality, convince decision makers to back your effort. Internal employees typically encounter different hurdles than external consultants. The former need to persuade; the latter need to sell.

Though your relationship to stakeholders may vary, many of the arguments are the same. To convince decision makers, know the objections, provide evidence, find a champion, and run a pilot to demonstrate the value. Also, create a pitch that you can recite at will.

Know the objections

If you get pushback, be ready with persuasive arguments. Table 4-1 lists some typical objections, the underlying error made, and potential counterpoints to make for each.

Provide evidence

Know the benefits of alignment diagrams outlined in Chapter 1. But also be able to provide convincing evidence to support your effort. For instance, find examples and case studies in the literature. Be able to point to those examples and integrate them into your discussion.

One such example is Forrester Research, a leading technology industry research company, that has been writing full reports on the benefits of customer journey mapping in particular. Locate their studies or similar reports that show strong evidence in favor of mapping.

Evidence on the return of investment is even more compelling. For instance, Alex Rawson and colleagues show concrete increases in revenue when companies design experiences end-to-end rather than optimizing individual touchpoints. In their article "The Truth About Customer Experience," they write:

Companies that excel in delivering journeys tend to win in the market. In two industries we've studied, insurance and pay TV, better performance on journeys corresponds to faster revenue growth: In measurements of customer satisfaction with the firms' most important journeys, performing one point better than peer companies on a 10-point scale corresponds to at least a two-percentage-point outperformance on revenue growth rate.

Objection	Error	Argument
We don't have time or budget.	Creating diagrams takes too long and is expensive.	Mapping needn't be expensive or time consuming. Even a formal project can be done in a few weeks for about the cost of a usability test or marketing survey.
Each department has its own process map.	Functional silos work efficiently individually.	Fine. But do they show interaction across channels and touchpoints? Great customer experiences cross our department lines.
We already know all of this.	Implicit knowledge is enough.	Great—then we're off to a good start. But by making that knowledge explicit we can keep the conversations going. Also, we don't lose insight when someone leaves. And if someone new joins the team, we can ramp them up quickly.
I was in that target group. Just ask me what's valuable.	Customers are viewed from an inside-out perspective rather than outside-in.	Your input will be invaluable to get an initial hypothesis. We want to supplement that with a grounded external perspective as well. That's where the best insights for growth and innovation are found.
Marketing already does research.	Marketing and experience research are the same.	That's a good thing, but not enough. We need to uncover unmet needs and unexpressed feelings and show them in the context of the overall experience.

TABLE 4-1. Typical concerns that may be posed before you get started, the error behind each objection and arguments you can make against them.

Mapping customer journeys, the authors conclude, provides the insight for the design of better experiences. This in turn contributes to revenue growth.

Finally, if possible, find out what competitors are doing. Search for competitors along with keywords like "customer journey map" or "experience map." Showing that others are doing this kind of work goes a long way in convincing decision makers.

Find a champion

Identify stakeholders who might best champion a mapping effort. The more influential, the better.

For external consultants, this may be a client with whom you have a longer, ongoing relationship. Internal employees need to know how to navigate decision making in their organization. In both cases a quick stakeholder analysis may help.

Run a pilot effort

If possible, run a small pilot project. Diagrams need not be complex or detailed to be effective.

Alternatively, try creating a diagram as part of another effort. For instance, if you are running a traditional usability test, add simple follow-up questions to elicit their steps in a given process. Map these together in a draft version of an experience map, and use that as a discussion point. Demonstrating value with first-hand results is often the most persuasive argument.

Create a pitch

Finally, create a succinct statement that you can readily recite. Include the business problems you'll address. Why should a decision maker invest in a mapping effort of any kind? Here's an example pitch:

> You'd like to grow beyond your current offerings. By mapping the entire experience, you'll have a better understanding of the needs and emotions of new markets and segments quickly.
>
> Mapping is a modern technique to improve customer understanding that more and more companies are using, such as Intel and Microsoft.
>
> By visually aligning various aspects of the customer experience with business processes, you'll be able to see how to best create and capture value across channels. It will also yield insight into innovative products and services that outperform competitors.
>
> With relatively little investment, mapping provides you with the strategic insight we need in today's fast-changing marketplaces.

Mapping customer journeys provides the insight for the design of better experiences. This in turn contributes to revenue growth.

Decide on a Direction

There are several questions to answer from the outset of a project. These may be a simple matter of self-reflection, or they may need investigation. The two key areas of concern to address are the organizational goals and the types of experiences you should map. After determining those, select the appropriate diagram to create.

Identify the Organization's Strategy and Objectives

Remember: alignment diagrams must be relevant to the organization. They need to answer open questions or fill current gaps in knowledge. Diagrams are most effective when congruent with the organization's strategy and objectives.

Some questions to explore in this step are:

- What is the mission of the organization?
- How does the organization create, deliver, and capture value?
- How does the organization want to grow?
- What are the strategic goals?
- What markets and segments are served?
- What are the gaps in knowledge?

Determine Which Experiences to Map

Most organizations have relationships with multiple parties: suppliers, distributors, partners, customers, and customers' customers. To determine what experiences to map, first understand the *customer value chain*: a depiction of key actors and the flow of value to individuals.

Figure 4-2 shows a simple example of a customer value chain for a news magazine. In this diagram, journalists provide content to publishers, who make money from advertisers. Stores distribute the publisher's magazine to readers, who form the

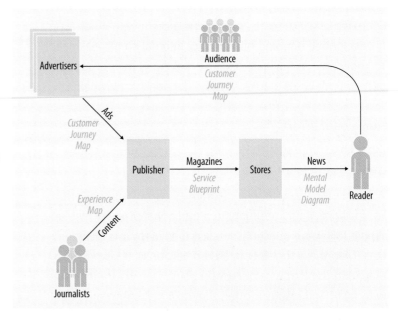

FIGURE 4-2. This example customer value chain for a news magazine shows the flow of value to end consumers.

audience for the advertisers. Overall, value flows from left to right in this diagram, from journalists to readers.

- Customer value chains are similar to what are also referred to as *stakeholder maps* or *ecosystem maps*. You may come across these terms in other sources on mapping. The difference here is the inclusion of the flow of value.

- There is no right or wrong way to create customer value chain diagrams. They are simple concept maps of the actors and entities involved in an experience. Ultimately, it's about coming up with a model the fits your purpose. The process is straightforward:

- List all actors and entities involved in the experience being investigated.

- Place the primary actor and primary provider in the center, with the provider to the left.

- Place other actors and entities around the two in a way that shows their basic relationships.

- Finally, reorder the elements as needed to show how value moves from providers to customers.

- Once completed, use the customer value chain map to examine various relationships that are possible to map. For instance, in Figure 4-3 the relationship of the advertiser to the publisher is unlike that of the publisher's relationship to the stores. And the relationship of the journalists to the advertisers is different from the readers to the store.

Alignment diagrams must be relevant to the organization. They need to answer open questions or fill current gaps in knowledge.

- A customer value chain helps set expectations with your clients. You can clarify which experiences to map and which to exclude. For instance, in the previous example, if the publisher is interested in learning more about the distribution of magazines to stores, and you were considering mapping the relationship of readers to advertisers, there's a mismatch in expectations.

- Customer value chains can generally be completed quickly—in a matter of minutes in some cases—and it's worth the effort to get a view of the ecosystem. This will help you scope the effort, select an appropriate diagram type, and also guide recruiting for research.

- Figure 4-3 also indicates some possible diagram types that might best illustrate the relationship. A *service blueprint* makes sense to map the relationship between the publishers and the stores to help optimize backstage processes. But a *customer journey map* might be better to illustrate the experience readers have with advertisers. And from the publisher's perspective, an *experience map* could be a good way to understand the journalist's relationship to the magazine's content.

Thomas Brauer

Architect, Partner
'I strive to use my expert knowledge of the architecture to lead successful client projects.'

Pain Points
- Maintaining a large network of professionals
- Travel to sites
- Managing many projects at once
- New business generation
- Keeping up on regulations

Background & Skills
- 42 years old, married, 2 children
- Practicing for 15 years
- Accredited building inspector

Company & Role
- Mid-size firm: 16 architects, 6 support staff
- Location in New York and Minneapolis
- Specializes in commercial property
- Oversees 3-5 projects at once
- Coordinates marketing activities for firm

Tools & Usage
- Professional drafting and architecture software
- Regularly work on-the-go with mobile devices
- Plotter and printers used frequently
- Maintains electronic and paper files and calendars
- Finds learning new programs and tools cumbersome

Motivations
- Building a successful business
- Looking good in front of clients
- Professional recognition in the industry
- Creating an attractive place of work for employees
- Growing talent from within the firm

Work Activities
- Managing projects and project teams (40%)
- Consult, communicate, present to clients (35%)
- New business development (15%)
- Manage marketing activities of firm (5%)
- Research and monitoring industry (5%)

Sources: 1.) Interviews 2.) Survey 3.) Monster.com

FIGURE 4-3. This example shows a persona for an architect.

Key questions when determining which experiences to map are:

- Which relationships in the customer value chain do you want to focus on?
- What point of view do you want to understand in that relationship?
- Which types of users or customers are most relevant?
- Which experiences are most appropriate to include?
- Where do those experiences begin and end?

Create Personas

Personas are narrative descriptions of user archetypes reflecting common patterns of behavior, needs, and emotions. They reflect details about a target group in a way that is easy to grasp.

Personas are generally short—not longer than a page or two each. Figure 4-3 shows an example of a persona document I created for a past project.

When you're illustrating a specific person's experience, it's common to include the persona or a shortened form of it on a diagram itself. For instance, Figure 4-4 shows a customer journey map created by Jim Tincher, founder of the Heart of the Customer, a consultancy specializing in journey mapping. In this example, you can see the persona of Passive Pat along the top of the diagram. It reflects basic demographic information, motivations, and a quote Pat might say.

Creating personas is not creative writing. Personas should be based on actual data. The process consists of the following steps.

1. Identify the most salient attributes that distinguish one segment from another. You can usually find three to five primary attributes to focus on.

2. Determine the number of personas that you need to represent the range of attributes included. Collect data that supports and describes those attributes. Of course, your investigation may reveal new attributes to include along the way.

3. Draft the personas based on the primary attributes. Also include some basic aspects to flesh out the persona such as demographics, behaviors, motivations, and pain points.

4. Finalize the persona. Create a compelling visualization of the persona on a single page. Develop various formats and sizes for different contexts.

5. Make the personas visible. Hang them up in brainstorming sessions and include them in project documents. It's your job to make them come alive.

6. Of course, creating personas is also a collaborative process. Include others so that the resulting documents are reminders of shared knowledge.

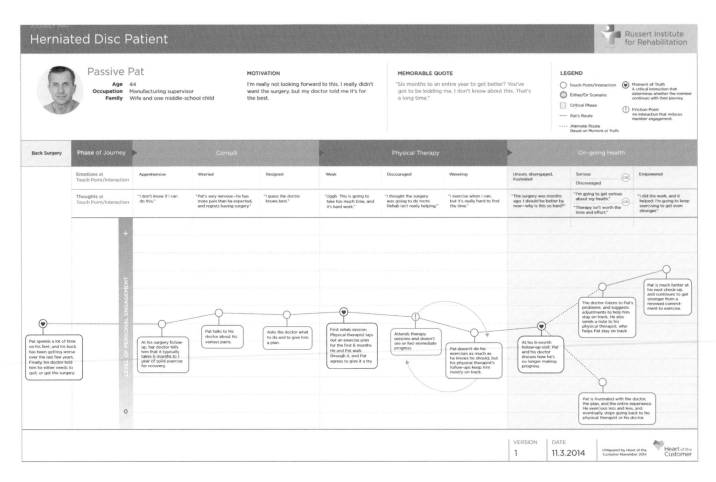

FIGURE 4-4. Diagrams often represent a persona at the top, as seen in this example of a customer journey map.

Proto-personas

⚡ Creating formal personas can be a lengthy endeavor. If you don't have existing personas or the scope to create them, rely on *proto-personas,* a term coined by Jeff Gothelf, author of *Lean UX*. He describes them as follows:

> *Proto-personas are a variant of the typical persona, with the important difference that they are not initially the result of user research. Instead, they originate from brainstorming workshops where company participants try to encapsulate the organization's beliefs (based on their domain expertise and gut feeling) about who is using their product or service and what is motivating them to do so.**

Proto-personas are lightweight representations of actors in the value chain that don't require you to go through a costly research process. They are depictions of who you believe your target audience is, based on what you know today. They are also sometimes referred to as *assumption personas* or *provisional personas.*

Proto-personas can be created on a simple grid with four squares, as shown in Figure 4-5. There are four main elements:

Name and sketch
Pick a name that is memorable and include a sketch of what the person might look like or find an image representing them.

Demographic and psychographic details
Include only those factors that are relevant to the subject at hand.

Behaviors and actions
Briefly indicate the key behaviors the person takes in the field you're focused on.

Needs and pain points
Indicate what the person needs and what difficulties he or she encounters.

The proto-persona gives the team an easy way to refer to the individuals involved in the mapping effort early on. Instead of saying *reader*, you can refer to *Mary*, for instance. Fully fledged personas can then be created later as the project unfolds, if needed, after you've completed more in-depth research.

---

* Jeff Gothelf. "Using Proto-Personas for Executive Alignment," *UX Magazine* (May 2012).

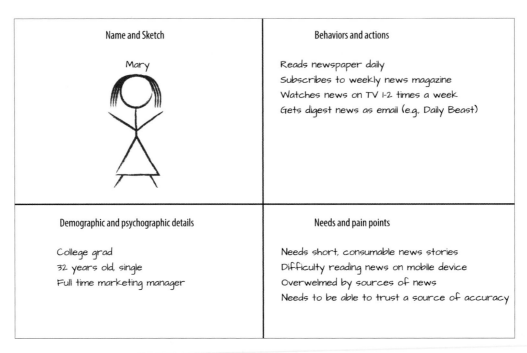

Name and Sketch	Behaviors and actions
Mary	Reads newspaper daily Subscribes to weekly news magazine Watches news on TV 1-2 times a week Gets digest news as email (e.g. Daily Beast)
Demographic and psychographic details College grad 32 years old, single Full time marketing manager	Needs and pain points Needs short, consumable news stories Difficulty reading news on mobile device Overwelmed by sources of news Needs to be able to trust a source of accuracy

FIGURE 4-5. The template for creating quick proto-personas is simple. Use it to represent the actors in the customer value chain you'll be targeting.

Select Diagram Type

The diagrams included in this book have a similarity: they all focus on value alignment. But recognizing the differences between them allows you to apply an approach that makes the most sense for your situation. Don't rule out any one technique over another *a priori*.

After understanding the organization's objectives and the experiences you want to map, select the type of diagram that's most appropriate. To do so, consider the primary elements of mapping discussed in Chapter 2.

Table 4-2 summarizes some of the common diagram types and the differences between them along these dimensions.

Type	Point of view	Scope	Focus	Structure	Uses
Service blueprint	Individual as the recipient of service	Concentrated on service encounters and ecosystems, frequently in real time	Real-time actions, physical evidence across channels Emphasis on service provision, including roles, backstage actors, processes, workflows	Chronological	Front-line personnel, internal teams, and managers to improve an existing service or brainstorm new ones
Customer journey map	Individual as a loyal customer, often making purchase decision	Usually from becoming aware, through purchasing, to leaving a company and returning	Emphasis on cognitive and emotional states of the individual, including moments of truth and satisfaction	Chronological	Used by marketing, PR, sales, account management, customer support, brand managers for optimizing sales, customer relations, and brand equity
Experience map	Individual as an actor behaving in the context of a broader activity	Beginning and end by definition, given by the specific experience or context	Emphasis on behaviors, goals, and jobs to be done Typically includes actions, thoughts, feelings, pain points	Chronological	Product managers, designers, developers, strategists; used for product and service design improvements, innovation
Mental model diagram	Individual as a thinking and feeling human within a given domain	Breadth of experience by definition, emerges from the data	Emphasis on fundamental motivations, feelings, and philosophies	Hierarchical	Product managers, designers, developers, strategists; used to gain empathy for individuals; inform product and service strategy and innovation
Spatial map	Individual as part of a multifaceted system of interaction	Given by the size, capabilities, and constituents of an organization	Highlights the flow of information and relationships between various aspects and components of a system	Spatial	Useful to managers, content specialists, employees to understand the flow of information for optimization and process innovation

TABLE 4-2. A comparison of different diagram types along the various elements of diagrams.

How Many Diagrams Are Needed?

People often ask me how many diagrams they should create. To some degree this depends on how you've framed the effort. There is no clear-cut answer.

A diagram of the entire experience may not reflect a single persona's experience, but rather aggregate all possible experiences in one map. To show the detail of someone's individual journey, on the other hand, you'll need a separate diagram for each target segment. Refer to the customer value chain and determine the difference in relationships you're mapping.

For instance, eBay may target two distinct experiences: those of buyers and those of sellers. One approach to mapping would be to create separate diagrams for each. It's possible to illustrate separate experiences as two interlocking experiences, as shown in Figure 4-6.

If the scope of your effort, however, focuses on sellers only, you may still need to consider different types of experiences. For instance, casual sellers on eBay have significantly different experiences than professional sellers. Two different diagrams are probably needed in this case.

In the end, it really depends on the factors detailed in Chapter 2: point of view, scope, focus, structure, and use. Generally there's a desire to reduce your effort as well as the number of artifacts you create. So, I advise creating multiple diagrams only if necessary to illustrate significant differences.

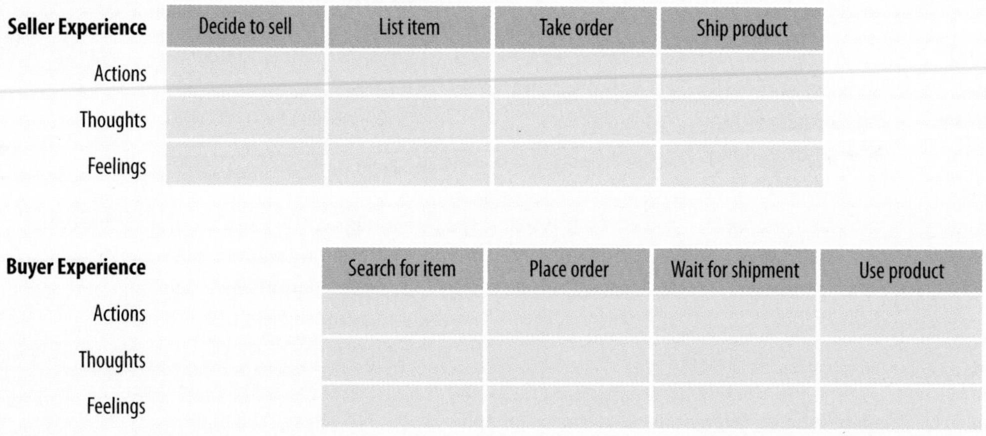

Seller Experience	Decide to sell	List item	Take order	Ship product
Actions				
Thoughts				
Feelings				

Buyer Experience	Search for item	Place order	Wait for shipment	Use product
Actions				
Thoughts				
Feelings				

FIGURE 4-6. It's possible to align different experiences that overlap in two separate maps within a single document.

What's the Difference? Customer Journey Maps, Experience Maps, and Service Blueprints

The types of diagrams most often conflated are *customer journey maps*, *experience maps*, and *service blueprints*. These are all chronological maps, so the mix-up is understandable: they have a similar form and similar use. But there are distinctions between these commonly used diagrams.

A key difference is the point of view and the relationship of individuals to the organization.

Customer journey maps typically view the individual as a customer of the organization. There is often a decision involved: to purchase a product or service and become a loyal customer. Service blueprints view how a service—usually a real-time encounter—is experienced by a customer. Both diagrams seek to show how the customer fits into the services provided by the organization. Experience maps, on the other hand, look at a broader context of human behavior. They reverse the relationship and show how the organization fits into a person's life.

Breadth and depth vary for each as well, providing a different focus. Figure 4-7 shows a skeleton for a generic chronological map. The chevrons at the top show phases of interaction. The top half represents a description of the individual's experience, and the bottom represents the service an organization provides. In the middle are touchpoints.

Customer journey maps tend to focus on the experiential side of the equation, with only a brief description of the service provision processes. Service blueprints focus on the backstage processes. An experience map focuses on the broad customer experience but could also include detailed descriptions of the organization's actors and processes.

Contrasting examples of each are shown in the following three figures to illustrate these differences. Figure 4-8 shows a customer journey map created by Macadamian, a full-service software and design firm. The rows in the center of this map clearly focus on the positive and negative experiences of the individual as a customer of the organization. There is a decision point in the middle of the journey.

The next example (Figure 4-9) is an experience map for pregnancy. This was created by Beth Kyle, a Senior Technical Analyst at Cornerstone Information Systems, during her graduate work in Human-Computer Interaction at Indiana University.

The focus here is on human experience, not on a particular company or business. There is no purchase decision or point of purchase. The organization in this case is not explicitly represented, but implied. As a result, multiple organizations could benefit from this diagram, such as a doctor's office or a pregnancy planning service.

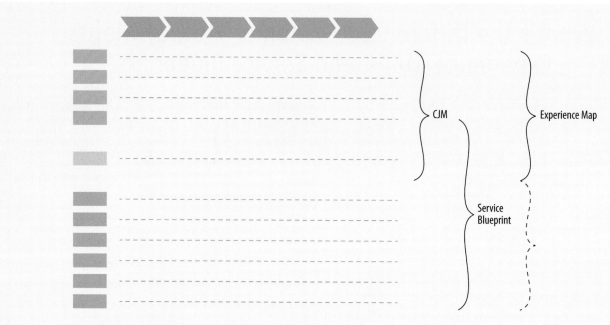

FIGURE 4-7. Depth and breadth differ across diagram types.

Service blueprints tend to focus on real-time interactions. They typically show more detail of the backstage service provision mechanisms and lack depth in describing the person's experience. Figure 4-10 shows an example of a service blueprint created by Mary Jo Bitner and colleagues from their landmark article "Service Blueprinting: A Practical Technique for Service Innovation."

Understand the nature of the diagram type you are targeting before beginning an effort. But don't get hung up on labels—they are less important at the end of the day. Instead, focus on how you'll show value alignment visually to engage others in your organization in a conversation.

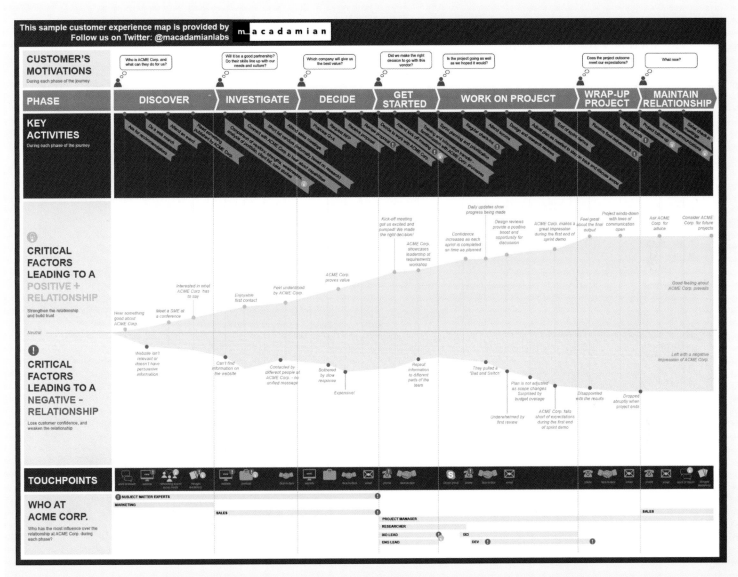

FIGURE 4-8. This customer journey map for a fictitious company, "Acme Corp," focuses on positive and negative emotions.

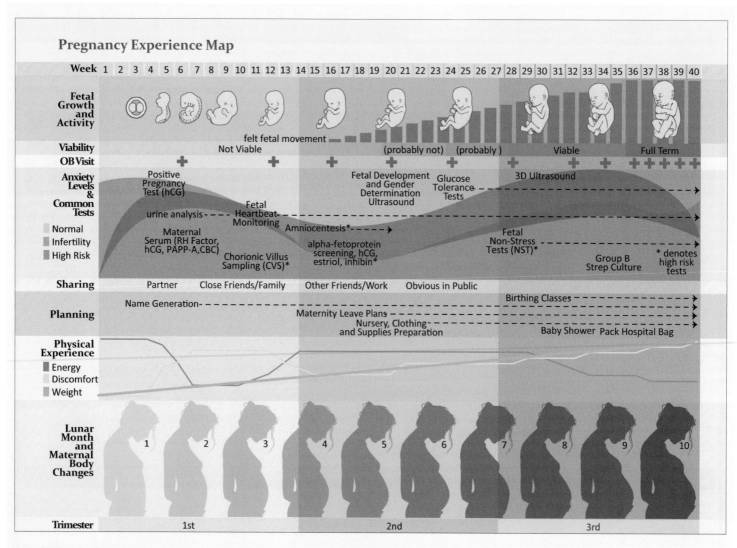

FIGURE 4-9. This pregnancy experience map created by Beth Kyle focuses on a human experience.

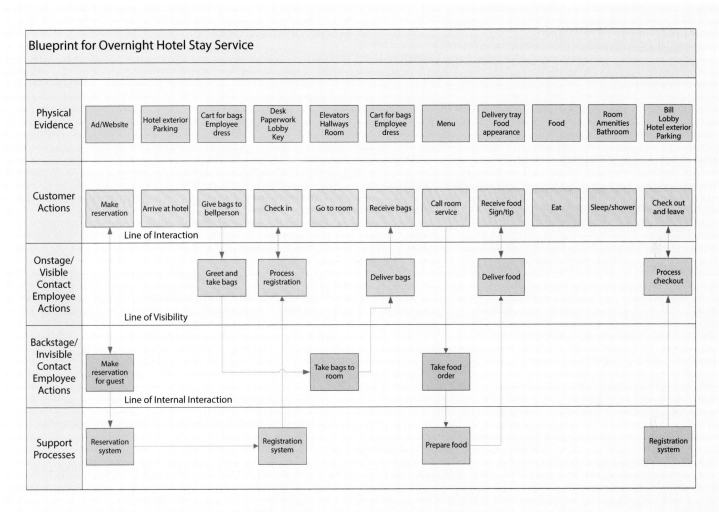

FIGURE 4-10. This service blueprint for an overnight hotel stay was created by Mary Jo Bitner and colleagues.

Define the Effort

Once the overall direction of the effort is outlined, assess the amount of time needed and approximate costs. In this step you'll also want to ensure you have the appropriate skills, equipment, and resources.

Estimate Duration

The time frame for mapping efforts varies greatly. It depends on the formality of the project, type of map you're targeting, and the depth of information it contains. Small startups, for instance, may be able to quickly create a map in a matter of days. Formal projects typically run anywhere from a few weeks to a few months in duration.

Below are some relative time frames of various types of efforts to give a rough sense of durations.

- Rapid effort: one to two days
- Short, full project: one to two weeks
- Average initiative: three to six weeks
- Generous program: more than six weeks

The time estimate is primarily a factor of the extent of your investigation, as well as how many revision cycles and meetings with stakeholders are needed.

> *Don't rule out any one technique over another a priori.*

Assess Resources

The primary resource needed for a mapping effort is staff time: someone to do the investigation, create a diagram, and facilitate workshops.

Skills needed to complete a diagram include:

- The ability to organize a wealth of information and abstract concepts
- The ability to collect data and conduct primary research
- The ability to model and visualize complex information

Other project requirements include:

- *Access to internal employees.* You will need access to internal members of the organization. Multidisciplinary teams are ideal. Diagrams are not a give-and-go deliverable: they necessarily involve people within the organization throughout the process. Their active participation is required.

- *Ability to recruit customers.* You will need the ability to recruit external participants in your research activities (as outlined in Chapter 5).

- *Ability to travel.* Depending on your industry and location of target groups, some travel may be necessary for research.

- *Transcription service.* Finally, depending on your research approach, you may want to record interviews with participants and have them transcribed.

Estimate Costs

Costs can vary greatly. Table 4-3 shows high and low estimates for an alignment project. The main driver is the staff month estimate. This will vary depending on your resource cost per month. The high estimate assumes one person working two full months. The low estimate assumes a person completing the project in two weeks.

	HIGH	LOW
Staff Month	2 × $15,000 = $30,000	.5 × $15,000 = $7,500
Incentives	10 × $50 = $500	6 × $25 = $150
Transcriptions	10 × $150 = $1500	None
Travel	$500	None
TOTAL	$32,500	$7,650

TABLE 4-3. Example of high and low cost estimates for an alignment project. Figures can vary greatly in both directions, depending primarily on the cost of a staff month.

Of course it's also possible to have larger or smaller efforts. These estimates are just median guidelines to give a sense of approximate cost ranges.

Write a Proposal

Informal efforts may not require a proposal at all. Formal projects will likely have a written statement of intent. Don't be put off. A proposal need not be time consuming or extensive. Keep it light by simply listing responses to each of these elements:

- *Motivation.* Include the reason why you're embarking on the project with the organization at this time.
- *Aim.* Include a statement about the aim of the effort and the overall timeline.
- *Goals.* List the objectives and measurable outcomes of the project.
- *Project participants.* List everyone involved and their roles. Mention that you will need access to internal stakeholders and their involvement throughout.
- *Activities, deliverables, and milestones.* Describe the sequence of activities and the expected outputs.
- *Scope.* Indicate the experiences you're intending to map. You can determine these from the customer value chain, like the one shown in Figure 4-3.
- *Diagram type.* If you have a target diagram type in mind, indicate that in the proposal.
- *Assumptions, risks, and constraints.* Highlight aspects of the project that may be out of your control, as well as the factors that may constrain the effort.

In total, a proposal doesn't have to be more than two pages. See an example in Figure 4-11.

Proposal: Acme Customer Experience Project

The Acme Corp. has successfully extended its product and service offerings over the past decade, capturing a significant market share in the process. However, the experience customers actually have with Acme has grown organically and become disjointed, resulting in declining customer satisfaction. This effort intends to align internal activities to the customer journey in order to design a more cohesive experience across touchpoints and ultimately increase customer satisfaction and loyalty.

AIM

Complete a customer journey mapping project by the end of Q1

GOALS

1. Involve stakeholders from at least 5 different departments throughout the project, from the creation of the maps to running experiments afterwards.
2. Generate and prioritze at least 100 new ideas to increase customer satisfaction.
3. Develop action plans and experiments to test 5 new services that demonstrate an increase in customer satisfaction.
4. Increase customer satisfaction scores by 5% by the end of the year.

PARTICIPANTS

- Core Project Team
  - Jim Kalbach, Project Lead
  - Paul Kahn, Designer
  - Jane Doe, User Researcher
  - John Doe, Project Sponsor
- Stakeholders
  - Sue Smith, Head of Product Development (+product developers)
  - Joe Smith, Customer Support (+customer support agents)
  - Frank Musterman, Marketing Lead (+marketers)
  - Sales and ecommerce representatives, TBD

ACTIVITIES

- Investigate: Recruit and research, internal and external participants
- Illustrate: Create customer journey map
- Align: Hold workshop and generate hypotheses
- Experiment: Run experiments to test hypotheses

DELIVERABLES

- Customer Journey Maps
- Accompanying documents, such as personas and typical day illustrations
- Catalog of prioritized ideas
- Detailed plan for experiments, included measurements of success

SCOPE

- This effort will focus on two customer personas:
  1. Our current paying customers
  2. Their customers (i.e., customers of our customers)
- The experiences should look at touchpoints from end-to-end, starting with the first contact customers have until when they decide to end the service.
- 5 hypothesis experiments with the given resources (to be confirmed depending on the nature and scope of the experiments)

MILESTONES

- Jan: Recruiting and research
- Feb: Complete journey maps and run workshops
- March: Conduct experiments to increase customer satisfaction

FIGURE 4-11. A proposal for a mapping project does not have to be long.

Summary

Initiating a mapping project begins by framing the effort. Start by assessing the required level of formality. Generally, larger organizations striving to design holistic experiences across a system of touchpoints have a greater need for a formal effort than an individual person designing the interface of a single product.

Both internal employees and external consultants may need to overcome potential barriers to get started. Know the objections and be prepared with evidence to make convincing counterarguments. Also, identify a champion to pilot a project with. Demonstrating first-hand results goes a long way toward winning over others.

The concept of alignment diagrams opens up possibilities for you: there is more than one way to address a given problem. You'll need to understand the organization and its goals to shape the effort in the way that has the most impact.

It's up to you to determine which experiences to map. Examine various relationships in the *customer value chain* to narrow down possibilities and set the right expectations. Then select the diagram type that is most appropriate. Again, there are no right or wrong answers here. You'll have to form a perspective that works best for your situation.

For formal efforts, define the project and summarize it in a written proposal. This should include motivations, goals, participants, resources, and approximate costs of the project. Be prepared to negotiate the details of the proposal with stakeholders to arrive at an appropriate, well-defined effort. Informal efforts may not require a proposal or much documentation at all.

Further Reading

Tim Brown. *Change by Design* (Harper, 2009)

> This full-length book is the definitive work on design thinking. Based on years of experience at IDEO, one of the most innovative companies in the world, Brown lays out an argument in favor of design thinking in detail. The theories are grounded in stories and case studies from the field. Though mapping plays only a minor role in the book at best, it advocates a change in organizational perspective—one that favors empathy for users and a general outside-in philosophy core to alignment diagrams.

Ram Charan. *What the Customer Wants You to Know* (Portfolio, 2007)

> Ram Charan is a highly acclaimed business leader, having worked with top executives at Fortune 100 companies. He is able to make business concepts very accessible. This book discusses value creation from the customer's perspective in detail, including specific aspects such as customer value chains.

Forrester Research. *www.forrester.com*

> Forrester has been researching and publishing reports about customer experience and journey mapping for nearly a decade. To find reports, search their website for "customer journey" and "customer journey mapping" or similar terms. Be warned: these are expensive, with each report costing hundreds of dollars or more.

Alex Rawson, Ewan Duncan, and Conor Jones. "The Truth About Customer Experience." *Harvard Business Review* (Sep 2013)

> This is an excellent article on the value of end-to-end experience design, appearing in a leading business magazine. The authors mention mapping activities only briefly and provide no details on how to create them. They do, however, provide hard evidence on the positive effects of end-to-end experience design on the bottom line. Citing articles like this one can help convince stakeholders to embark on a mapping project.

Diagram and Image Credits

Figure 4-3: Example persona, created by Jim Kalbach.

Figure 4-4: Customer journey map created by Jim Tincher of the Heart of the Customer (*www.heartofthecustomer.com*), used with permission.

Figure 4-8: Customer journey map created by Macadamian (*www.macadamian.com*), used with permission.

Figure 4-9: Experience map created by Beth Kyle, a Senior Technical Analyst at Cornerstone Information Systems, during her graduate work in Human-Computer Interaction at Indiana University, used with permission.

Figure 4-10: Service blueprint created by Mary Jo Bitner and colleagues, originally appearing in: Bitner, Mary Jo, Amy L. Ostrom, and Felicia N. Morgan. "Service Blueprinting: A Practical Technique for Service Innovation," Working Paper, Center for Leadership Services, Arizona State University (2007). *http://files.g51studio.com/parsons/ServiceBlueprinting.pdf*

"You can observe a lot just by watching."

— Yogi Berra

IN THIS CHAPTER

- Reviewing existing information
- Interviewing internally
- Creating a draft map
- Contextual inquiry and analysis
- Quantitative research
- Case Study: Music Curation: User Research and Diagramming at Sonos

CHAPTER 5

Investigate: Researching the Experience

I'm often stunned by how little some organizations know about the people they serve. Sure, they may have detailed demographic data and comprehensive purchasing statistics and the like. But they fail to understand the fundamental needs and motivations of their customers.

Part of the problem is that people's behaviors are often irrational. They act on emotions and subjective beliefs. These are harder to understand and quantify, and are generally not part of the business vernacular.

I've come across many organizations with low appetites for understanding the customer experience. These same organizations might be willing to spend tens of thousands on market analysis reports. But getting out, speaking with customers, and observing them directly receives little funding.

It's not just a matter of money. I've worked with plenty of companies that simply avoid in-depth investigations of the customer experience. Uncovering deep emotional connections to products and services is a messy endeavor. Instead, they focus on things like operational efficiency and short-term gains.

Creating diagrams of experiences breaks this pattern of organizational navel gazing. It shifts the mindset from inside-out to outside-in. Of course, the diagrams themselves don't create empathy, but they spark and guide the conversations that do.

It all begins with investigation. Research is necessary to inform and provide confidence. Otherwise, conclusions and decisions are made based on conjecture.

What's more, research into the customer experience is typically eye-opening. There's a healthy reality check for everyone involved. I tend to uncover insights that the organization didn't know about or even suspect.

For instance, on one project for an educational testing service, my research team found several educators doing extra calculations with spreadsheets and sometimes even by hand on paper. Adding a mechanism to do these online was simple, but no one was aware of this need until we observed it. It wasn't something users ever complained about or asked for: they just accepted the system the way it was.

People use products and services in unintended ways. They find hacks and workarounds. They invent novel uses and applications of the offering. In doing so, they may fabricate their own satisfaction.

Peter Drucker, the renowned "father" of modern management, famously wrote:

> The customer rarely buys what the company thinks it sells him. One reason for this is, of course, that nobody pays for a "product." What is paid for is satisfaction.

Strive to uncover the value customers *believe* they are getting. Understanding how your offering gets their jobs done is a source of opportunity. Target your solutions to fulfill unmet needs.

This chapter covers the five main steps of investigation in an alignment diagram project.

1. Reviewing existing sources of information
2. Interviewing internal stakeholders
3. Creating a draft map
4. Conducting research externally
5. Analyzing the data

Creating diagrams of experiences breaks this pattern of organizational navel gazing. It shifts the mindset from inside-out to outside-in.

The steps outlined in this chapter present a logical sequence to follow. You may find yourself moving back and forth between these activities fluidly. The process is typically more iterative than linear.

Note also that some specific techniques, such as the methods for creating a mental model diagram, may start with external user research as well. The order of activities in the process outlined in this chapter is descriptive rather than prescriptive.

Survey Existing Sources

Take advantage of existing sources of information as a starting point. Begin by reviewing insight for patterns across various resource types, such as:

Direct feedback
: People typically can contact an organization in a variety of ways: via phone, email, contact forms, online comments, face-to-face service encounters, and chat. Obtain a sample of data for review—for instance, customer emails or call center logs for the past month.

Social media
: Get a sense of what people are saying in social media channels about your organization and about your service. Obtain a cross section of posts that refer to your organization on sites like Facebook and Twitter.

Reviews and ratings

Tap into reviews and ratings for relevant insight. Amazon.com is famous for their reviews and ratings; so are services like TripAdvisor.com for travel and Yelp.com for restaurants. Even comments and ratings in the Apple App Store can be a source of insight.

Market research

Many organizations regularly conduct surveys, questionnaires, and focus groups—details that could inform your effort.

User testing

If your organization has performed tests in the past, review them for insight into the overall experience they are having.

Industry reports and whitepapers

Depending on the industry you are working in, there may be reports available from analysts in the field.

Consolidate Findings

You probably won't find a single, existing source of information about an end-to-end customer experience. Most industry reports and whitepapers focus only on slices of an overall experience. And unless your organization has already done work mapping experiences, it's unlikely you'll have any preexisting research in house.

Instead, you'll have to pick through and identify the relevant bits. This is a bottom-up process that takes patience and tolerance for irrelevant information. An industry report, for instance, may only include a few facts useful for your particular project.

To help comb through existing data, use a common format to review findings across source types. Organize user research findings using a simple progression of three steps—*evidence*, *interpretation*, and *implications* for the experience:

Evidence

First, note any relevant facts or observations from the sources of information without any judgment. Include direct quotes and data points to illuminate the evidence.

Interpretations

Explain potential causes for the evidence you identified: why did people behave or feel the way they did? Consider multiple interpretations of the observed behavior.

Implications for the experience

Finally, determine the impact of the finding on the individual's experience. Strive to include the emotional factors motivating their behavior.

For each source, consolidate insights in a separate table. Table 5-1 shows this type of consolidation from two different source types for a fictitious software service.

The consolidation tables help sort through various information types. They then normalize findings for comparison across sources.

Evidence	Interpretations	Experience implications
Many emails indicate trouble with installation, e.g.: *"After going through the instructions and process several times, I gave up."* – Trial customer	People lack the skills and knowledge to complete the installation process and get frustrated. People don't have the time or patience to read the instructions carefully.	Installation is a problematic phase in the journey.
There were frequent questions about having admin rights to install the software, e.g.: *"I got the message 'Please contact your IT admin' and didn't know what to do."*	For security reasons, many companies don't allow employees to install software. It may be difficult or time consuming for employees to contact an IT admin.	For users without admin rights, installation ends their experience: it's a showstopper.
Some emails praised customer support, e.g.: *"The customer service agent I spoke with was really knowledgeable and helpful!"*	People like to be able to speak with a "real" person. People feel like they are getting personal attention with live agents.	Customer support is a positive aspect of the current experience.

Source 2: Marketing survey

Evidence	Interpretations	Experience implications
Respondents indicated that the top ways of becoming aware of the magazine are: 1. Word of mouth (62%) 2. Web searches (48%) 3. Internet ads (19%) 4. TV ads (7%)	Customers seek input from others in their decision to purchase our software. Advertisements may not be as effective as previously assumed.	Word of mouth plays the greatest role in becoming aware of our service.
64% of customers indicated they regularly switch between a computer and mobile while using our service.	People have a need to use the software on-the-go.	Customers experience our software across devices.
A majority of customers indicated installation was difficult or very difficult.	Installation is not straightforward for some users. Instructions for installation are not easy to follow.	Installation is a source of frustration.

TABLE 5-1. Examples of consolidation of two different existing sources of information for a fictitious software service

Make Conclusions

Next, collect all the implications for the experience in a separate list. Then group these by topic. Patterns then emerge that bring your investigation into greater focus. For instance, from the tables in Table 5-1, the implication statements are shown in the simple list that follows.

- Installation is a problematic phase in the journey.
- For users without admin rights, installation ends their experience: it's a showstopper.
- Customer support is a positive aspect of the overall experience.
- Word of mouth plays the greatest role in becoming aware of our service.
- Customers experience our software across devices.
- Installation is a source of frustration.

Some of your findings from this exercise will be straightforward and not need much validation. For instance, you may find that the ways in which people become aware of a service may not need much further research. From the example in Table 5-1, you could conclude that word of mouth is the leading way people hear about your service. If you are creating a customer journey map, you can readily include this information in the diagram.

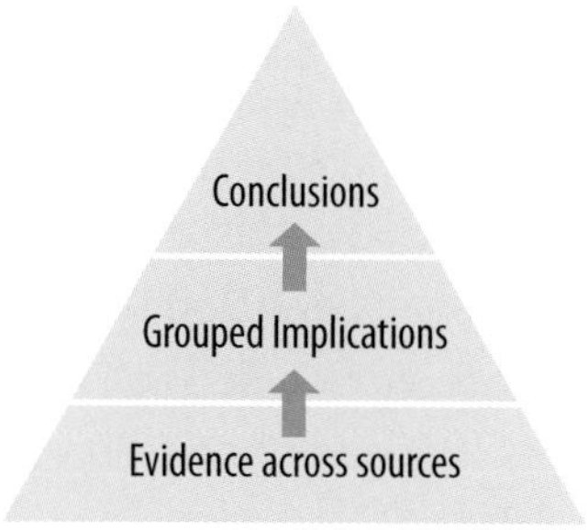

Other points you uncover may reveal gaps in knowledge. For example, from the list of implications in Table 5-1, it's apparent that frustration during installation is already emerging as a theme. But you may not know *why* this is the case. You may need to research the causes of this frustration further.

Overall, the process is grounded in evidence, moving from individual facts to broader conclusions (Figure 5-1). By breaking down findings in a common format, you can then compare themes across different sources.

FIGURE 5-1. Comb existing sources for relevant evidence, group the implications on the experience people may have, and make conclusions.

Reviewing existing sources of information not only informs the creation of a diagram, it also sets up your research agenda for the following steps in this investigation phase. You'll have a better sense about what to ask in your next phases of research, starting with internal stakeholders.

⚡ This step need not take long. Depending on the number of sources to review, it may only take a day or less to complete. Try distributing the review of sources across several members to work even quicker. Then come together and discuss the key findings in a brief meeting.

Interview Within the Organization

Alignment diagram efforts necessarily involve investigation with people within the organization. Seek out a range of people to interview. Don't stop with the primary sponsors of the project. Include decision makers, managers, sales representatives, engineers and technicians, and frontline personnel.

At this point, your investigation is exploratory: you want to uncover the main themes to research further. The sample of people you have access to may be fairly small—only a half dozen or so in total. This also means you may only get one or two people to interview per function within the organization. If this is the case, assume your interview partner can speak on behalf of others in a similar function.

Conduct Interviews

Internal stakeholder interviews can be informal and take anywhere from 30 to 60 minutes. If many of them work in the same location, it may only take a day to complete them. Phone interviews are also possible if you can't get with everyone face-to-face.

Open questioning works best since you'll be talking with different types of people. This is a technique that allows you to have a free-flowing conversation. Your interviews should not be a questionnaire but rather guided discussions with participants. The goal is to explore and learn, not to take a quantitative poll. See the sidebar, "A Brief Guide to Interviewing,"

for more on interviewing qualitatively with open questioning. There are three key areas to include:

Role and function

Start by getting the background of the participant. What do they do within the organization? How is their team organized? Get a sense of where they fit into the value creation chain.

Touchpoints

Everyone in an organization has some impact on the experience people have when interacting with them. In some cases, stakeholders have direct contact with customers. In this case, ask them directly about their perspective on the customer experience. Others may only have indirect contact. Either way, probe to understand their role in the user experience and the touchpoints most relevant to them.

Experience

Find out what participants *think* people experience when interacting with the organization. Start by understanding the flow of actions: What do customers do first? What happens after that? Also probe on how the participant *believes* customers feel along the way. When are they most frustrated? What delights them? When are potential moments of truth? Keep in mind their understanding may not match what customers actually experience. At this point, your investigation will generate assumptions that need to be validated with subsequent field research.

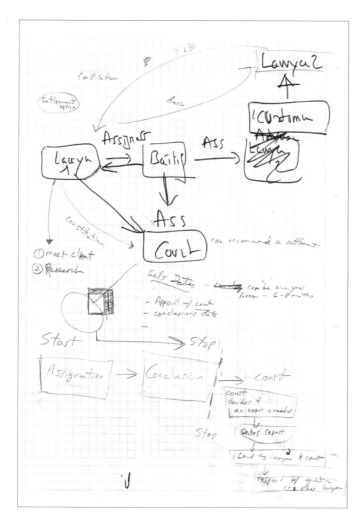

FIGURE 5-2. Have participants sketch during stakeholder interviews.

Ask participants to draw a diagram of the experience or parts of it as they describe it. Figure 5-2 shows an example of such a diagram from my own work. The sketch evolved over the course of the conversation, and allowed us to point to specific parts of the experience and dig deeper. This drawing then served as a basis for creating a diagram.

Alternatively, try using a template to have a guided conversation about the user experience. For instance, Figure 5-3 shows a PDF template created by John Kembel at Designing CX (*www.designingcx.com*). It outlines a generic customer journey.

⚡ Present a template to your interview partners and have them fill it in. This allows you to collaboratively understand the experience from end to end very quickly. This visual aid guides the conversation and keeps participants engaged. To conclude, ask participants if you can contact them again with follow-up questions. This is usually not a problem with internal stakeholders.

FIGURE 5-3. A simple mapping template can be used to gather existing knowledge about an experience.

Create a Draft Diagram

At this point you should be able to draft an initial diagram. This serves as a preliminary hypothesis of the experience. At a high level, consider some of the basics of creating a map discussed in Chapter 2: the point of view, scope, focus, and structure.

The draft diagram will guide future research. From it, you should be able to identify key research questions. At a minimum, a draft map will also help organize your thoughts.

Include others in the creation of a draft map. Assemble a small group of stakeholders to create a model of the experience together. The goal is not to analyze the experience and add data points. Instead, get agreement on the underlying model of the experience.

Use sticky notes to work out a preliminary structure of the diagram together. You should end up with something similar to the diagram shown in Figure 5-4. The aim is to think about how to tell the story of alignment and value creation for your situation. Some inference may be involved, and you may have to fill in gaps by making educated guesses at this point.

There may be a tendency to come up with solutions in such an initial workshop. Let this happen, and be sure to capture those ideas. But don't make the focus of the workshop brainstorming. Instead, concentrate on the diagram and generating questions for research.

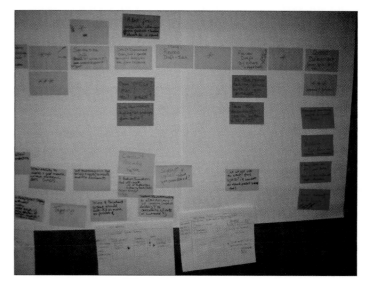

FIGURE 5-4. Create a simple, draft diagram in a team workshop.

Note that, in startups and "lean" efforts, creating a draft map may be all you need to do. Remember: you're looking for a common understanding within your organization of how you'll create value for customers. If a small team is focused on how they will create user value, more formal activities may not be needed.

Touchpoint Inventory

After you have an initial framework for your diagram, take inventory of current touchpoints.

One way to do this is with a type of role playing or so-called "mystery shopping." With this, you'll step through a defined process or flow as an individual would experience it. Then record the artifacts and evidence they come in contact with, including:

- Physical evidence, such as regular mail sent home, or even packaging.
- Digital touchpoints, including everything from emails, to online marketing, to use of software.
- One-to-one contact, such as a phone call with a sales representative or chat with customer care.

Mystery shopping might not touch on edge-case and exception flows, however. Go back and find alternative touchpoints to complete your inventory. For instance, the emails that a solo trial customer gets might be different from those for a paid account with multiple users. Look at the broader picture so that the breadth of touchpoints is accounted for.

Figure 5-5 shows an example of a touchpoint inventory from Chris Risdon of Adaptive Path. This was created for the Rail Europe Experience Map shown in Chapter 1 (see Figure 1-5). It's a simple table with a list of touchpoints per channel.

In this example, each touchpoint is described with text. You may want to also include a screenshot or photo of the touchpoint for higher fidelity. If there are many images to capture, this can get unwieldy to manage in a single document: the images take up a lot of real estate and make the document unnavigable. In that case, you may just want to include a sample of images that represent key touchpoints to accompany the text descriptions.

Both the draft diagram and a touchpoint inventory will help you understand the domain within which you are working. This will guide future research. Keep in mind that mere inspection of existing touchpoints will not provide a complete picture of the customer experience. For that you need to do research with actual users.

Rail Europe Touchpoints by Channel

Stage	Research & Planning	Shopping	Booking	Pre-Travel (Documents)	Travel	Post-Travel

Channels

	Research & Planning	Shopping	Booking	Pre-Travel (Documents)	Travel	Post-Travel
Website	Maps Test intineraries Timetables Destination Pages FAQ General product & site exploration	Schedule look-up Price look-up Multi-city look-up Pass comparison	Web booking funnel - Pass - Trips - Multiple Trips	Select document option (from available options) - station e-ticket - home print e-ticket - mail ticket	Contact page for email or phone	
Call Center	Order brochure Planning (Products) Schedules General questions	Site navigation help	Automated booking payment Cust. Rep booking Site navigation help	Call re: ticket options Request ticket mailed Reslove problems (info, payment, etc.)	Call with questions regarding tickets General calls re: schedules, strikes, documents	
Mobile	Trip ideas	Schedules	Mobile trip booking		Access itinerary Look up schedules Buy additional tickets	
Communication Channels (social media, email, chat)	Chat for web nav help	FB Comparator Email questions Chat for website nav help	Chat for booking support	Email confirmations Email for general help Hold ticket	Ask questions or resolve problems re: schedules and tickets	Complaints or compliments Survey
Customer Relations						Request for refund, escelation from call center.
Non-REI Channels	Trip Advisor Travel blogs Social Media General Google searching	Airline comparison Kayak Direct rail sites	Expedia		Travel Blogs Direct rail sites Google searches	Trip Advisor Review sites Facebook

Non-linear, no time restrictions   Linear process   Non-linear, but time based

FIGURE 5-5. Take inventory of existing touchpoints.

A Brief Guide to Interviewing

Open questioning is a qualitative approach to interviewing that is well suited for creating alignment diagrams. With this, you'll strive to hold in-depth conversations with participants on their terms. Don't read directly from a questionnaire, but instead probe in a nondirected way on topics relevant to the effort.

The idea is to embrace the uniqueness of the participants and their particular situation. What makes them special? What concerns do they have in particular? How do they feel while experiencing your offering?

This type of interviewing is an art. The challenge is balancing between a nondirected conversation and getting feedback on the specific topics you need to learn about. It's the interviewer's job to drive the conversation, letting go of control at times, and jumping in and steering the session at others.

Use a discussion guide, such as the one shown in Figure 5-6. This is a one- or two-page document to refer to during the session, in this case for interviewing journalists. It's a prompt for the interviewer, not a survey.

A discussion guide typically begins with a standard greeting to set expectations. The body of the discussion guide consists of questions to prompt a conversation about the topics relevant to the study. These prompts should address the questions, assumptions, and gaps in knowledge you have.

Journalist Interviews – Discussion Guide

Thank you for agreeing to talk with us today. We want to take the next **1 hour** to understand your work and how you interact with the publisher. We'll first ask a few questions and then have you do typical tasks using some tools around you.

It's important that we hear how you do work from **your** perspective.

We're going to record the audio of this session. It's completely anonymous and just for our own reference later.

We may take some photos—of course with your permission. If there's anything that is confidential, just say so—we'll respect that at all times.

1. **Background** (5 mins): Tell us a little bit about yourself and your work as a journalist. How long have you been doing it? What are your interests and areas of expertise?

2. **Tell us about the last piece you wrote for the publisher** (20 mins)
   a. What were the triggers? What concerns do you have initially? How do you feel at the very beginning about a new assignment?

   b. How did you get started? What do you do to prepare to write?

   c. What background investigation did you do, if any? What prerequisite knowledge is needed?

   d. What is the writing process like? What concerns you most at this point?

   e. How do you interact with your editor? What is the most difficult part?

   f. What does it feel like when it's published? Do you take any follow up actions?

3. **What does a typical day look like for you** (15 mins)? (If the participant answers "it depends," ask: "What was yesterday like?")

4. **Social media**
   a. What role does social media play in the creation of a story? What are your experiences with social media?

   b. What role does social media play after a story has been published? How do you feel about it?

FIGURE 5-6. A sample discussion guide for a fictitious interview with journalists.

The discussion guide is more of a reminder of topics than a script to read from top to bottom. In fact, it's rare you'll cover the themes in the same order as in your guide. That's OK. If a participant immediately starts talking about one of the topics further down on your list, go with the flow, and shift to that section of the guide.

General Interviewing Tips

- **Create a rapport.** Establish a bond with the participant and try to gain their trust and confidence.

  Avoid yes-or-no questions. Strive to ask open-ended questions that keep the participant talking.

- **Follow the conversation.** Use eye contact and affirmative gestures, such as nodding and feedback, to show you're actively listening. Agree with them, when appropriate (e.g., "Yes, I can see how that could be frustrating for you" or "Yes, that does sound like a lot of work for one person").

- **Listen.** Let the participant do most of the speaking. Do not lead participants and put words in their mouth. Follow their line of thought and use their language.

- **Dig deep.** Try to understand participants' underlying beliefs and values. They may not offer this information immediately. Dig further with simple phrases like: "Why do you think that is?" and "How do you feel about that?"

- **Avoid generalizations.** People often generalize when talking about their own behavior. To avoid generalizations, ask questions like: "How do *you personally* accomplish that task or feel when doing it?"

- **Minimize distractions.** People may get calls or be interrupted during the session. Try to restore focus on the interview as quickly as possible.

- **Respect participants' time.** Be sure to start on time. If the interview starts running late, acknowledge that fact first and ask if it's OK to continue.

- **Go with the flow.** The setting for the interview may not be what you expected and may not be the best condition for interviewing. Try to make the best of the interview nonetheless.

Conduct Research Externally

Research for alignment diagrams typically focuses on qualitative *interviews and observations* as a primary source of data. The draft diagram you co-created with the team helps identify your assumptions and open questions about the individual's experience. Structure your research to fill in your gaps in knowledge.

Conducting interviews and observation on location is the gold standard for this type of research. This provides face-to-face interaction with participants and allows you to see their environment firsthand.

In some cases, however, conducting remote interviews by phone or teleconferencing software is a viable option. (See the case study at the end of this chapter for an example.) Remote investigation speeds the process up and reduces the need to travel, but may miss some of the richness of data you can collect on location. Determine the level and type of research you need to understand the experience before you begin.

The next section outlines a formal approach for *field research*, involving on-site interviews and observations. Remote interviews follow a similar pattern, but involve less direct observation.

Field Research

One of the best techniques for investigation is a qualitative method called *contextual inquiry*, pioneered by Hugh Beyer and Karen Holtzblatt in their book *Contextual Design*. This type of interviewing involves visiting participants on location, in the context of their experiences.

Formal contextual inquiry can be time consuming and expensive. Full-blown research of this sort is not required for mapping efforts. However, understanding the principles of contextual inquiry is valuable for the type of field research required in general.

Onsite interviews and observations typically last between one to two hours. Longer sessions are possible, but are typically not needed. Plan on conducting four to six interviews per segment are needed.

To gather feedback more rapidly, try sending several teams into the field simultaneously to collect data. Then debrief together at the end of the day.

Field research can be broken into four steps: preparing, conducting the interview, debriefing, and analyzing the data. Each is outlined below. Refer to the resources at the end of the chapter for more in-depth discussions on the technique.

Prepare

Interviewing participants on location adds complexity to the preparation. It's not like conducting a survey or remote interview. You'll want to pay particular attention to recruiting, incentives, scheduling, and equipment:

Recruiting

Be sure to brief the participants and set expectations. Remind them that you will be at their workplace or in their home during the interview and that you shouldn't be interrupted. Also be sure that it's OK to record audio of the session. Use a screener to make sure you recruit the appropriate participants and that they approve of the conditions.

Incentives

Going on location may require higher incentive than other research techniques, such as a survey. It's not unusual to offer several hundred dollars. Generous incentives typically make recruiting easier, so it's not advisable to save money here.

Scheduling

Since you'll be going on-site, be sure to schedule interviews with enough time to travel between them. Finding multiple participants in a single location is ideal, but not always possible. Typically you'll only be able to do two to three on-site interviews a day comfortably.

Equipment

Prepare thoroughly for each interview. Be sure to go out into the field with everything you'll need:

- Discussion guide (see the sidebar, "A Brief Guide to Interviewing")
- Notepad and pens to take notes
- Sheets of paper for the participant to draw on (optional)
- Digital voice recorder or audio recording app
- Camera (ask permission before taking any photos)
- Business cards
- Incentives

Parts of an interview

Since you'll be on location for the interview, you don't want to overwhelm the participant with interviewers and observers. Research in pairs—no more than two people at a time. More than two researchers can create an unnatural atmosphere, which in turn can affect participant behavior and the insights you get.

Determine clear roles for each researcher. One is the primary interviewer; the other acts as an observer. Maintain these roles. This allows the lead researcher to build a rapport with the participant and steer the conversation. The observer may ask questions at the end or when asked.

There are four parts to an interview.

1. Greet the participant

Greet the participant, explain who you are, and set the stage for the interview. Keep this brief. Confirm that it's OK to record the session before starting the audio.

Begin by having the participants introduce themselves and describe their background as it relates to the study.

2. Conduct the interview

Use a discussion guide for open questioning. Have a naïve curiosity. The relationship you want to assume is one of master-apprentice: the interviewer is the apprentice, and the interviewee is the master. In other words, don't instruct or correct them, even if the behaviors they describe seem inefficient. You want to learn what they actually do in the situation you're investigating, not what the assumed "correct" way is. Make the interview about them and their experiences, not about you or your organization.

When asking broad, open questions, you may often get the response "it depends." If that's the case, try to qualify the question by asking about the most common situation or a typical situation.

One technique to keep the session moving is called the *critical incident* technique.

With this, there are three simple steps to follow.

1. Recall a critical incident. Have the participant remember an event that happened in the past that went particularly badly.

2. Describe the experience. Ask them to describe what happened, what went wrong, and why. Be sure to also ask how they felt at the time.

3. Finally, ask what *should* have happened and what would have been ideal. This typically reveals their underlying needs and expectations of the experience.

The critical incident technique not only avoids generalizations but also gets deep insight into useruseremotions and philosophies people have about their experiences. In general, you want to bridge the gap between what people say or think they do and what they actually have done or would do.

3. Make observations

Take advantage of being on-site and make direct observations. Take note of the physical arrangement of the space participants are in, what artifacts are present, and how the participant interacts with them.

If appropriate, ask participants to show you how they might do a representative task. Keep in mind that some things may be confidential. Once they begin, simply observe with as little interjection as possible.

Take photographs. Make sure to ask permission first and avoid including confidential information or artifacts in the photo.

Video recording the session is also possible, but this is more involved. The angle of the camera, the sound quality, and lighting may distract you at the beginning of the interview. What's more, analysis of full-length interviews can take a very long time. Don't video the session if you don't have the resources to review the recordings afterward. Instead of the entire session, try video-recording short testimonials or responses to a few predetermined questions.

4. Conclude

At the end of the session, summarize the main points to confirm your understanding. Keep this short. Ask any follow-up questions for clarification. Ask if participants have any final thoughts about anything that was discussed.

If you're recording the session, keep the recording going during this part of the session. Often people interject important details they previously left out. Even while walking toward the door, you may hear a new insight you'll want to record.

Make sure you give the participant his or her incentive. It may be uncomfortable for them to have to ask you directly. The incentive is your way of saying "thank you." Be sincere and appreciative as you hand it to them.

Finally, ask if you can contact them later for follow-up questions or clarification.

Debrief

Schedule time to debrief immediately after each session or two. Review notes with your interview partner. Take the time to complete and complement each other's understanding of what the participant said and did. You can start to pull out some main themes and highlights as well.

It also helps to make a brief description of the customer's environment immediately after the interview. If you were interviewing someone at their workplace, for instance, sketch a map of their office. Include tools and artifacts around them, as well as interactions they had with others.

⚡ Create an online space to capture thoughts, particularly if there are multiple researchers involved. An online collaboration board such as MURAL (Figure 5-7) provides an excellent format to accumulate findings quickly. Each interview can add photos and notes from the field. The intended structure of the diagram and elements it will include are already reflected.

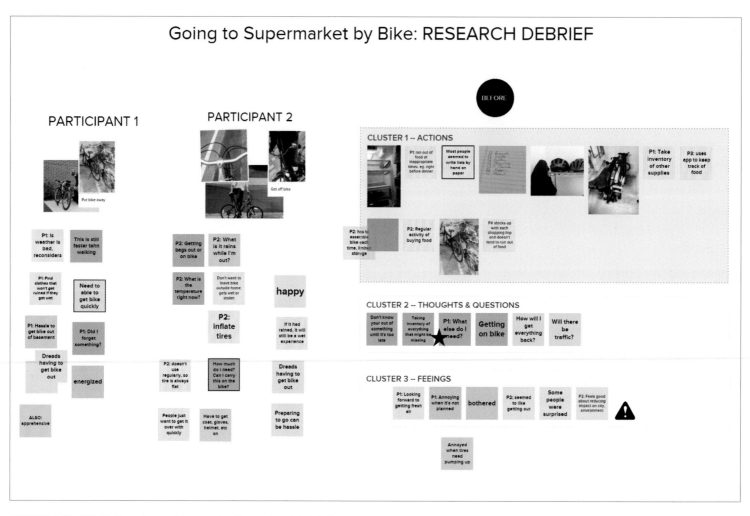

FIGURE 5-7. MURAL (*http://mur.al*) is a good online tool to debrief after interviews.

Analyze the Data

Qualitative research uncovers tacit knowledge—a clear strength of the approach. However, the data you collect does not come organized. Instead, you'll be left with a wealth of unstructured notes and recordings to plow through. Don't be daunted. Let the overall story of interaction defined in the Initiation stage guide your analysis.

Diagrams of a current experience are aggregate pictures of the people and organizations you are investigating. When synthesizing the data you've gathered, seek out the common patterns. Create a single storyline for each target group.

From each interview, extract relevant findings. Group these by theme. Then align the conclusions into a flow or pattern of your diagram. Figure 5-8 shows the progress of moving from unstructured texts to common themes to sequences of experiences.

Informal analysis

⚡ One informal way to analyze the data is to cluster sticky notes on a wall. Figure 5-9 shows the creation of a mental model diagram using sticky notes. This can be done alone, or collectively in a small group.

Alternatively, you may start analyzing data in a simple spreadsheet. Figure 5-10 shows a spreadsheet used to capture research findings. This is a modified version of a data collection sheet I used on a past project investigating a chronic illness. It allowed multiple people to contribute independently.

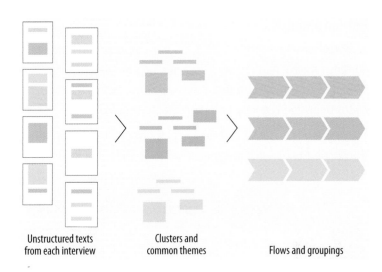

Unstructured texts from each interview   Clusters and common themes   Flows and groupings

FIGURE 5-8. During analysis you'll move from unstructured texts to clusters, and then to the flows that make up a diagram.

FIGURE 5-9. Informal analysis using sticky notes can be done on a large wall.

Formal analysis

A more formal analysis requires full transcripts of the audio recordings for each interview. A 60-minute interview may yield 30 pages of transcribed text. Consider outsourcing this step, as transcription is a very time-consuming process.

Then, use a qualitative text analysis tool to comb through the transcribed texts—for instance, MaxQDA, shown in Figure 5-11. First, upload interview texts (upper left), create a list of themes to code passages (lower left), and apply the codes to the interview texts (center). Finally, view all coded passages across interviews for a given theme in one place (right).

Reading the coded passages for a particular theme then allows for grounded conclusions about the experience. Compare the themes to your open research questions and incorporate your findings into the draft map.

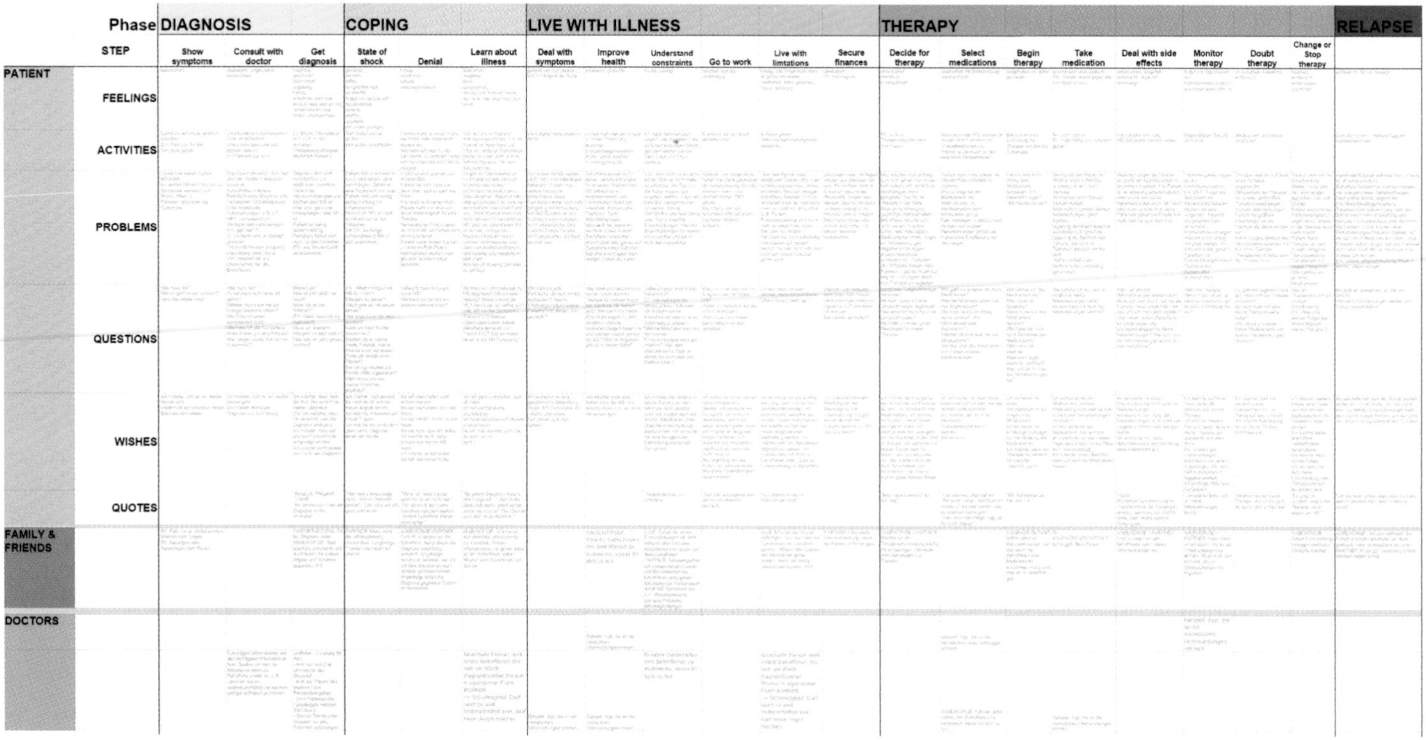

FIGURE 5-10. Use a simple spreadsheet for an informal analysis of your research.

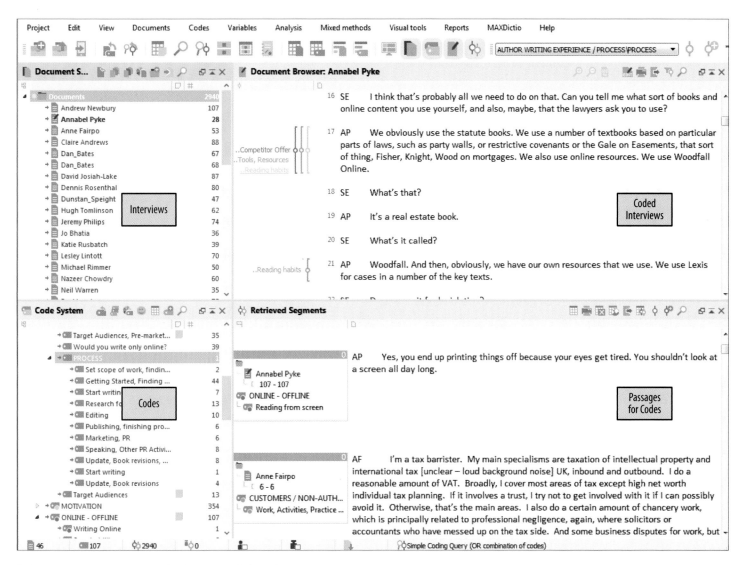

FIGURE 5-11. MaxQDA is a qualitative text analysis tool.

Quantitative Research

When you are creating an alignment diagram, a survey is the primary tool to get quantitative data. This will allow you to measure the same aspect across phases or touchpoints.

At a basic level, try to understand *what types* of experiences people are having. For instance, a question could list a series of touchpoints and require respondents to select the ones they encounter. This would allow you to indicate the percentage of people who encounter a given touchpoint.

Asking questions on a scale is more powerful. This allows you to indicate *how much* of an aspect people experience, including such things as:

- Frequency in which phases or steps are experienced
- Importance or criticality of a given touchpoint
- Satisfaction at each touchpoint or phase

When you create the survey, use a consistent scale throughout. If you ask participants to rank satisfaction on a scale of 1 to 5 for one question, don't change to a different scale for the next.

Creating a bespoke survey is no easy task. Consider using a standardized survey instead. For instance, *NPS* (Net Promoter Score) is a popular measure for customer loyalty, introduced by Fred Reichheld in his book *The Ultimate Question*. Or, in software and web applications, there are surveys such as *SUMI* (Software Usability Measurement Index, *http://sumi.ucc.ie*)

and *SUS* (System Usability Scale)[*] that have been around for decades. There are also newer measurements such as the *UX Score*, a proprietary measure created by market research giant GfK.[†]

Other sources of quantitative information include:

Usage metrics
: Electronically enabled services—everything from online software to computer chips in cars—can capture actual usage data. Things like web analytics and software telemetrics allow for very detailed measurement of usage.

Call center reports
: Most call centers record the volume of calls and general traffic patterns. There is often a quantitative classification of call types as well.

Social media monitoring
: Quantitative measures of social media activity can be considered for a diagram. This may include such things as traffic for each social media platform or the volume of a hashtag use or mentions.

---

[*] For a thorough description of SUS, see Jeff Sauro's article: "Measuring Usability with the System Usability Scale (SUS)," *Measuring U* (Feb 2011).

[†] For more on the UX Score, see *http://www.gfk.com/products-a-z/ux-score/*.

Industry benchmarks

Depending on the sector and industry you are working in, there may be benchmark data available. This will show how your current service compares to others in the same field.

As you collect data from these sources, think about how you might incorporate them into your diagram. There are many approaches that depend on the type of diagram you're targeting, its structure, and its depth. Chapter 6 discusses some specific ways to represent quantitative information in an alignment diagram.

Summary

An experience is something that is constructed in the mind of the perceiver. It's not something an organization owns. To map experiences, investigation into those experiences from the perspective of the individual is necessary.

Begin by *assessing existing sources* of information. This can include email feedback, phone calls, blog comments, social media activity, formal marketing studies, and industry reports. Extract relevant information that can inform the creation of a diagram. This information may be hidden or buried in existing sources.

Also create a *touchpoint inventory* of existing physical, digital, and person-to-person interactions. Note the channel and means of interaction as you complete the inventory, and collect images of each touchpoint.

Create a *draft diagram* together with the project team and stakeholders. This provides an initial picture of your current understanding of the individual's experience. It also provides an overview of knowns and unknowns, which guides subsequent research. In some cases, this may be all that is needed for your team to get aligned.

Next, *interview people internally* within the organization. Get a mix of roles across functions and levels. Try to include frontline personnel in your initial interviews as well: service desk agents and call center workers, for instance, often have a clear perspective on a client's experience because they are serving them.

Conduct field research to fill in gaps in knowledge and to deeply understand the individual's experience. Go on location to the place where participants interact with the service in question. Engage them in interviews, but also observe their surroundings. Remote research using teleconferencing solutions speeds up the process, but loses the richness of face-to-face interaction.

Qualitative research can validate assumptions. Surveys and questionnaires work best here. The results of these methods can be included in an alignment diagram for greater impact.

All of this data needs to be analyzed and reduced to just the key points. Only then can you start drawing a map of the experience with confidence. The next chapter discusses how to take the findings from your research and illustrate a map.

Further Reading

Hugh Beyer and Karen Holtzblatt. *Contextual Design* (Morgan Kaufmann, 1997)

> This is the original, landmark book that introduced a formal technique for contextual inquiry to the design community. This is a thorough, well-structured book with step-by-step guidance into their process. The first part discusses interview and inquiry techniques in detail. The latter parts of the book outline a method of translating findings into concrete designs. This is a highly recommended book everyone should have.

Karen Holtzblatt, Jessamyn Burns Wendell, and Shelley Wood. *Rapid Contextual Design* (Morgan Kaufmann, 2004)

> This is a follow-up book to Contextual Design. It outlines ways to do contextual research quickly. There are many templates, tools, and examples that bring the subject to life. The level is not too advanced, and this is a great place for beginners to get started.

Mike Kuniavsky. *Observing the User Experience* (2nd ed., Morgan Kaufman, 2012)

> Experience mapping requires some type of primary investigation. This is an excellent resource into the ins and outs of user research.

Steve Portigal. *Interviewing Users* (Rosefeld Media, 2013)

> Steve Portigal is a recognized expert in user research. This book is a must-read for anyone engaging in contextual interviews or ethnographic research. There is a wealth of practical information and tips in this volume, with a wealth of examples.

Giff Constable. *Talking to Humans*, *self-published* (2014)

> This thin volume of only 75 pages provides an excellent overview to getting in front of customers and talking to them. The approach the author takes is clearly within the Lean Startup movement, featuring discussions of assumption and hypothesis testing. There is a wealth of practical information for getting starting and conducting quick interviews.

Music Curation: User Research and Diagramming at Sonos

By Amber Brown

Sonos is a leading provider of wireless home audio products. From the customer's point of view, the service is simple: you connect your speakers to your home WiFi and then play music through your phone, tablet, or computer.

The app for Sonos speakers enables control for multiple services, multiple rooms, and multiple people. While these components are important in making the service work, nothing really matters more to the users than playing music. The goal of this effort was to illustrate the complexity involved.

Before attempting to diagram how people curate music, Sonos had to first understand *how* and *why* people used the product. Our research consisted of a series of extensive interviews with ten Sonos households over the course of two weeks.

At first, we conducted interviews remotely. Using teleconferencing software and webcams we were able to get participants to demonstrate how they use the Sonos application on their phones. All sessions were recorded to show other stakeholders not present during the interviews.

After that, we asked participants to record interactions with the product in a daily dairy. The weekly check-ins with each household made for the most eye-opening insights. We found that when participants recounted stories they often revealed their deeper goals.

Next, we examined all of the data we collected to find common themes. Using sticky notes and a whiteboard, we arranged our findings into a model that served as the basis for a diagram.

Finally, we created a complete diagram reflecting the key insights from our research, shown in Figure 5-12. This simplifies the user's experience by focusing on five key elements:

- *User goals.* We sought to uncover underlying motivations: what are customers trying to achieve when playing music? In each interview, we asked the customer *why* they did what they did.

- *Supporting features.* Recalling Indi Young's process of creating mental model diagrams, we mapped features of our app to the goals. This helped stakeholders understand what features people used to get the job done. In our case, we found there was too much weight on the queue functions of the app, for instance.

- *Benefits of features.* The *benefits of the features* reveal the value of your current features. This also helps with stakeholder buy-in. Instead of focusing on only negative feedback, they also show what is working well.

- *Obstructions of actions.* The most important aspect of the diagram showed that the app *didn't* support people's goals. The obstructions got our stakeholders' attention.

- *Unused items.* This section showed features that are not used when people are playing music. The list helped us decide what could be removed without having an impact on user goals.

Once the model was created, we found that it could be used in multiple ways to engage with the stakeholders.

- *Show the diagram during meetings and workshops.* The model is simple enough that others don't get overwhelmed. I showed it in a paper form and in electronic form. This helped create a common understanding of user motivations.

- *Print out the model for colleagues to use at their desk.* Having the model distributed around the office and kept near colleagues' desks help socialize the insight and keep the conversation going.

- *Map new concepts to the model.* Once stakeholders saw what the problems were, they came up with solutions. They saw how they could exchange the supporting features with the new concept's supporting features.

- *Use the new benefits to write user stories.* New (or sometimes existing) benefits served as a basis for writing user stories for development teams.

- *Creating simple models allows stakeholders to easily engage.* It encourages people to use them as a reference and leverage them for various different activities to help improve the design.

We saw product managers, engineers, and designers use this diagram to help them understand what problems they were addressing and how they can solve them. Since the model was based on firsthand investigation, we also had confidence that our decisions were grounded in actual customer needs.

About the Contributor

Amber Brown is a UX researcher at Sonos. Her areas of specialty include contextual interviews, mental models, and workshop facilitation. Amber holds a degree in human-computer interaction from Iowa State University.

User goals

1. Get music ready for later
2. Create a playlist for a party
3. Share music with someone next to me
4. Keep the music going (DJ)
5. Turn on a mix of music
6. Play what I found right now
7. Take requests (DJ)
8. Look at what is going to happen
9. Repeat same song for kids
10. Refer to what I listened to before
11. Avoid mixing listening history with current listening
12. Create immediate access to music I am currently listening to
13. Turn on music so I can do something else
14. Play a song
15. Feels turning on a lot of music is time consuming

Supporting features

1. Add to queue; Add to playlist
2. New playlist; Play next
3. Play now; Play now; Play now
4. Add to queue; View queue; Play now
5. Add to queue; View queue; Play now; Play next
6. Play now
7. Play now; Add to queue
8. View queue; Up next
9. View queue; Previous track
10. View queue; Save queue; Sonos favorites
11. Clear queue; Replace queue
12. Add to favorites
13. Play now; Play all tracks
14. Play now
15. Play now; Play all tracks

Benefits of the features

1. I have music ready to go that fits what I am in the mood for
2. I can add songs/albums/playlists that I want to a playlist
3. The menu choices for what I am doing are at the top; I can continue to change what I am playing
4. I can play songs as the requests come in; I can add to a list of songs so the music keeps going
5. I can build a queue of all the different music I like
6. I can play songs as I find them
7. I can choose to play a request now or later
8. I can go into the queue and view what is in there
9. I can go into the queue and view what else is in there; Once the song ends, I can go back to the song
10. The queue tells me what I put in there before; I can turn the queue into a playlist; I can mark things I want to listen to frequently
11. I can choose a song and erase irrelevant music at the same time
12. I have easy access to the music I listen to regularly; I can get rid of the old music I don't want to listen to
13. I can easily get a radio station going; All tracks makes it easy to get an album or playlist going
14. When I find a song I like I can play it right away
15. I can get all the tracks from a previously made playlist

Obstruction of action

1. Required to select from a menu for each song
2. Required to select from a menu and playlist for each song
3. Pulled into the now playing but still looking for music; The song will drop to the bottom of the queue
4. Required to select from a menu for each song; The song will drop to the bottom of the queue
5. Required to select from a menu for each song; The song will drop to the bottom of the queue; Required to choose one song or the whole album
6. The music will stop after this song plays; A song will appear in Now Playing and not play; Required to choose one song or the whole album
7. Music stops when I do not expect it to; The song will unexpectedly drop to the bottom of the queue
8. This changes when I add music, but I can't see the change; When I move around the queue, time is unknown; I only have a quick glance at the very next song
9. I get lost trying to find what I just added; I can only repeat the song if it's the only one in the queue
10. The old queue disappears; Random music is mixed in with what I listened to before; Required to navigate to the queue
11. I didn't realize music was in the queue; I heard a random song that is in the queue; Accidentally erased someone's queue
12. I have to remember to pick the content as my favorite
13. The music stops when I did not expect; I have to start the album/playlist from the beginning; I have to select a menu each time I turn on a station
14. Music stops after a song is played; It's required to go through a menu for each song
15. It's required to go through a menu for each song

Unused "Curation" items

Delete track from My Library · View reviews · View all tracks on album · Add album to my library · Search for this everywhere · Artist info · Add to favorites · More albums like this · Album info

FIGURE 5-12. A simplified curation model for Sonos.

Diagram and Image Credits

Figure 5-2: Sketch by Jim Kalbach reflecting feedback from interview participants

Figure 5-3: Journey map template created by John Kembel at Designing CX (*www.designingcx.com*)

Figure 5-4: Photo of a simple diagram during a workshop by Jim Kalbach

Figure 5-5: Touchpoint inventory created by Chris Risdon, appearing in his article "The Anatomy of an Experience Map," *Adaptive Path Blog* (Nov 2001)

Figure 5-9: Image from *Mental Models* (Rosenfeld Media, 2007) by Indi Young, retrieved from flickr: *https://www.flickr.com/photos/rosenfeldmedia/sets/72157603511616271/*

Figure 5-10: Example of an online spreadsheet for data collection in Google Sheets, modified from the original version

Figure 5-11: Image of MaxQDA, by Jim Kalbach

Figure 5-12: Model for curating music with Sonos, created by Amber Brown

"Graphical excellence is that which gives to the viewer the greatest number of ideas in the shortest time with the least ink in the smallest space."

— Edward R. Tufte
The Visual Display of Quantitative Information

IN THIS CHAPTER

- Layout and form of a diagram
- Consolidating the content
- Designing the information
- Tools and software
- Case Study: Mapping the Lab Test Experience

CHAPTER 6

Illustrate: Drawing the Diagram

"I'm not a graphic designer and can't draw. How can I possibly create a diagram?" I get that reaction a lot in my classes and workshops on alignment diagrams.

There's good news: creating an alignment diagram is not primarily about artistic talent. The task at this point is to compile all of your findings into a single, cohesive story. In some respects, creating an insightful storyline is the hard part.

⚡ Consider the diagram in Figure 6-1, created by Eric Berkman, a design strategist and author of *Designing Mobile Interfaces* (O'Reilly, 2011). It's visually minimal, but reveals key insights about both negative and positive service aspects at a Starbucks coffee shop.

Or, review the diagram in the case study at the end of Chapter 5 created by Amber Brown. This simple arrangement of colored boxes had an impact on the organization and provided valuable insight.

Yes, graphic design plays a role in creating a diagram. Depending on your skills and the level of formality of the effort, you may need to involve a professional designer. But understanding a few principles of design goes a long way toward creating a compelling diagram. This chapter discusses three interdependent factors in the mapping process:

Layout
> The form of the overall diagram

Content
> The information contained in the diagram

Design
> The representation for the information and graphic design

There may be movement back and forth between these aspects. Be prepared to iterate. After this chapter, you should be able to transform the insights from your investigation into a meaningful diagram.

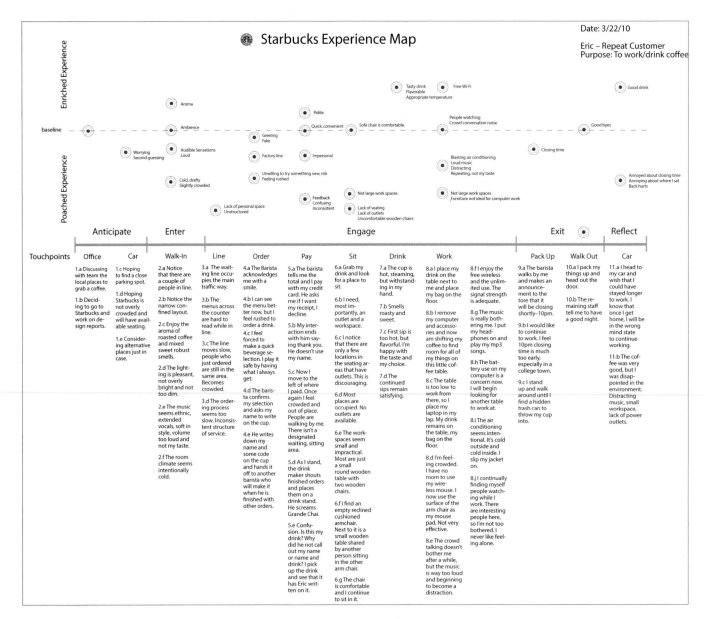

FIGURE 6-1. This simple but effective diagram for a visit to Starbucks reveals key insights.

Lay Out the Diagram

As discussed in Chapter 2, typical organization schemes are chronological, hierarchical, spatial, or a network. The choice of organizational scheme has an impact on the layout of your diagram. Some methods prescribe the layout *a priori*. Mental model diagrams, for instance are organized hierarchically into towers. Or, a formal service blueprint will have a table-like form by default. At this point, you probably already know how your diagram will be laid out.

But it's worthwhile considering alternative forms as well. Used correctly, the layout itself enhances the overall message. Figure 6-2 shows some possible layouts.

For instance, Sofia Hussain, a leading design strategist in Norway, created the diagram in Figure 6-3. She intentionally chose a circular form to show that success of this event planning app relies on *repeat use*. The form amplifies the message.

A table or timeline form will usually work in most situations. I recommend starting with those layouts to be on the safe side. Consider alternative layouts only if it enhances your overall message.

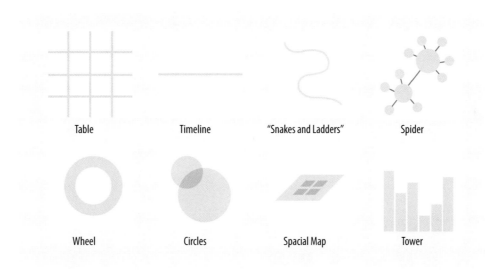

FIGURE 6-2. A summary of possible layouts for alignment diagrams of various kinds.

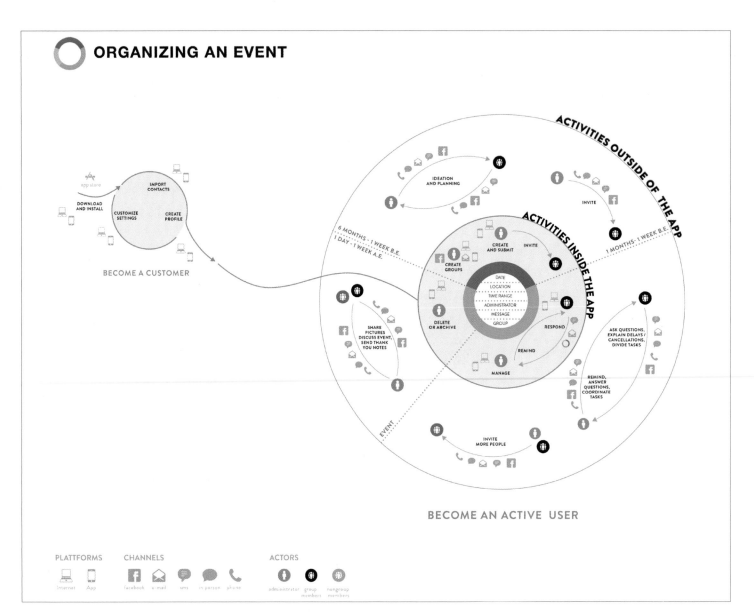

FIGURE 6-3. A circular diagram reflecting a desire for repeat use of an event planning app.

Displaying Chronology

Chronological maps—the most common type of diagram—are simple for others to grasp. But this strength also presents a challenge: not all aspects of an experience are sequential. Some events are ongoing, some may have a variable order, and others may have different subflows.

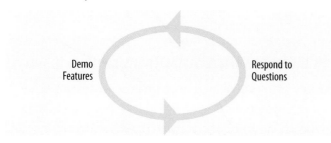

FIGURE 6-4a. REPEAT BEHAVIOR: Some aspects of an experience repeat. For instance, during a sales call, the salesperson may alternate between showing a product and responding to customer questions. Use arrows and circles to show repeating actions.

FIGURE 6-4b. VARIABLE ORDER: There may be a variable order of events: the sequence could be one way or the other. For instance, a sales person may generate new leads, maintain existing relationships, and maximize reach all at the same time. If that is the case, indicate that the order is variable. The use of nonlinear shapes, such as a cloud-like form, indicates that activities don't happen sequentially.

There are several ways to handle the limitations of presenting asynchronous activities on a single timeline, shown in Figures 6-4a–d.

FIGURE 6-4c. ONGOING ACTIVITY: Some aspects of an experience may be ongoing. For instance, a salesperson may continually look for new leads. One way to handle this is to indicate the first time that a behavior occurs. Then, note that it is ongoing and/or extend a line across the rest of the diagram. Avoid repeating the behavior over and over again in the diagram.

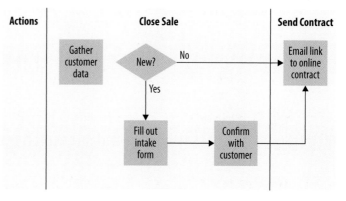

FIGURE 6-4d. ALTERNATE FLOWS: You may come across distinct subflows in the experience you're mapping. It's possible to insert a decision point and divide the flow. Keep this to a minimum to avoid overcomplicating the diagram. For instance, a sales person may have distinct activities based on the customer type.It's OK to have a temporary split, but try to bring branches of the flow together again.

Compile the Content

At this stage, your aim is to map the current state of an experience. From your investigation you should have a good sense of the narrative you want to tell. Mapping future states and coming up with solutions comes later, as outlined in Chapters 7 and 8.

An alignment diagram shows the current experience of an individual. After conducting research and doing investigation, you should have a sense of what that experience is and how to describe it. Looking at future states and solutions comes in the next step, alignment (discussed in Chapter 7).

Reduce the data you've gathered to the most salient points and find common patterns. Work both from the bottom up and from the top down, alternating between the two (Figure 6-5).* Start by working *bottom up* by clustering and grouping

FIGURE 6-5. Work iteratively from the bottom up and from the top down to consolidate your research findings.

---

* Note that a top-down process doesn't apply to creating mental model diagrams. They are created from the bottom up. For more, see Chapter 12.

findings repeatedly until you've reduced your research to just key insights. At the same time, work from the *top down* using your draft map to help direct your consolidation.

Be prepared to shift things around. Your goal is first to create a prototype of the diagram, taking qualitative and quantitative information into account.

Qualitative Information

A majority of information to describe experiences is qualitative—rich descriptions of the *why* and the *how*, rather than quantitative data about *how many*. The following are the primary qualitative elements to include.

Create phases, categories, and divisions

Determine the major "joints" of the model you're creating. In chronological maps, this means creating phases, e.g., *become aware*, *purchase*, *use*, *get support*. There are typically anywhere from four to twelve phases. For spatial maps and hierarchical diagrams you need to create categories and groups by theme. There are many possible ways to divide the elements in your map. Try to find what feels natural for you and for stakeholders.

Describe the experience

Decide what aspects to show to describe the experience. Core elements include actions, thoughts, and feelings. Consider ways to make the description as rich as possible.

For instance, include direct quotes from customers from research. Or incorporate photos from on-site visits. Demonstrate what is valuable to the individual.

Reevaluate the divisions in your diagram as you go. Strive to balance and distribute information evenly. Let the content influence the categories from the bottom up.

Show touchpoints

Include interfaces between the individual and service for each phase. Think about their context of use. Remember, a touchpoint takes place within a given set of circumstances. Be sure that the information in the map surrounding the list of interfaces provides the context for those touchpoints.

Include aspects of the organization

Indicate which roles or departments are involved at each touchpoint. Other elements you can map are the goals of the organization, strategic imperatives, and even policies. Show what is valuable to the organization.

Format the content

Formatting the content is one of the trickiest parts of mapping. After being steeped in data and research, it's likely you'll want to include everything you found. Resist this urge. Favor brevity. It takes practice to be able to express information in a compact form.

Table 6-1 lists some of the guidelines to follow at this stage. It shows two examples through the process of iteratively transforming research insights into concise content for a diagram. Notice how insights from research at the top of the table reduce down to concise statements to include in a diagram. In this example, assume you are creating a customer journey map for a hypothetical software company.

It's important to keep the same syntax for each facet of information. A cohesive system of content will make the diagram more readable and self-evident. Here are example formats for some of the most common information types:

- *Actions:* start each with a *verb*, e.g., download software, call customer service.

- *Thoughts:* phrase as a *question*, e.g., Are there hidden fees? Who else do I need to involve?

- *Feelings:* use *adjectives*, e.g., nervous, unsure, relieved, delighted.

- *Pain points:* start each with a *gerund*, e.g., waiting for installation, paying invoice.

- *Touchpoints:* use *nouns* to describe the interface, e.g., email, customer hotline.

- *Opportunities:* begin each with a verb that shows change, e.g., *increase* the ease of installation, *eliminate* unnecessary steps.

Guideline	Description	Example 1	Example 2
Start with insights	Start with clusters of findings from your research.	Research cluster 1: People indicated they sometimes hesitate and reconsider during the customer acquisition phase because of our premium pricing model.	Research cluster 2: There is a clear pain point around deploying the solution, primarily due to lack of necessary technical knowledge.
Use natural language	Use language that reflects the individual's experience in terms they would use.	People reconsider when making a purchase because they may be nervous or anxious about the high cost.	Users struggle to install the software for the first time if they don't have the required technical skills.
Keep voice consistent	Rewrite the insights in either the first person or third person (pick one), but don't mix voice.	I reconsider when making a purchase because I'm anxious and nervous about the high cost.	I struggle to install the software for the first time because I don't have the necessary technical skills.
Omit pronouns and articles	To save space, omit articles and pronouns, which are implied.	Reconsider when making purchase due to anxiousness and nervousness over high cost.	Struggle to install software for first time without the necessary technical skills.
Focus on the root cause	Reduce the information to reflect underlying motivations and emotions.	Feel anxious and nervous when making purchase due to high cost, and then reconsider.	Struggle during installation due to lack of necessary technical skills.
Be concise	Rewrite the descriptions to use as few words as possible. Use thesaurus if needed.	Feel anxious during purchase about cost, and then reconsider.	Struggle due to lack of technical skills during installation.
Use abbreviations sparingly	Abbreviations can be OK if they are widely used and accepted.	Feel anxious during purchase about cost, and then reconsider.	Struggle due to lack of *tech* skills during installation.
Rely on context of map	Some information can be inferred from its position. Rely on the row and column headers if you have a table-like diagram.	anxious about cost *(In the cell for the column for "purchase" and row for "feelings")* Reconsider *(In the cell of a column for "purchase and a row for "actions")*	Struggle due to lack of tech skills OR Lack tech skills *(assuming a column for "installation" and a row for "pain points")*

TABLE 6-1. Guidelines for formatting content based on a fictitious example of a customer journey map for a software company.

Quantitative Information

Including quantitative content—information that reflects an amount or magnitude, usually represented by numbers—adds validity to your diagram.

During investigation, look at metrics and survey results, and consider how to include the data in the diagram. There are several ways to represent quantitative data, shown in Figures 6-6a through 6-6d.

1. Word of mouth
2. Web searches (48%)
3. Internet ads (19%)
4. TV ads (7%)

FIGURE 6-6a. SHOW NUMBERS AS TEXT: Include numbers and figures to show absolute values. For instance, you may have quantitative data on how people find your service. If so, you can list those figures (Figure 6-6a).

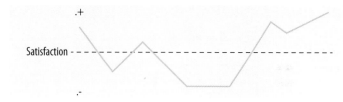

FIGURE 6-6c. PLOT VALUES ON A GRAPH: Quantitative data can also be plotted on a graph. This is good if the goal is to track the rise and fall of a given measure across a diagram. For instance, you may have quantitative data for customer satisfaction at the end touchpoint in a journey. A simple line reveals at a glance where high and low points are on this curve (see Figure 6-6c).

FIGURE 6-6b. USE BARS TO AMOUNTS: Bars typically show relative quantities. Absolute values can be included in text, but it's not common to have an axis with values as with a bar chart. Vertical bars are easier to compare than horizontal bars in most diagram forms, as shown in Figure 6-6b.

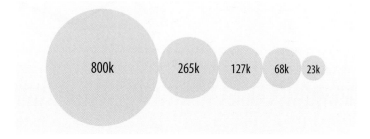

FIGURE 6-6d. USE SIZE TO INDICATE QUANTITY: It's also possible to show quantity with the size of a shape, as shown in Figure 6-6d. For instance, the example in this figure could be used to indicate the number of customers that move through a typical purchase funnel. Working with size to show quantity may have an impact on your overall layout, particularly if the differences between the sizes is great. Use size with caution when showing quantity.

Sankey Diagram

Sankey diagrams are a specific type of flow diagram that use different sizes and thicknesses of lines to show quantity increases or decreases.

Perhaps the most famous Sankey diagram is Charles Minard's maps of Napoleon's march to Russia in 1812, shown in Figure 6-7.

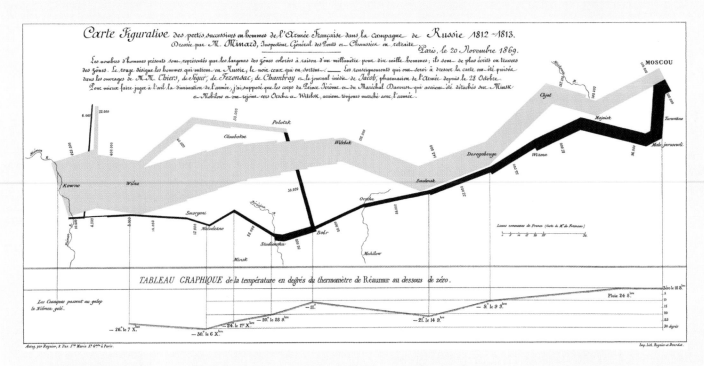

FIGURE 6-7. Minard's famous map of Napoleon's Russian campaign in 1812 is a type of Sankey diagram.

Example Diagram: Prototype Version

Figure 6-8 shows a fictitious diagram for organizing a conference event. It reflects a first pass at a consolidation of information. Thought has been given to the phases of interaction, the wording and format of text, and the balance of content in general. In the next step, you'll be looking at how to design the information to tell a more compelling narrative.

Event Organizer

| | BEFORE THE CONFERENCE | | | | DURING THE CONFERENCE | | | | AFTER THE CONFERENCE | |
	Plan	Promote	Invite Attendees	Prepare	Initiate Event	Start Main Presentations	Engage Audience	End Event	Follow-Up on	Improve Event
ACTIONS	· Set budget, costs · Determine topic · Create agenda · Set date and time · Set success criteria · Figure out reporting	· Create materials · Reach widest audience · Decide where, when · Cross promote · Track data on promotion · (Re-)evaluate promotion	· Maintain contact lists · Figure out who to invite · Create calendar entry · Send save the date notices · Send invitations and follow-up reminders	· Co-create materials · Organize materials · Make materials accessible · Discuss handoffs · Check equipment	· Show up early · Go over ground rules · Communicate time · Monitor attendance · Greet audience	· Welcome attendees · Give overview, timings · Set expectations · Instruct attendees on environment, tools	· Integrate social media · Gauge attentiveness · Take breaks · Network	· Wrap up · Thank people · Stay for questions · Debrief · Plan next steps	· Address unanswered questions · Send out materials · Collect feedback · Launch survey	· Analyze survey results · Review metrics, compare to goals · Gauge effectiveness · Update materials
THOUGHTS	Who is this for? Will they come? What does success look like?	Who do I target? How do I best promote? Is promotion effective?	Who am I attracting? What are their needs? Will everything go as planned? Will I remember everything?	Will anyone come? What does success look like? How do I best promote? Is promotion effective?	Who is signing up?	Will everything go as planned? Will I remember everything?	Is the audience engaged? Are they getting their money's worth?	Was it well-received? A success?		
FEELINGS	creative indecisive	hopeful uncertain	relieved worried		MoT! excited panic (high uncertainty)	relieved overwhelmed	relieved exhausted	forward looking discouraged	proud	
PAIN POINTS	· Figuring out when to schedule an event	· Determining social media channels · Managing social media promotions · Unprofessional looking material	· Having to reschedule the event · Updating meeting details, agenda, etc.	· Locating materials · Consolidating materials · Setting up hardware · Coordinating staff	· Unexpected technical difficulties	· Unexpected technical difficulties	· Maintaining focus · Gauging attendee understanding		· Lack of time to follow-up right after	· Lack of motivation to update materials · Lack metrics collected · Inability to show effectiveness of event
OUR GOALS	· Maximize reach to the widest audience	· Maximize reach to the widest audience	· Maximize the number of people that attend · Increase the likelihood that the right people attend	· Increase the likelihood audience will be engaged · Maximize professional appearance	· Increase the likelihood of a smooth start	· Increase the likelihood that attendees have a positive experience · Maximize utilization of time while not "on stage"	· Maximize audience engagement · Reduce the likelihood that attendees get distracted	· Maximize overall satisfaction	· Maximize the length of the relationship with attendees	· Increase the quality of future events · Maximize buzz around the event and topic
CURRENT SATISFACTION		7.1 / 10	4.2 / 10		8.2 /10	6.5 / 10	5.5 / 10		8.7/10	

FIGURE 6-8. A consolidated model of an event organizer's experience.

Design the Information

People like information that is rich in presentation. Content that is presented with color, texture, and style has relevance to our lives and our work. The visual presentation of a diagram influences how others understand the information.

Strive to create a consistent visual language that amplifies your storyline. What insights should be highlighted? What are the key messages you wish to communicate? How can you make the diagram approachable, aesthetically pleasing, and more compelling?

Even if you are not a graphic designer, there are some basic decisions you can make to help the clarity of the diagram. First, stay true to these principles:

- *Simplify.* Avoid frivolous and decorative graphics. Strive for efficiency in display.

- *Amplify.* Keep the goals of project and expectations of the sponsors in mind. The design should intensify the overall message.

- *Clarify.* Strive to be as clear as possible.

- *Unify.* The information should form a cohesive whole. Maintain consistency in the display of information for a well-rounded appearance.

The key aspects to pay attention to are typography, graphics, and creating a visual hierarchy, each discussed in the following sections.

Typography

Typography refers to the selection of letter forms and the general design of text. Alignment diagrams comprise mostly text. As a result, the typography of your diagram is paramount to facilitating its practical use.

Variations in typeface, size, case, and emphasis (bold, italic) are critical in creating a visual hierarchy in the diagram. When these differences encode information, they support the meaning of the diagram.

Options with typography can overwhelm. Let function and purpose guide your choice. When in doubt, favor legibility and intelligibility over flair and expression. Consider typeface, size and width, case, and bold and italic styling (Figures 6-9a through 6-9d).

Serif

The quick brown fox jumps over the lazy dog.	Times New Roman
The quick brown fox jumps over the lazy dog.	Georgia
The quick brown fox jumps over the lazy dog.	Courier

Sans Serif

The quick brown fox jumps over the lazy dog.	Arial
The quick brown fox jumps over the lazy dog.	Verdana
The quick brown fox jumps over the lazy dog.	Trebuchet

FIGURE 6-9a. SELECT A TYPEFACE: There are two major categories of typefaces: serif and sans-serif. Serifs are those short lines at the end of a main character stroke. Typically, diagrams make use of sans-serif typeface for the bulk of the information. You may also find a serif typeface being used for a headline. It's best to use only one or two different typefaces in a diagram.

Different font widths

The quick brown fox jumps over the lazy dog.	Verdana
The quick brown fox jumps over the lazy dog.	Frutiger
The quick brown fox jumps over the lazy dog.	Frutiger Condensed
The quick brown fox jumps over the lazy dog.	Arial
The quick brown fox jumps over the lazy dog.	Arial Narrow
The quick brown fox jumps over the lazy dog.	**Franklin Gothic**
The quick brown fox jumps over the lazy dog.	**Franklin Gothic Condensed**

FIGURE 6-9b. CONSIDER FONT SIZE AND WIDTH: You will be motivated to use a small font size to get more information into the diagram. Avoid making the size so small it can't be read. Instead, work with the content to reduce it to its most meaningful essence.

Also, be aware of the overall width of the font you're using. For instance, Verdana is a very wide font and not recommended. Instead, try a condensed or narrow font. The characters are slimmer and closer together. Pair these with their regular versions for greater consistency. Make sure a narrow font is readable at a distance if you use one.

All caps: full sentence vs. short label

✕ THE QUICK BROWN FOX JUMPS OVER THE LAZY DOG

✕ CONTACT CUSTOMER SUPPORT FOR HELP

✓ BECOME AWARE

✓ DECIDE

FIGURE 6-9c. PAY ATTENTION TO CASE: Generally, longer texts are harder to read in capital letters than in mixed case. They will take up more space as well. Single words or short phrases, however, such as the title of a phase in a journey, may work well in uppercase. Use all caps sparingly to add emphasis or show differences.

Different font styles for emphasis

The quick brown fox jumps over the lazy dog.	Frutiger
The quick brown fox jumps over the lazy dog.	Frutiger Ultra Black
The quick brown fox jumps over the lazy dog.	Frutiger Light Italic

FIGURE 6-9d. EMPHASIZE WITH BOLD AND ITALIC STYLES: Use bold and italics to help distinguish different information types, but use them sparingly. Generally, the information will be more readable if you keep the same weight and style. A mix of bold and italics can get messy quickly.

Legibility also changes with bold and italics. Making a text large and bold may not necessarily make it more readable. For instance, Frutiger UltraBlack draws attention but doesn't make the text easier to read. Likewise, long texts in Frutiger Condensed italics are less legible.

Graphic Elements

After you have compiled the content, consider how to represent it visually. Graphic elements play an important part. You may not be able to create the graphics yourself, but being aware of a few basics helps plan and critique the outcome. Figure 6-10 shows some of the key elements to consider.

Show relationships with lines

Lines are a principal means of showing visual alignment. They have four primary functions in alignment diagrams: dividing, containing, connecting, and showing paths.

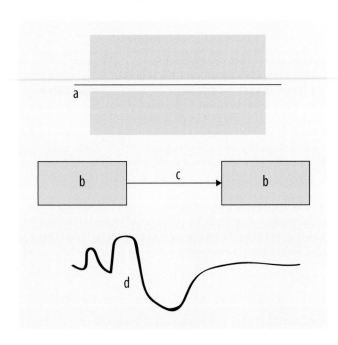

Divide (a)

Lines demarcate fundamental sections of a diagram. A service blueprint, for instance, has several lines integral to the technique, e.g., the line of visibility and the line of interaction. Similarly, a mental model diagram has a thick horizontal center line separating the experience from the support for that experience.

Contain (b)

Lines create regions and shapes. They contain information and set it off from other information in the diagram.

Connect (c)

Arrows and lines relate two pieces of information to one another. Lines show important connections between elements in the diagram. The steps in a workflow, for instance, may be connected by arrows.

Show paths (d)

Lines can also show a path. Often we see lines in a diagram representing a journey or an experience.

Be careful of unnecessary lines. If every cell in a table-like diagram has a line border, for instance, the overall diagram will become unnecessarily heavy in feel. As a general rule of thumb, use as few lines as possible, and only use lines that carry meaning to the diagram.

FIGURE 6-10. Show relationships with lines.

Convey information with color

Color is more than just decoration. It helps create a sense of priority and facilitates overall understanding. Two key uses of color in alignment diagrams are color coding facets of information and showing background regions, as shown in Figure 6-11.

- *Color coding* allows viewers to see individual facets of information across the diagram. This is crucial for creating a sense of visual alignment. For instance, pain points or moments of truth may have a consistent color throughout the diagram, as shown below. Even if they are not on the same line of sight, color will visually connect different facets of information throughout the diagram.

- Use color to create *backgrounds* within the diagram. This avoids unnecessary use of lines. For instance, the phases of a journey may each have a different color to distinguish them. You can accomplish dividing and containing by using values of a single color, rather than introducing new colors. The background regions in this image, for instance, are different shades of the same grey tone.

The use of too many colors can have diminishing returns. Use color purposefully for emphasis, and use it consistently.

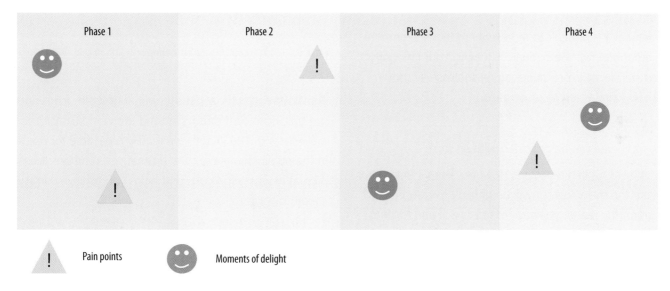

FIGURE 6-11. Convey information with color.

Add icons for efficiency

Icons communicate a great deal of information in a small amount of space. They also add visual interest. But not all information types can be represented as icons. Typical icons found in alignment diagrams include (see Figure 6-12):

People (a)

It's common to see figures for people in diagrams to indicate the actors in an experience.

Physical evidence (b)

Touchpoint interfaces often can be clearly represented as graphics without labels or keys.

Emotions (c)

In general, it's difficult to represent emotions. (For more on emotions, see the sidebar "Showing Your Emotions.") However, facial expressions can be successfully shown with an icon, as a type of emoticon.

Moments of truth (d)

Key moments can be indicated with an icon.

Create a key to explain the icons. However, keep in mind that if there are too many icons it will be difficult to comprehend the diagram: the reader will have to refer back and forth to a key to understand the information. Strive to represent the content of the diagram so it can be read without reference to a key or further explanation.

FIGURE 6-12. Add icons for efficiency.

The Noun Project is a website that aggregates icons and symbols from contributors around the world (*http://thenoun-project.com*). The images are readily accessible for use, either in the public domain or with a Creative Commons license. It's a great resource for icons that helps you achieve consistency in your diagram.

Visual Hierarchy

Not all information in a diagram is of equal importance. Create a visual hierarchy to direct how the eye perceives the experience you're mapping.

Guide readers through the visual story with alignment, different visual weights, and layering (Figures 6-13a through 6-13c), as well as avoiding chartjunk (Figure 6-13d).

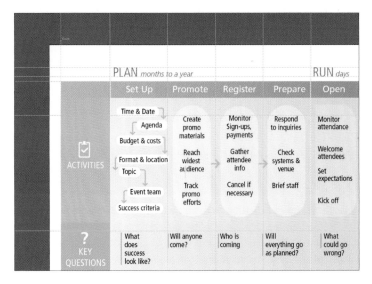

FIGURE 6-13a. ALIGN TEXTS AND GRAPHICS: Visual alignment is critical to your diagram. A grid is an invisible (i.e., not printed) structure of equally spaced lines. Elements of the diagram are then justified to the grid. This creates clear lines and guides readers' line of sight vertically and horizontally.

If you are using a spreadsheet to capture information, for instance, you may already start seeing alignment along a grid in the early stages. Even working with sticky notes on a whiteboard can benefit from vertical and horizontal alignment. This image shows the light blue guide lines used to align elements of the diagram.

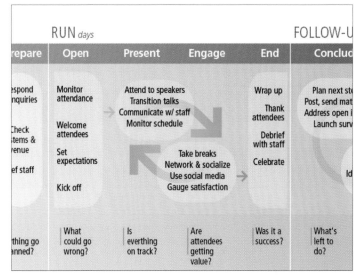

FIGURE 6-13b. CREATE EMPHASIS WITH WEIGHT AND SIZE: Weight and size of both text and graphic elements provide focus and differentiation. In Figures 6-13a and 6-13b, the phase headers (e.g., "PLAN," "RUN," etc.) are larger than the text body. This provides a sense of hierarchy.

There are also different weights and sizes of the arrows in this example. Small arrows show chronological forward motion; the large arrows emphasize a more critical iterative process in the experience.

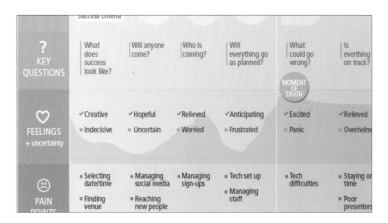

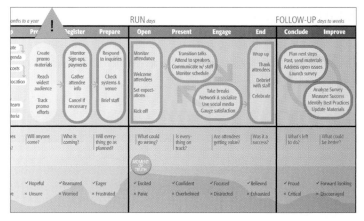

FIGURE 6-13c. LAYER INFORMATION: Create visual depth by layering information. Make some elements stand out more than others. You can achieve layering by using different sized texts, through the use of color, or by applying background shading.

In the middle of this diagram excerpt, for example, possible positive and negative feelings are indicated with text. Varying levels of uncertainty, however, are shown as a darker tone of the same color in this row. Combining elements in this way increases the density of information in the diagram without sacrificing readability or comprehension.

FIGURE 6-13d. AVOID CHARTJUNK: "Chartjunk" is a term coined by information design guru Edward Tufte. This refers to anything unnecessary in an information display. Don't assume you are enhancing information with added graphics and lines. Make every mark count.

A simple example of chartjunk is a table with dark grid lines. In this case, the table data is the focus, and lighter lines would allow the information on the page to be scanned and read more quickly. Or, perhaps no lines are needed at all and light-colored backgrounds can align the information as intended..

Example Diagram: Final Design

Figure 6-14 shows an updated version of the prototype diagram shown previously in Figure 6-13b. The final design was created by Hennie Farrow, head of design at Zignal Labs. Typography, graphic design, and visual hierarchy come together holistically in this example.

Typography

This diagram uses Frutiger and Frutiger Condensed, which is economical in terms of width. The weight of the text is fairly even throughout the diagram.

All capitals are used for row headers for emphasis and to set them off from other text.

Bold text is kept to a minimum. Italics are used to set off duration in the headers, but not used otherwise.

Hierarchy

Horizontal and vertical alignment create a sense of rows and columns across the diagram.

Graphic elements

Color is used to distinguish the different facets of information in the rows. The first column with the row labels has darker backgrounds, providing depth to the overall diagram and giving that information priority.

Icons are added for visual interest. Each information type also includes a unique element to help provide a sense of cohesion. For instance, the organizational goals have arrows to show desired direction of the outcome, pain points have a square bullet, and key questions have a line. The moment of truth in this experience is indicated with a graphic element in the middle.

Content

There is a consistent use of syntax—for instance, verbs for the main phase and adjectives for feelings. The voice is consistent as well.

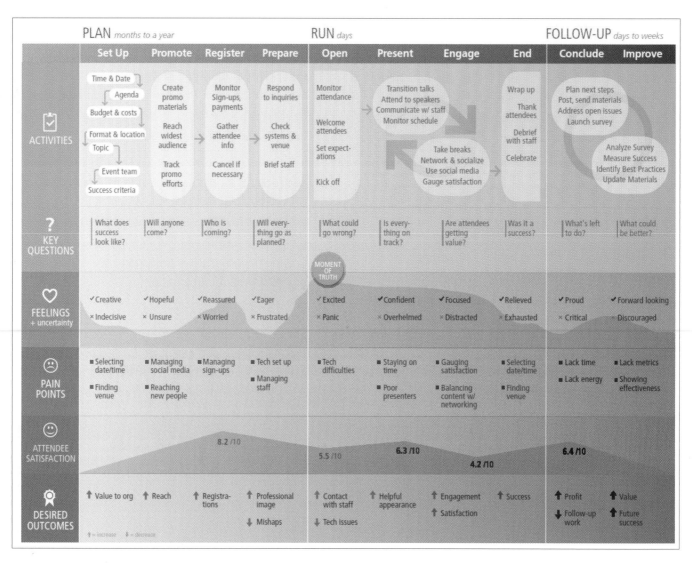

FIGURE 6-14. Final version of an experience map for organizing a conference.

Showing Your Emotions

Emotions play a critical role in the experiences we have. Mapping experiences necessarily includes some description of the individual's emotive state of mind. But describing emotions is difficult.

Part of the problem is that emotions are difficult to research and observe. They may not be immediately observable, subjective, and open to interpretation.

Pieter Desmet has done some of the leading research into measuring emotions.[*] He developed and tested a tool called Product Emotion Measurement instrument (PrEmo), an instrument to assess emotional responses to consumer products (Figure 6-15).

Various emotional states are portrayed with an animated cartoon character. Partici-

pants report their reactions to a product by self-selecting those animations that correspond with their felt emotions. With this tool, it's possible to gauge emotional states at each stage in a journey. Participants could be shown the characters, for instance, and chose the one that best matches their feelings at a given phase in the experience.

---

[*] See Desmet's full-length book based on his dissertation research, *Designing Emotions* (2002).

FIGURE 6-15. The PrEmo tool for measuring emotions uses universal facial expressions with animations. The PrEmo tool is owned and licensed by the SusaGroup: *http://www.premotool.com*.

Emotions also don't let themselves be easily represented in a diagram. The simplest approach is to indicate emotions with text. Mental model diagrams rely on this approach, for instance. Indi Young writes in her book on the subject: "Mental models capture not only the cognitive intent of a person but also the emotion, social environment, and cultural traits of a concept."

Icons and symbols may also be used. For instance, building on the PrEmo tool, the firm SusaGroup created a complementary tool called CapturEmo (Figure 6-16). This integrates the facial expressions in a simple journey map.

Typically, though, feelings are represented on a curve. Emotional ups and downs are shown over time. Figure 6-17 shows an early example of this approach. It comes from a 2004 report by Ed Thompson and Esteban Kolsky entitled "How to Approach Customer Experience Management." This example is for business passengers on a major US airline.

This plotted line style has become a convention in experience mapping. One problem with this approach is that it suggests some kind of quantification. However, rarely is this information derived from quantitative investigation—typically it's estimated intuitively.

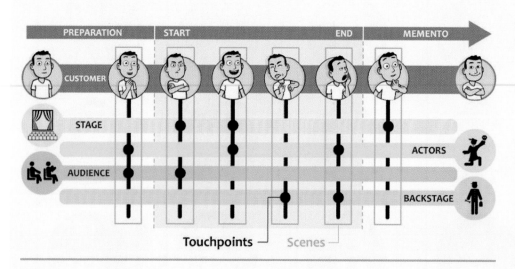

FIGURE 6-16. A snapshot of CapturEmo, a tool for showing emotions across a service encounter, created by SusaGroup (*www.capturemo.com*).

What's more, the plotted line approach oversimplified the emotions. Rarely do we just have one emotion at a time. For example, when checking out of a hotel resort after a two-week vacation, you may be *delighted* with the service, but at the same time *sad* to leave or even *anxious* about going back to work on Monday—all at the same time.

Capturing the multidimensional nature of emotions visual is illustrated in Figure 6-18. This diagram excerpt shows multiple emotions at once, each in a different color. See the key in the lower right for a list of the emotions included.

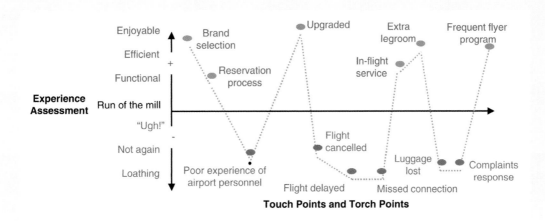

Source: Gartner Research (October 2004)

FIGURE 6-17. An early map of moments of truth from researchers at Gartner Research in 2004.

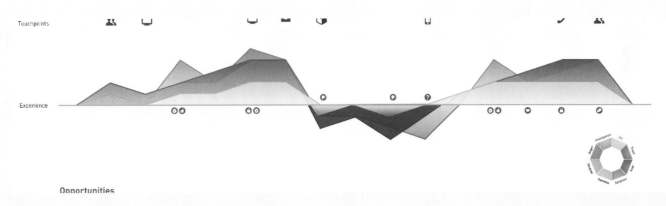

FIGURE 6-18. An excerpt from a customer journey map showing multiple layers of emotions.

But even showing multiple emotions at once that are either positive or negative doesn't show a complete picture. Both positive and negative emotions are possible at the same time. Figure 6-19 shows an excerpt from a journey with positive and negative factors possible in an experience. (This diagram is shown in full in Figure 4-8 in Chapter 4.)

Understanding and representing emotions is a challenge. Consider the tradeoff you'll have to make and how best to characterize the emotional aspects of the experience you're illustrating.

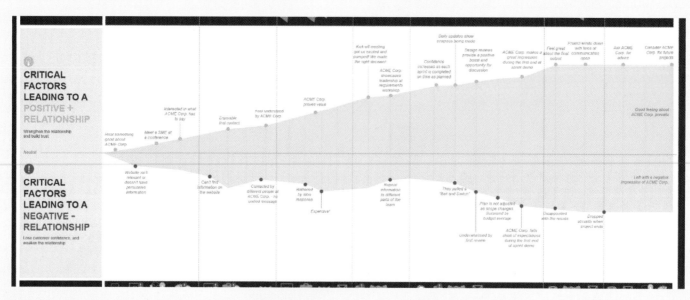

FIGURE 6-19. Positive or negative emotions may be possible in any given experience, sometimes simultaneously.

Tools and Software

There are a range of tools and software you can use to illustrate a diagram depending on your skills and need. For informal efforts, a simple whiteboard with sticky notes may suffice. In other cases a more polished diagram may be presented to clients and stakeholders formally.

The following section reviews various types of tools you can use for mapping.

Desktop software

High-end graphics applications

The programs from Adobe Creative Suite dominate this type of software, including Illustrator, InDesign, and Photoshop. Figure 6-20 shows an image of Adobe Illustrator. These programs require training and practice to use properly.

Diagramming tools

Omnigraffle for Mac and Visio for Windows are often used to create workflow diagrams, flowcharts, and sitemaps. They have rich diagramming capabilities that can yield high-quality final diagrams.

Spreadsheets

It's also possible to create diagrams in programs like MS Excel. The important thing to look for in alternative programs like this is the ability to work on a large, near-limitless canvas. Presentation programs, such as PowerPoint or Keynote, generally don't extend far enough in width or height to be able to accommodate a full alignment diagram.

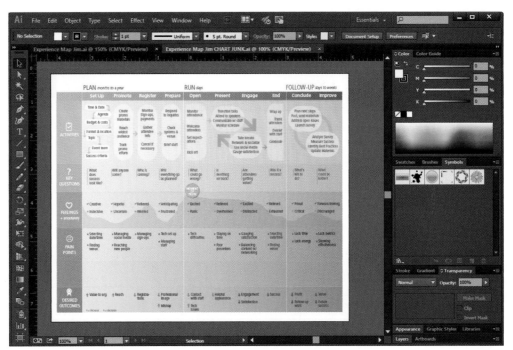

FIGURE 6-20. The experience map example in Figure 6-14 was created with Adobe Illustrator, a high-end graphics program.

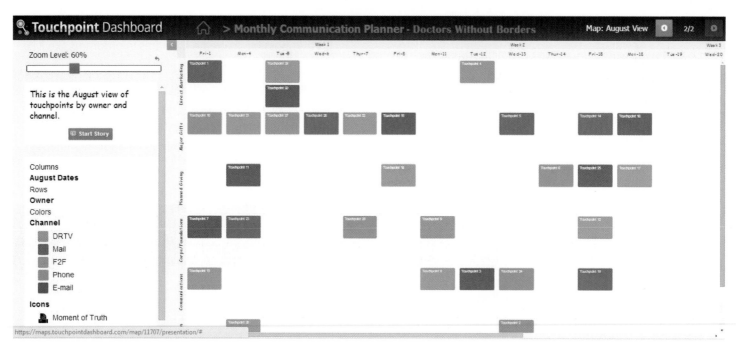

FIGURE 6-21. Touchpoint Dashboard is an online tool used to manage touchpoints.

Web-Based Tools

Web-based tools for mapping are becoming more powerful. They have the benefit of easy sharing and high portability. If you're working with people in different locations, an online tool can support remote collaboration.

Touchpoint management programs

Touchpoint Dashboard (*www.touchpointdashboard.com*) is a leading example of an online tool specifically for managing touchpoints (see Figure 6-21). This type of tool is best for tracking changes to touchpoints over time. Because it's database-driven, it also allows for multiple views of information. For instance, you can filter and change views to see your data from multiple perspectives. This isn't possible with graphics programs and other desktop software.

Online mapping tools

Smaply (*www.smaply.com*) and Canvanizer (*www.canvanizer.com*) are two online tools that help structure mapping work. Smaply.com is particularly designed for experience mapping. It includes a suite of related options, such as personas and stakeholder maps that are tightly integrated with each other.

Online diagramming tools

Lucidchart (*www.lucidchart.com*) is an online diagramming tool akin to Omnigraffle or Visio. It has the advantage of being integrated directly into Google Drive.

Online whiteboards

Online whiteboards such as MURAL (*http://mur.al*) or RealtimeBoard (*www.realtimeboard.com*) work well for all aspects of the mapping process. Their flexibility and large canvas area allow for the creation of detailed diagrams, all online. This opens up the process for active contribution from others on an ongoing basis.

Figure 6-22 shows a mapping exercise I completed using MURAL. First, you'll see that multiple activities can be included on one diagram: value chain mapping, personas, empathy maps, and experience maps. Second, the large virtual service allowed us to compare two different experiences—in this case, going to the supermarket by bicycle and by car. Finally, working online allows for the integration of images to make a description of the experience even richer.

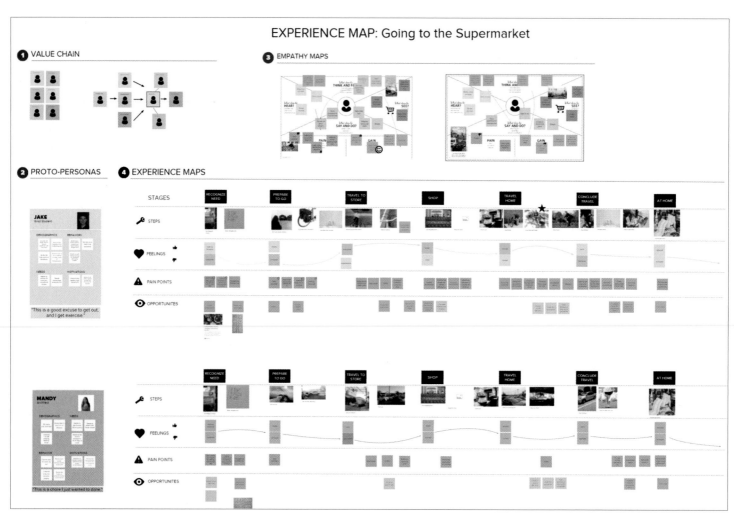

FIGURE 6-22. Several mapping activities and a comparison of different experiences all in one place using MURAL (*http://mur.al*).

Formatting and Printing

Keep the intended purpose of the diagram in mind as you create it. Who will ultimately make use of it? In what context will it be used?

Typically, there is a print version of a final diagram. In this case, be aware that things look different on paper than on screen. Colors may be darker on paper than on screen. This can adversely affect the contrast of the text against a background, for instance. Text may not be readable once printed.

A large printout requires a plotter printer. If you don't have access to one, most print shops can help. The cost of a single, large printout is generally not trivial, so get an estimate first. Otherwise, you may want to print out the diagram on several pages and tape them together. In this case, be conscious of page breaks.

Additionally, there may be multiple programs and formats you'll use throughout the process. This includes word processors, spreadsheets, presentation tools, and print versions. Consider how your diagram translates to different sizes and situations.

Summary

The goal at this stage in the process is to assemble the insights from investigation into a single diagram. An alignment diagram is a key way to capture a great deal of information in a compact space.

The form of your diagram conveys meaning. Typically, a chronological diagram will have a table-like or timeline layout. But there are alternative as well, such as circular layouts, spider-like networks, and "snakes and ladders." Consider how the form of the diagram amplifies the overall message.

Getting the content to fit in a condensed format is challenging. This is an iterative process of clustering and grouping and clustering the groups. Your goal is to reduce the information to representative aggregate behavior for the target group. Thinking from the top down helps this process. Use the form and structure of your diagram to guide compiling the content.

It is important to understand the basics of information design and importance of visualization, even if you are not a graphic designer. Typography is critical since much of the body is text. Graphic elements add visual interest and efficiency. Lines, shapes, icons, and color enhance comprehension.

Visual hierarchy also plays a role. Not all elements are of equal importance. Use layering and different sizes to bring some aspects to the foreground and to push others into the background. If you need to hire a graphic designer, you should be able to discuss some of these basics with him or her.

There are a variety of tools for illustrating a diagram. On the high end are desktop software applications like Adobe Illustrate, Omnigraffle, or Visio. But Excel is an alternative. There are more and more online tools available, such as Mural.ly and Lucidcharts. Other online offerings, such as Smaply.com and Touchpoint Dashboards are built specifically for experience mapping and touchpoint management.

Further Reading

Robert Bringhurst, *The Elements of Typographic Style*, version 3.2 (Hartley & Marks, 2008)

> *This is an attractive, extremely well-written book that is considered by many to be a "bible of typography." The illustrations and examples included are impeccable and engaging. There is a wealth of practical information, including a review of selected font specimens and a thorough glossary. This volume is a timeless reference to own.*

Pieter Desmet, *Designing Emotions* (2002)

> *Over a decade and a half ago, Desmet did some of the most important research in emotional responses to consumer products and services. The culmination of his work is this book, which is based on his dissertation thesis. Other papers and writings by Desmet on emotions and design can be found online via a web search. His company, Susa Group, specializes in the measurement and design of emotional consumer experiences.*

Joel Katz, *Designing Information* (Wiley, 2012)

> *This book broadly covers topics of information design, from display to structure. There are many excellent examples that bring the conversation to life and make it real. There are also studies included that vary the design of a given visualization and show how to fix issues in it.*

Dan Roam. *Back of the Napkin*, expanded edition (Portfolio, 2013)

> *Dan Roam made visual thinking accessible to anyone in business with this landmark book. It's a short book that breaks down drawing into simple elements. He conclusively shows that anyone can solve problems of any kind visually.*

"Service Design Tools" *http://www.servicedesigntools.org*

> *This website is a collection of tools for design, in general. A fair portion of it focuses on games and activities for groups to use in co-creation exercises. In addition to customer journey maps and touchpoint maps, there is a wealth of tools related to experiencing mapping, in general.*

Edward Tufte, *Envisioning Information* (Graphics Press, 1990), and *Visual Explanations: Images and Quantities, Evidence and Narrative* (Graphics Press, 1997)

> *Edward Tufte is the leading thinking in information design. These two books are a few of his many tomes outlining fundamental principles of information design. Understanding these concepts helps greatly in creating alignment diagrams.*

Mapping the Lab Test Experience

by the Mad*Pow Strategy and Service Design Team: Jon Podolsky, Ebae Kim, Paul Kahn, and Samantha Louras

Mad*Pow was approached by an international laboratory and diagnostics company to improve the patient's lab test experience. Our process for creating compelling user experience always starts with research. To improve a service, we need to understand that service from the customer's point of view.

We start by mapping out the current experience, using a combination of stakeholder and user interviews, along with direct exposure to the service, staff, and operations to produce the materials and insights.

From the research we build a narrative that describes how a customer interacts with the service. The narrative may be generic or may represent a scenario associated with a specific persona developed through the research. We organize the steps of the customer's experience in a chronological sequence, and then group the steps into stages that identify meaningful transitions.

For example, our research showed that several stages precede scheduling the appointment. The first stage is *Awareness of a*

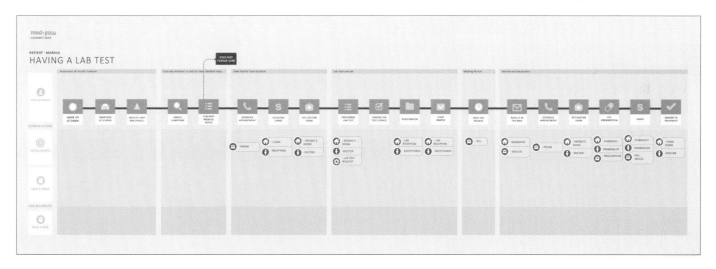

FIGURE 6-23. The first step is to map user journey stages and touchpoints.

Health Problem followed by *Evaluation of Whether or Not to Seek Medical Help*, when most users independently search for an evaluation of their symptoms. This approach produced a customer journey map showing the stages, steps, and patient touchpoints associated with each step (Figure 6-23). This allowed us to show our client how their service fit into their customer's larger healthcare journey.

The stages of the journey are also the structure for building individual customer scenarios. We can select a persona developed through the research (Figure 6-24), building a scenario for that character, and can add a layer of customer emotions to the journey.

These emotional responses help us identify steps where the experience could be improved. The persona's moments of concern, discomfort, and anxiety can be made visible through a combination of emotional symbols and quotes, bringing the customer's experience to the forefront.

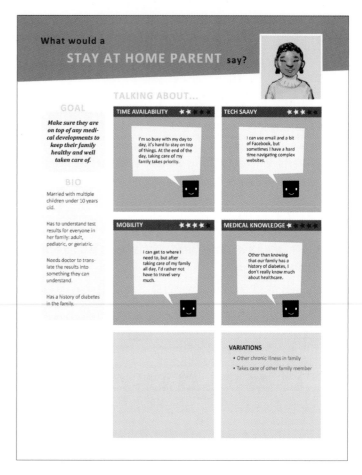

FIGURE 6-24. In the second step, select a persona to build an individual journey.

In this example, we have encoded the persona's emotions with a single color and variations of facial expressions. Color variation is used only to call attention to the two moments in the journey where changes could have a positive impact. We broke the anxiety-producing step of waiting for test results into three additional steps to emphasize the amount of negative activity and feeling the waiting period can produce for this persona (see Figure 6-25).

In this scenario, the customer is interacting with staff at the offices of both the healthcare provider and the testing lab. By adding frontstage processes for both locations, then aligning these with backstage processes needed to support the customer's touchpoints, the map can be expanded to include elements of a service blueprint (Figure 6-26).

This approach produces a highly readable and condensed customer journey map, with the option to add more complex service blueprint information as needed to illustrate current gaps and opportunities for changing the offering to produce the desired improvement.

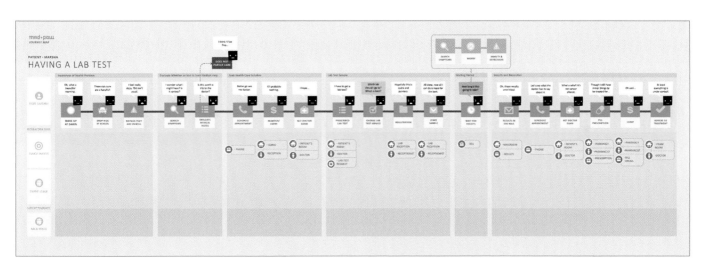

FIGURE 6-25. Third, map the persona's emotions at each step.

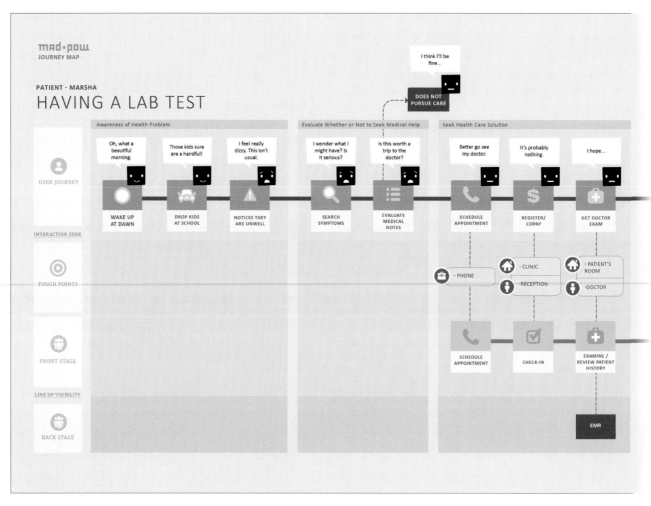

FIGURE 6-26. Finally, add the frontstage and backstage processes.

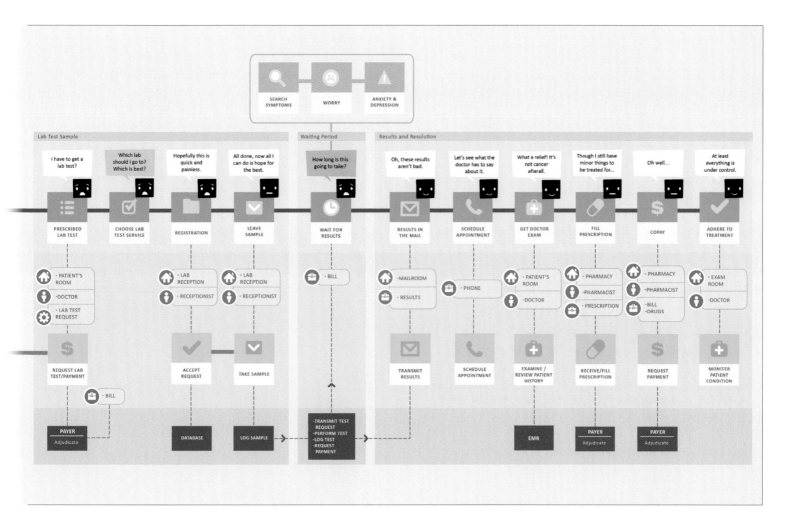

Diagram and Image Credits

Figure 6-1: Customer journey diagram for Starbucks created by Eric Berkman, used with permission

Figure 6-3: Diagram created by Sofia Hussain, appearing in her article "Designing Digital Strategies, Part 1: Cartography," *UX Booth* (Feb 2014), used with permission

Figure 6-7: Minard's famous map of Napoleon's Russian campaign in 1812, public domain

Figure 6-8: Consolidated model of research findings, created by Jim Kalbach

Figure 6-14: An experience map for organizing a conference, created by Jim Kalbach and Hennie Farrow

Figure 6-15: The PrEmo tool for measuring emotions, by Pieter Desmet, used with permission

Figure 6-16: The CapturEmo tool for showing emotions in a service encounter, by the SusaGroup, used with permission thanks to Lars Rengersen

Figure 6-17: Excerpt from a diagram appearing in Ed Thompson and Esteban Kolsky. "How to Approach Customer Experience Management" (Gartner Research Reports, 2004)

Figure 6-18: Excerpt from a customer journey map believed to be created by Ronald Peeringa

Figure 6-19: Excerpt from a customer journey map created by Macadamian (*http://www.macadamian.com*), appearing in full in Figure 4-8, used with permission

Figure 6-20: Screenshot of experience map created in MURAL (*http://mur.al*) by Jim Kalbach

Figure 6-21: Image of Touchpoint Dashboard from *www.touchpointdashboard. com*

Figures 6-23 to 6-26: Created by Jonathan Podolsky, Ebae Kim, Paul Kahn, and Samantha Louras at Mad*Pow, used with permission

"Visualizations act as a campfire around which we gather to tell stories."

— Al Shalloway

IN THIS CHAPTER

- Running an alignment workshop
- Using diagrams to gain empathy
- Envisioning new solutions
- Evaluating ideas and concepts
- Case Study: Rapid Online Mapping and Design Workshop

CHAPTER 7

Align: Designing Value

I'm lucky: for a majority of my career I've had the fortune to come in direct contact with the customers of the companies I worked for. I've observed hundreds of people at their workplaces or in retail stores or in their homes, across many industries. I've observed what they experience in context.

Ideally, everyone in an organization would get firsthand contact with customers. But for many this type of exposure is limited. Even frontline personnel, such as customer support center agents, may only see a few of the experiences customers have. Anecdotes come in without context, like notes in a bottle washed up on shore.

A broader picture is needed in order to connect the dots. Diagrams provide such a view. But creating a diagram is not the ultimate goal. Rather, it is a means to engage others in your organization in a discourse. It's your job to make this discourse happen. Consequently, your role switches from mapmaker to facilitator at this point in the process.

This chapter describes the main components of an *alignment workshop*, a primary event to bring others together. The session has three parts:

- *Empathize:* Gain an outside-in view of the individual's experience
- *Envision:* Imagine a future that provides meaningful value
- *Evaluate:* Articulate ideas quickly and test them for immediate feedback

You won't come out of the workshop with fully fleshed-out concepts ready to implement. In a final step, you'll *plan experiments*. Test your hypotheses and measure outcomes in the weeks that follow.

The overall process is illustrated in Figure 7-1.

By the end of this chapter, you should have a clear understanding of how to use a diagram to engage stakeholders and to chart a course forward.

FIGURE 7-1. The main parts of an alignment workshop are to empathize, envision, evaluate, and plan experiments.

Empathize

It's not enough that *you* empathize with the experiences people have. You need to ensure that others gain that same deep understanding. Strive to spread empathy throughout the organization.

Empathy is about seeing the world through someone else's eyes. It's about an implicit sense of what an experience is like, what people value, and what emotions are involved. Diagrams allow you to walk through an experience in slow motion, helping to create empathy within your organization.

The process begins by first understanding the current experiences. Then, assess how well you support those experiences before finally finding opportunities to create unique value.

Understand

To begin the workshop, review the findings from your investigation together as a group. Make the diagram the focal point. Complement it with other artifacts you've created, such as personas.

You can also play video clips from interviews to highlight a specific state of mind or pain point. Or, have co-researchers tell stories from the field that bring the experience to life. Portray a rich description of the world as you've observed it in a way that is relevant to the organization.

After setting the stage, have the group engage with the diagram. Display it prominently so a group of people can stand around it (Figure 7-2). Alternatively, place it flat on a table for the team to gather around. This has the advantage of offering the chance to sit but still be part of the workshop.

The aim is to immerse the team in the details of the experience by examining the diagram together. If there are many sections to the diagram, break the team up and have each group read through a different part.

FIGURE 7-2. Display the diagrams prominently for others to gather around.

The workshop is not a presentation for passive consumption. Instead, participants are active contributors. There are several techniques to achieve this:

Write on the diagram

Invite people to comment, correct, or add information directly on the diagram (Figure 7-3). Even if you have a polished graphic version of it, keep it open for feedback. For instance, create empty rows for people to make additions from their own observations.

Foster discussion

Prompt the group with directed thought exercises. For instance, have the group indicate moments of truth, and discuss the relative importance of each touchpoint.

Tell stories

Have everyone in the group recount stories from the field research. What have they heard people saying at each stage in their experience? What evidence can they add?

Empathy doesn't come from the diagram itself. Rather, the diagram serves as the hub for conversations that create a deeper understanding of an experience. Your job is to make sure that happens. I have found it is usually not difficult to get people talking, and conversations happen naturally.

> *Creating a diagram is not the ultimate goal. Rather, it is a means to engage others in your organization in a discourse.*

FIGURE 7-3. Invite everyone to contribute to the diagram.

Assess

Next, evaluate the organization's ability to support the experience at each step. There are several ways to do this quickly:

Grade performance

Have stakeholders give school grades at each division in the diagram. If you are working in multiple groups, compare the grades after you come back together.

Identify moments of truth

Collectively identify points in the experience that are most important to individuals. Give everyone some colored dot stickers, and have them indicate the most critical moments. Discuss the areas that got the most votes.

Vote on importance to the organization

Look at what's valuable to the organization. Use dot voting to find the most important points in the experience.

For instance, Figure 7-4 shows ratings from two separate groups working on the same section of a diagram in a workshop I once ran. The scale was 1 to 6, with 1 being the best score and 6 being the worst. At one point the scores between breakout groups diverged: one gave a 6, while the other gave a 3. The ensuing conversation was enlightening, building both consensus within the team and empathy for the customer.

Identify Opportunities

Next, look for opportunities. Insight into value creation emerges from the discussion about the diagram. Highlight some of the following aspects:

- *Weaknesses.* Look for points of failure. How can you better support users? When are their needs least satisfied?

- *Gaps.* Find where no support is offered. What pain points are not addressed? What moments of truth are potentially overlooked?

- *Redundancies.* Alignment diagrams point to potential duplication of efforts. Where can you eliminate redundancies?

- *Competitors.* Look at what other providers are doing at each step in the journey. Where are you underperforming? When do they provide more satisfying experiences?

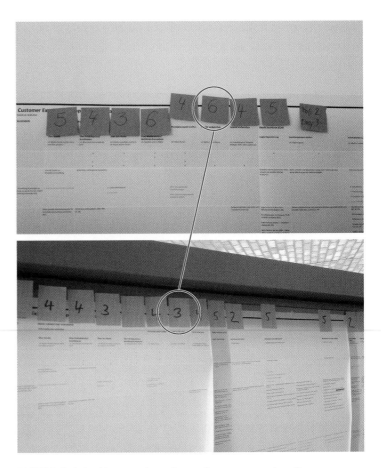

FIGURE 7-4. In this example, rating performance reveals a discrepancy between two workshop breakout groups.

Then, take a step back and consider the overall experience. Try to see what patterns emerge. For instance, I once consulted a large publisher to improve their relationship with their authors, existing and new. We noticed a trend during the workshop: the publisher didn't stay in close contact with authors after the manuscript was submitted.

Figure 7-5 shows this pattern overlaid on the experience map. The bars show our relative, estimated level of involvement at each stage. The team then focused on ways to increase contact with authors throughout the journey. How could they make authors feel more connected? How could they create a sense of belonging?

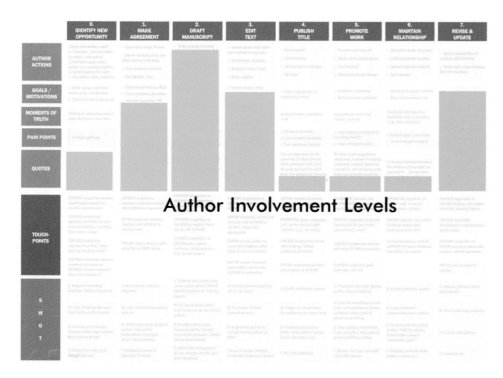

FIGURE 7-5. A simple pattern emerged from an experience map for authors: their involvement decreased during production phases.

Envision

In my experience, diagrams inspire ideas almost instantly. Typically, stakeholders are teeming with ways to enhance their offering. Ideas pour out. It's your job as the facilitator to direct their attention and focus this energy.

At this point in the session, move from understanding the current experience to envisioning possible solutions. The process is one of "going wide" in terms of ideas and concepts. This mode of working is commonly called *divergent thinking* (Figure 7-6).

First, set the right expectations with the team. Ensure that the transition from empathizing to envisioning happens. Communicate the rules of divergent thinking, which are:

- *Go for volume.* Aim to cover a breadth of ideas. Keep the details at a minimum at first. Avoid filtering ideas as you go.

- *Withhold judgment.* Create a safe place for people to be creative. Participants should be comfortable contributing ideas, even if they are not fully thought through.

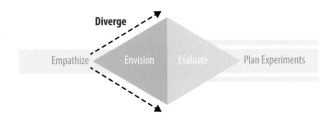

FIGURE 7-6. Envisioning starts with divergent thinking.

- *Build on ideas.* Get the group to say *Yes, and...* instead of *But* to ideas as they emerge. Find the underlying value of ideas and build on that.

- *Find alternatives.* Strive to come up with variations and alternatives on initial ideas. Don't discard them too soon.

- *Encourage crazy ideas.* Refrain from censoring yourself during ideation. There will be plenty of opportunities to prioritize and evaluate ideas later.

- *Be visual.* Work on whiteboards and flipcharts to map out ideas as they come. Uncover new relationships and connections as you brainstorm.

The intent is to protect ideas in their infancy. Create the environment that embraces a range of possibilities and that recombines ideas to arrive at innovative ideas.

Ideate

Start with a general brainstorming round. I find it helpful to let people get out their initial ideas quickly—even ideas they had before the workshop—so they are open to further ideation later on. Two key phrases you can use in conjunction with each other are:

How might we...?

Shifts attention from the current to the future state. For example, based on the pattern in Figure 7-5, I asked workshop participants, *how might we* better involve authors throughout the publishing process?

What if...?

Helps change direction and dig deeper. For example, in the above scenario, you might ask, "What if we focus only on face-to-face contact with authors?" Or, "What if we leverage alumni authors to help new authors?"

After collecting initial ideas from the group, conduct directed exercises for more innovative concepts. Three specific approaches I've had success with are:

1. Removing barriers

2. Challenging industry assumptions

3. Aspiring to transform

Barrier	Example	How to identify
Access: Some experiences are limited to specific times or places.	Mobile phones gave access to telephoning even on-the-go. Smartphones now give access to the Internet and data from anywhere.	Look at the instances in which an individual is not able to consume a product or service at all. Are they locked out of getting value?
Skill: People may lack the ability to perform a necessary task.	Computing prior to 1970 was reserved for trained users until the graphic user interface and mouse came along in 1982. Photography in the late 19th century before the Kodak camera simplified taking pictures.	Having to take many steps in a process is a sign that skill may be a barrier. How can you make tasks simple enough for anyone to complete?
Time: Interacting with a product or service may simply be too time consuming.	Prior to eBay, buying and selling collectibles was prohibitively time consuming.	Look for high drop-out rates within a process and assess if lack of time is the root cause. What can you do to shorten the process?
Money: People may lack the financial means to afford a product or service.	Airline travel prior to 1970 was only for the wealthy.	Identify points where a service has high costs. Ask, how might you offer that same service for free?

TABLE 7-1. Types of barriers that prevent individuals from getting value

1. Remove Barriers

To find opportunities for innovation, look at what's holding people back in their experience. Identify the obstacles to getting the jobs done at each stage. Table 7-1 summarizes key types of barriers to overcome, with examples and how to identify each type.*

Be sure to consider emotional and social aspects as well. For instance, if you are looking at the experience of attending a conference, you may find that people fear embarrassment when asking a question of a speaker. How might you overcome this emotional and social barrier?

At each stage in the diagram, consider how to remove the primary barriers people have from getting the value they need. As you move through the diagram, pose the question: how might we overcome obstacles? This focuses the collective energy of the group and points to sources of deeper change.

---

* This table is adapted from *The Innovator's Guide To Growth* (2008) by Scott Anthony and colleagues. See this book for more on barriers to innovation.

2. Challenge Industry Assumptions

Meaningful change comes from breaking the rules. To help foster a disruptive mindset, identify the prevailing industry assumptions, or those unwritten rules that define an industry.

First, generate industry assumption statements using this formula:

Everyone in the <industry or category> knows that <assumption>….

Then, think of ways to change or overturn each. In his book *Disrupt*, Luke Williams points to three ways to twist assumptions (which he calls *clichés*):

- *Invert.* What can be turned upside down? Take the assumption and do the opposite.

- *Deny.* What can you get rid of completely? Try intentionally denying some aspect of the assumption by simply removing it from the equation.

- *Scale.* What is scarce that could be made abundant and vice versa? What is expensive that could be cheap? Challenge assumptions of quantity and scope.

Finally, brainstorm possible solutions that invert, deny, or scale the industry assumption statement (Figure 7-7). Try forcing the group to do each for the most important assumptions.

Here are some examples of game-changing innovations and how they broke industry assumptions:

FIGURE 7-7. Challenge industry assumptions in a workshop.

- Everyone in the mop category knows that a mop was a one-time purchase, until P&G introduced disposable mops with Swiffer. (Invert)
- Everyone in architecture knows that plumbing, electrical services, and air vents go on the inside of buildings, until the Pompidou Center in Paris put them on the outside (Figure 7-8). (Invert)

FIGURE 7-8. The Pompidou Center inverts conventional architecture.

- Everyone in the airline industry knows passenger seats are preassigned, until Southwest made seat selection first come, first served. (Deny)
- Everyone in the luxury hotel business knows that offering a wide range of premium services justifies a high price, until Citizen M omitted many of the typical 5-star hotel services so they can offer accommodations at a lower price. (Deny)

- Everyone in the car rental business knows you have to see the customer, rent by the day, and complete a lot of paperwork, until Zipcar made it possible to book online without paper and pay by the hour. (Scale)
- Everyone knows that doctor's offices treat a wide range of conditions, until CVS's Minute Clinics treated a limited number of conditions that don't require a doctor to diagnose. (Scale)

To change the game, you have to first know what game you're in. This exercise forces your organization to consider doing the opposite of what the rest of the market is doing. This increases your ability to provide unique, meaningful value.

3. Aspire to transform

Products and services that merely connect, delight, and provide positive experience don't go far enough. What's needed is a better way to envision users as they *may* act.

Enter *The Ask*, a single question outlined by MIT Professor Michael Schrage in his book *Who Do You Want Your Customers to Become?* Successful innovations, Schrage contends, don't merely ask users to do something different: they ask them to *become* someone different.

For example, George Eastman didn't just invent an affordable, easy-to-use automatic camera at the end of the 19th century; he created *photographers*. His innovation allowed everyone to do something only trained professionals could previously do.

Through the lens of The Ask, Google is not just a sophisticated search algorithm. It lets everyone become *expert researchers*. Or consider eBay. The popular trading platform has created a new breed of *entrepreneurs*.

However, innovations that ask people to become something they don't want to become typically fail. Take the Segway. What does it ask us to become? A mad, helmeted scientist racing down the sidewalk? Or an authority figure (e.g., a police-woman) extending a few feet above other pedestrians? Or maybe just a *weirdo on a scooter* (Figure 7-9)?

McDonald's "super size me" campaign is another example. From a business standpoint it was very effective. For a few extra cents in cost to the organization, customers got what appeared to be a good deal. But it asked them to become *unhealthy*. That ended up hurting the reputation of the company.

Table 7-2 summarizes the preceding examples. It shows the transformations these products and service had on people, both positive and negative.

FIGURE 7-9. The Segway asks us to become someone we don't want to.

Kodak	= Camera	> Photographers
Google	= Search engine	> Expert researchers
eBay	= Trading platform	> Entrepreneurs

but...

Segway	= New vehicle	> Weirdo on scooter
Super size	= Value for money	> Unhealthy person

TABLE 7-2. A summary of the transformations selected innovative products and services had on people, both positive and negative.

Here is how to apply The Ask to alignment diagrams.

1. At each major division in the diagram, pose the question, *Who do we want our customers to become?*
2. Collect potential answers and decide which is best.
3. Continue for each major division of the diagram.
4. Finally, brainstorm solutions.

For example, Figure 7-10 shows the service blueprint from the previous chapter, created by Brandon Schauer. Overlaid on top of it are hypothetical answers to The Ask at each phase in the journey.

The Ask opens up the doors for truly aspirational thinking and transformative innovation. It starts with the outcome, not the solution. Brainstorming around those outcomes generally yields new ideas that stand out from previous exercises in the alignment workshop.

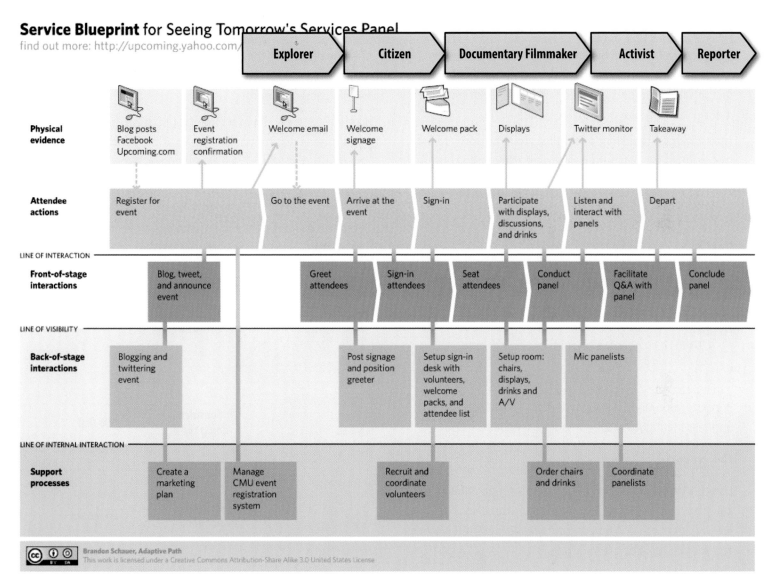

Service Blueprint for Seeing Tomorrow's Services Panel

find out more: http://upcoming.yahoo.com/

Explorer → Citizen → Documentary Filmmaker → Activist → Reporter

Physical evidence
- Blog posts Facebook Upcoming.com
- Event registration confirmation
- Welcome email
- Welcome signage
- Welcome pack
- Displays
- Twitter monitor
- Takeaway

Attendee actions
- Register for event
- Go to the event
- Arrive at the event
- Sign-in
- Participate with displays, discussions, and drinks
- Listen and interact with panels
- Depart

LINE OF INTERACTION

Front-of-stage interactions
- Blog, tweet, and announce event
- Greet attendees
- Sign-in attendees
- Seat attendees
- Conduct panel
- Facilitate Q&A with panel
- Conclude panel

LINE OF VISIBILITY

Back-of-stage interactions
- Blogging and twittering event
- Post signage and position greeter
- Setup sign-in desk with volunteers, welcome packs, and attendee list
- Setup room: chairs, displays, drinks and A/V
- Mic panelists

LINE OF INTERNAL INTERACTION

Support processes
- Create a marketing plan
- Manage CMU event registration system
- Recruit and coordinate volunteers
- Order chairs and drinks
- Coordinate panelists

Brandon Schauer, Adaptive Path
This work is licensed under a Creative Commons Attribution-Share Alike 3.0 United States License

FIGURE 7-10. An example of a service blueprint shows possible responses to The Ask at each phase.

Evaluate

Integrate evaluation activities directly into the workshop. You will be making presumptions at this point, but that's OK. In fact, it's better to presume and fail than to overrationalize the merit of an idea based on its face value alone.

After divergent thinking, select ideas to move forward. At this point you'll switch from divergent thinking to convergent thinking (Figure 7-11).

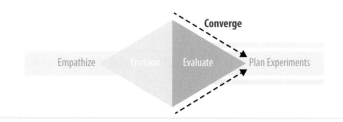

FIGURE 7-11. After divergent thinking, converge ideas into concepts and prioritize them.

Prioritize your ideas, articulate the details of each concept, and test them quickly for immediate feedback.

Prioritize

Use the "feasibility versus value" matrix for an initial prioritization, shown in Figure 7-12. On the one axis, consider how easy an idea is to implement, or its *feasibility*. On the other, consider its *value* to the individuals.

The idea is to sort the output of ideation into these quadrants. Once sorted, you can then do subsequent prioritization within each quadrant.

Figure 7-13 shows an example of a prioritization matrix from a workshop I once conducted. We used the window frame for the matrix grid. We quickly identified five high-impact ideas that the engineering team could implement immediately—literally the next day—with no extra funding or resources.

From the obvious things to implement, move to the ideas that are of high value but are harder to implement. These generally take planning, design, and development effort. Select the concepts to develop further that have the most potential and that people feel passionate about. Have a product owner make these selections or do dot voting to get group consensus.

FIGURE 7-12. A simple prioritization scheme looks at value to the customer and feasibility to deliver.

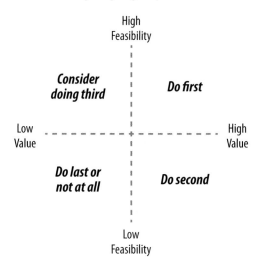

FIGURE 7-13. Prioritization of ideas by feasibility and value to the customer can be done on a simple grid.

Articulate

Innovation often comes without epiphany. Don't expect to be able to recognize an innovation as such immediately. You'll have to first develop your ideas iteratively.

⚡ As quickly as possible, articulate the ideas you want to test. Even within a few hours you can create representations of your leading ideas for evaluation. This "debugs" your thinking and can prove or disprove the value of an idea quickly. Here are a few techniques:

Write scenarios

Write out the details of a concept in prose. Be as detailed as possible in terms of the anticipated experience. Even the simplest of concepts can easily fill multiple pages of text. Let others read and critique it.

Create storyboards

Represent the intended experience in a series of graphic panels. Then critique the idea as a group. Figure 7-14 shows an example of a series of storyboards created during a workshop, with comments from the team surrounding it. In this case, we decided to put one concept on hold based on this initial assessment.

FIGURE 7-14. Storyboards represent ideas visually.

Draw a flowchart

Quickly express the steps of your idea as steps in a flow-chart. This will help you make connections and see all of the moving parts at once.

Sketch ideas

Quickly draw an image of the product or service to share with others.

Wireframe solutions

Create simple greyscale versions of screens for interaction (Figure 7-15).

Build a prototype

With easy-to-use online prototyping tools such as InVision, it's very simple to simulate working software. You can create a convincing prototype in a matter of hours (Figure 7-16).

Even physical products can be prototyped in a day-long workshop. In one workshop I conducted, we targeted an idea for improving the shipping experience with a large ecommerce website. We went to the local postal supply store, bought a box with the approximate dimensions we needed, and mocked it up to look like we had envisioned it. This was then used to get immediate feedback from potential customers.

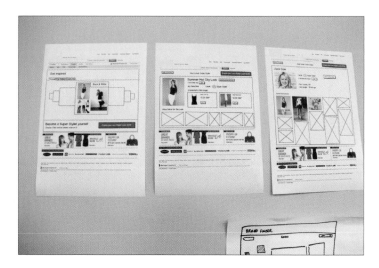

FIGURE 7-15. Wireframes created during an alignment workshop quickly bring ideas to life.

FIGURE 7-16. Create a clickable prototype quickly for testing with potential users.

Test

⚡ Get feedback on your ideas as quickly as possible, even during the workshop. This will not be controlled, scientific research. Instead, the aim is to understand your assumptions better. Are you solving the right problems? Does your idea address the problem in the right way?

Once you've articulated and represented your ideas, there are many lightweight ways to evaluate it, including some of the following.

Hallway testing

Get feedback from people close by who are not part of the workshop. Colleagues in other departments can provide quick, initial reactions on your concepts, for instance.

Online tests

There are many online services that provide feedback on concepts and prototypes—for example, Usertesting.com. You'll usually get results within a matter of hours.

Focus groups

Recruit people in advance of the workshop to give direct feedback. Present the concepts to a small focus group of two or three people and watch how they react.

Innovation often comes without epiphany. Don't expect to be able to recognize an innovation as such immediately.

Concept tests

Moderated tests ask participants to think aloud as they interact with your prototype or artifact. As with focus groups, you have to recruit participants in advance. Figure 7-17 shows a concept test during a workshop. The tests were conducted in a separate room, viewable by the workshop team via video camera.

FIGURE 7-17. Test concepts during an alignment workshop for immediate feedback.

Hold discussions on the feedback you gather. Determine what you will change in the next iteration of the concept prototype. Or, you may decide to put the concept on hold. Either way, be sure that you integrate the learning from the evaluation rounds into your thinking.

Facilitating an Alignment Workshop

Diagrams don't provide answers; they foster conversations. As the facilitator of the workshop, it's your job to make those conversations happen (Figure 7-18). Your role begins with careful preparation, then moves into moderating the session, and continues with a strong follow-up.

FIGURE 7-18. The author facilitating an alignment workshop.

1. Prepare

Organize the alignment workshop well in advance. Include it in your initial proposal, and schedule the event early.

Invite a range of stakeholders. The alignment workshop is an inclusive activity. Invite a range of participants for broad buy-in and input from diverse perspectives. Groups of 6–12 partici-

pants work best. Larger groups are possible but make moderation more difficult.

Assign roles. An alignment workshop is a creative endeavor that results in designed artifacts:

- Facilitator: This is the person moderating the workshop, who ideally is also the mapmaker.

- Designers: Include designers and others that can help articulate the envisioned concepts.

- Test moderator: Also include someone who can moderate user tests, if needed.

- Outside industry experts: Consider inviting industry experts from outside of the organization for a fresh perspective.

- Stakeholders: To the degree possible, include senior decision makers in the mix.

Find a date and time. Book the alignment workshop early. In many organizations, getting people to commit for a whole day or multiple days is difficult. Schedule it before you have started creating the diagram.

Reserve a room. The alignment workshop is a working session. You will be moving around and standing much of the time. Book an oversized room for the number of people you've invited.

Go offsite. Try to find a space outside of the normal workplace. Participants can get distracted by daily tasks and interactions with other colleagues.

Plan logistics. Secure equipment and supplies in advance: a projector, Internet connection, flipcharts, whiteboards, sticky notes, pens, markers, paper, and tape. You will also need several large, printed copies of the diagram.

Arrange catering. It's important to take breaks and have snacks. Plan for coffee in the morning and breaks in the afternoon. Get out of the workshop room for lunch, but try to stay close by.

Create an agenda. Plan an agenda for the workshop, including time for breaks. It's OK to improvise and go off schedule, but having an agenda will keep the session on track.

Hold a pre-workshop meeting. Schedule a meeting or call a week before the alignment workshop. Distribute materials and set expectations. Include information about the location, times, and travel. You can also start some of the initial workshop activities ahead of time.

2. Run the Workshop

Think about the shape of the session, as outlined in this chapter.

- *Set the stage.* Explain the parts of the workshop: empathizing, envisioning, and evaluating. Set expectations that the outcome will be a plan for running further experiments. Remind people that the conversation does not end with this workshop—it's ongoing.

- *Engage with the diagram.* Plan exercises that make people absorb the information in the diagram. Have them read through and assess the experiences people currently have.

- *Facilitate divergent thinking.* Brainstorming is the principal way to generate new ideas. Use the diagram as a springboard into new concepts with some of the techniques discussed in this chapter.

- *Create artifacts.* Sketch, draw, and prototype your ideas quickly. The room should be more like a project war room than a board room (Figure 7-19). Alignment workshops are messy affairs.

- *Select concepts.* Focus on ideas that have high value to customers and to the organization.

- *Run tests.* Quickly evaluate the leading concepts, outlined above.

FIGURE 7-19. An alignment workshop is a working session to prototype and test ideas immediately after they are conceived.

Additionally, plan social activities. In many cases, the group of people you bring together may have never been in the same room together. Include a social event such as an evening dinner. It's important for continued collaboration that people get to know one another on a personal level. This helps build trust and respect, which goes a long way for the success of the effort.

3. Follow Up

Alignment activities do not end with the workshop. Make sure that you keep the momentum going after the session has ended. Consider ways to continue working with the team.

- *Get feedback on the session.* Follow up with a brief survey on the effort itself. This can be done verbally at the end of the workshop or by a short online survey. The intent is to learn how you can improve this type of effort in the future.

- *Update the diagram.* Take the feedback you get from the session and update the diagram. Include on it the additions and comments others made. You can also map other outcomes from to the diagram.

- *Distribute materials.* Collate the output of the workshop and distribute it to others who didn't participate. Schedule a meeting to present the workshop results to a wider group of stakeholders.

- *Make the diagrams visible.* Create different forms of the diagram and make them visible. Print out large copies for the office space. Create flyers or handouts of

the diagram that colleagues can keep by their desks. Integrate it into presentations and other documents internally.

Finally, the effort does not end with the workshop. Ensure that the experiments are actually conducted. Keep the momentum going with an action plan and assigned owners of each experiment. Hold weekly checkpoints to track progress.

Single-Day and Multiday Workshops

The process for an alignment workshop outlined in this chapter—empathy, envisioning, and evaluating—has no time frame. It can be done in a matter of hours or extend for days. I have found that multiday workshops are effective for gaining momentum quickly.

For instance, I have been able to run two or three tests with external test subjects within a few days. The three scenarios in Figures 7-20a–c show approximate schedules for workshops across one, two, and three days, respectively.

Diagrams don't provide answers, they foster conversations.

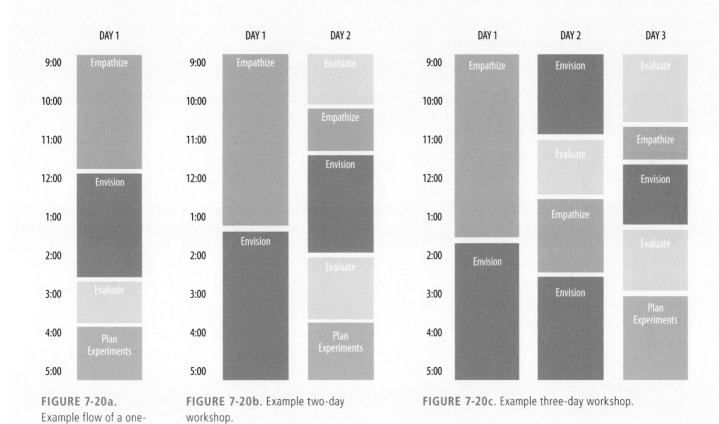

FIGURE 7-20a. Example flow of a one-day workshop.

FIGURE 7-20b. Example two-day workshop.

FIGURE 7-20c. Example three-day workshop.

Plan Experiments

Creating new value brings uncertainty. Although you already have initial feedback on your ideas, you still don't know how the market will react to the proposed innovation in the proposed context of use. It may or may not be adopted.

To address this risk, plan for ongoing experiments. Start by creating hypotheses statements for each of the concepts you've decided to move forward. Structurally, there are three parts:

> *We believe that providing [solution, service] for [individual, customer, user]*

> *Will likely result in [desired outcome, assumed effect]*

> *We will know this when we see [result, measurable impact]*

Notice that the hypothesis is phrased as a *belief*. You won't know the impact until you introduce it into the market. Also note that if there is not a measurable outcome, you don't have a testable hypothesis. Be sure to include a metric. Then plan experiments to be conducted over the following weeks. Some specific approaches include the following:

- *Explanatory video.* Create a video explaining your service and circulate it on the Internet. Measure interest via traffic and response rates.

- *Landing page* (sometimes called a "fake storefront"). Creating a landing page. Announcing the fictitious launch of your proposed service.

- *Prototype testing.* Simulate a functioning version of your concept. Test this with potential customers and measure concrete aspects such as task completion and satisfaction.

- *Concierge service.* Start with a simulated version of your service. Invite a very limited set of potential customers to sign up, and then provide the service manually.

- *Limited product release.* Create a version of your service with only one or two functioning features. Measure the success and appeal of those features.

Combinations of the above are also possible. For instance, after one recent workshop I conducted, we developed both an explanatory video and a landing page (Figure 7-21). Visitors could view the video and then sign up to be notified for a beta release. There was a short, three-question survey we introduced after signing up as well.

From these touchpoints we were able to measure traffic to the website over a given period of time, the number of sign-ups, and responses to our survey. We also spoke with selected individuals to better understand their motivations and what excited them about our value proposition.

Those familiar with the current literature on "lean" techniques will recognize some of these approaches. Other techniques and tests are also possible. For more on defining and running market experiments, see Eric Ries *Lean Startup* and Ash Maurya's *Running Lean*. Also recommended are *Lean UX* by Jeff Gothelf and *The Innovator's Hypothesis* by Michael Schrage.

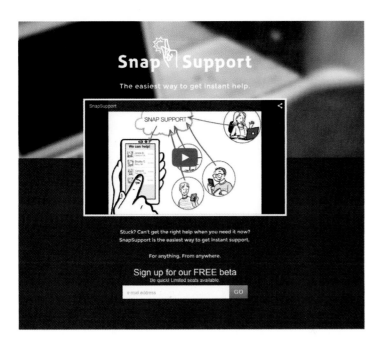

FIGURE 7-21. SnapSupport began as a concept video and landing page to test market reactions to the idea before a working prototype was built.

Summary

A diagram is a means to an end—to get team alignment. But diagrams don't provide the answers; instead, they spark conversations. They are like campfires that people gather around to share stories and to make sense of the experiences they create.

In this stage of the process, your role switches from map-maker to *facilitator*. The goal is twofold: align the internal perspective of the organization to the outside world, and use that insight to generate new ideas. In an alignment workshop you'll alternate between three modes of activity: empathizing, envisioning, and evaluating.

Think of a diagram as a prototype of an experience. It allows team members to put themselves in the user's shoes. In the alignment workshop, first read through the diagram together and assess your performance at each stage. Then find opportunities by looking at weaknesses, gaps, and redundancies, as well as where competitors perform well.

Envision possible solutions. Use techniques like *The Ask* to consider how you might transform customers. Pose the simple question: who do we want our customers to become? Ideate and brainstorm solutions resulting from these discussions and the diagram.

Select ideas with the most potential and represent them in some way. This can be done quickly with scenarios, storyboards, and wireframes. Use these artifacts to get input from others. Evaluate the results, and iterate.

Even within a single-day workshop you can run lightweight tests. Invite a few outsiders to critique storyboards and sketches, for instance. Iterate as many times as possible, and plan to continue iterating after the workshop.

Finally, plan experiments. The ideas you come up with are hypotheses, not ready-to-implement requirements. Build a culture of learning in your organization by following "lean" practices.

Running a workshop is not an easy task. It requires a lot of planning. Alignment doesn't stop with the diagram or with the workshop. After you generate excitement, consider how to keep the momentum going.

Further Reading

Chris Ertel and Lisa Kay Solomon, *Moments of Impact* (2014)

> This book is about how to design effective meetings within organizations. The authors' advice will help you shape your time with others. You will better understand the dynamics of real-time group collaboration and be able to run more effective workshops.

Leo Frishberg and Charles Lambdin, *Presumptive Design: Design Provocations for Innovation* (Morgan Kaufmann, 2015)

> Presumptive Design details a radical approach to design research. Taking the standard Discover, Define, Design, Deliver design-thinking cycle, PrD starts with design. The book is divided into three parts: the importance of PrD, the principles and risks involved, and how to execute the PrD process. Over 10 case studies bring the process to life.

Dave Gray et al., *Gamestorming* (O'Reilly, 2010)

> Gamestorming is an indispensable collection of activities for interactive workshops. There are detailed instructions and examples of each. The introduction provides a good overview for running workshops.

Luke Hohmann, *Innovation Games* (Addison-Wesley, 2006)

> Like Gamestorming, this is a collection of workshop techniques. Many of the game-like exercises use metaphors (e.g., Speedboat, Design The Box) and interactive techniques (Buy A Feature) that get results through serious play.

Michael Schrage, *Who Do You Want Your Customers to Become?* (Harvard Business Review Press, 2012)

> This is a short ebook with a powerful message. Rather than looking at who your current customers are and trying to delight them, strive to transform them: enable them to become somebody or something they currently are not. The simple question, "Who do you want your customer to become?" reframes your focus to go beyond providing incrementally better services.

Elisabeth Bjørndal Skjelten, *Complexity and Other Beasts* (Oslo School of Architecture and Design, 2014)

> This thin volume focuses specifically on facilitating mapping workshops. Skjelten offers many practical tips and advice. The approach to mapping is one of co-creating a diagram rather than working with research-based diagrams. The hand-drawn illustrations throughout make this a fun and accessible resource. It has a limited circulation with only 1,200 copies printed.

Russ Unger, Brad Nunnally, and Dan Willis. *Designing the Conversation* (New Riders, 2013)

> This is an excellent book for facilitating collaboration sessions of various kinds. The techniques range from interviewing users to holding workshops. It is a perfect companion to mapping efforts.

Rapid Online Mapping and Design Workshop

by Jim Kalbach

MURAL (*http://mur.al*) is a leading virtual whiteboard for design collaboration. It's a cloud-based service that lets you work visually online, from wherever you are. I joined the MURAL team in March 2015.

We used our own product to examine the onboarding experience of MURAL and make improvements. To do this, we held a one-and-a-half day workshop in Buenos Aires with a group of eight people with different roles. The workshop had three parts.

Part 1: Empathize

The aim was to first understand the user's experience. To do this, I mapped out elements of the experience using MURAL in advance of the session (Figure 7-22). There were three main sections to mural I created:

- Value chain (upper left). To understand the flow of value, I mapped the customer value chain. This provides an overview of the actors involved and their relationships to one another.

- Proto-personas. In the upper right of Figure 7-22 you'll see three proto-personas. These were based on the actors in the value chain diagram. Sophia, the design lead, was our primary persona for this exercise.

- Experience map. In the middle was an experience map. It is based on prior research I conducted on team collaboration, as well as recent customer interviews. The circular shapes represent repeat behavior.

As a group, we discussed each of these elements to understand the broader experience. The digital format of the diagram allowed us to add and update it on-the-fly. For instance, we added details to the proto-personas as we discussed them.

Part 2: Envision

We then brainstormed about barriers to consumption. We asked, "What is keeping the primary persona from using our service repeatedly?"

With a large virtual area to work on, it was easy to record answers right below the experience map. These were clustered and prioritized using the dot voting feature built into MURAL.

We then conducted an exercise to find solutions, called a design studio. For each barrier we identified, participants individually sketched possible solutions. The sketches were photographed and uploaded to another mural for everyone in the workshop to see (Figure 7-23).

ONBOARDING EXPERIENCE

1 VALUE CHAIN

2 PROTO-PERSONAS

3 EXPERIENCE MAP

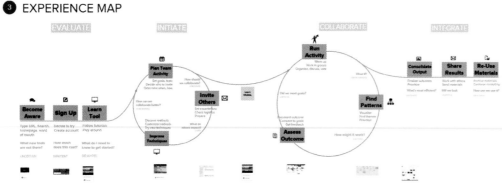

BRAINSTORMING

What are the barriers to consumption?

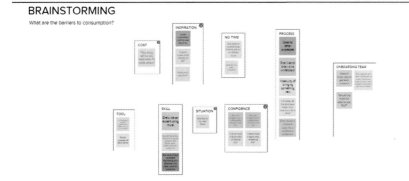

FIGURE 7-22. A combination of value chain, proto-personas, and experience fit in one mural, as well as the results of an initial brainstorming session.

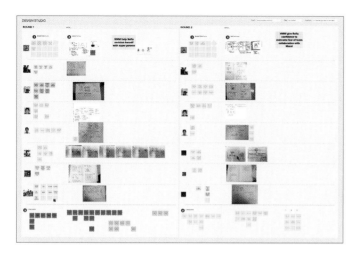

FIGURE 7-23. The results of a design studio using MURAL.

Part 3: Evaluate

After lunch the team broke into two groups. Each focused on consolidating the sketches into a single solution. Our aim was to create testable artifacts by the end of the day.

Using Usertesting.com, an online unmoderated remote testing service, we quickly got feedback on our proposed solutions. The tests ran overnight, and by the next morning we had initial results.

Some of our assumptions were validated, while others were disproven. We took the test feedback and iterated on the proposed designs. In a final step we created a concrete plan for implementation over the next few months.

Conclusion

This rapid approach allowed us to go from understanding the experience to prototyping to testing in less than two days. There were no written proposals, reports, or other documents.

Experience mapping does not have to be a lengthy process. Using an online tool like MURAL makes the process even quicker. More than that, working online also allowed us to combine elements in one place for a better overview.

Finally, we were also able to loop in others later who were not present at the workshop. Creating the experience map online makes the process ongoing rather than a static, one-time event, regardless of where people are.

Diagram and Image Credits

Figures 7-2, 7-3, 7-4, 7-13, 7-14, 7-15, 7-16, 7-17, 7-19: Photos by Jim Kalbach

Figure 7-5: Diagram created by Jim Kalbach

Figure 7-8: Photo of the Pompidou Center in Paris uploaded to Wikipedia by Reinraum, CC BY-SA 3.0

Figure 7-9: Photo by Scott Merrill, *https://skippy.net*, used with permission

Figure 7-10: Service blueprint created by Brandon Schauer of Adaptive Path, used with permission

Figure 7-18: Photographer unknown

Figures 7-22 and 7-23: Online maps and murals created by Jim Kalbach in MURAL (*http://mur.al*), used with permission

*"If you don't know where you are
going, any road will get you there."*

— Lewis Carroll

IN THIS CHAPTER

- Storyboards, scenarios, and storylines
- Design maps and user story maps
- Business model canvas and value proposition canvas
- Case Study: Customer Journey Mapping Game

CHAPTER 8

Envisioning Future Experiences

In the preface, I urged you to empathize with the people you serve. The advice is clear: view your offering from the outside-in rather than the inside-out.

But it's important to first develop empathy before conceiving new solutions. Distinguish *gaining* empathy from *applying* empathy, a point Indi Young makes in her book *Practical Empathy* (Rosenfeld Media, 2015). She writes:

> You can't apply empathy until you've developed it by listening deeply to a person...People try to act empathetic—to take someone's perspective, to walk in his shoes—without first taking time to develop empathy.

I've experienced this trap in the past. At a prior company I worked for, for example, a small team spent two months behind closed doors developing a new concept that helped people plan events. They had virtually no contact with potential customers.

To anyone who had already gained empathy for the target users it was clear this solution had serious flaws. It didn't address actual user needs, and it didn't match their mental model. Despite the team's passion, the concept was doomed from the outset. They would have better spent their time developing empathy first.

⚡ Note that I am not advocating big, upfront research. Ideally, empathy building is a regular ongoing activity. But grounding yourself in reality first saves time and reduces risk later. It need not take long, and visualization tends to make the process go quicker.

The process of mapping helps teams acquire develop common understanding of a person's experience. For this reason, this book has focused on *current state* visualizations—diagrams of the world as it exists today. After gaining empathy, then envision a future as you think it should be.

One approach to represent the intended experience is to create *future state* maps of the experience—separate, full-fledged illustrations akin to those described throughout this book. However, this is time consuming and is often not needed.

Instead, it's typically possible to include future experiences within the current state map, for example at the bottom of a diagram (see Figure 8-1). This highlights the transition needed to move from the present to the future. Both cause and cure are captured in one place.

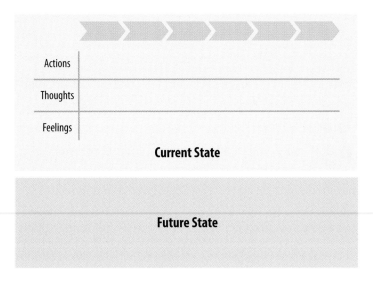

FIGURE 8-1. Mapping the current state to the future state shows the relationship between the two.

But also, it's more efficient to use complementary techniques to illustrate the future state creates greater impact. This chapter deals with some of these techniques, including storyboards, scenarios, storylines, and design maps, as well as user story mapping. By the end of the chapter you should have a good idea of how to visualize future experiences with complementary techniques.

Storyboards

Storyboards come from filmmaking. The process organizes a series of illustrated panels to represent the flow from scene to scene. A storyboard allows creators to experiment with different sequences of action.

The technique is also used in product and service design. Each step in the experience is given a panel with a rough description of what should happen at that moment. Storyboarding is a way to quickly flesh out concepts before building a prototype.

As a modeling tool, storyboarding helps you put personas in action, taking various constraints and context into account. If an alignment diagram is a map of the landscape, storyboards are specific routes through that landscape.

Storyboards let you focus on the emotional highs and lows of a *specific* experience. They also allow you to focus on extreme cases. For instance, you can create a storyboard for a novice user of a system and compare it to what a power user might experience in another storyboard.

More than that, storyboards allow you to test ideas and "debug" them conceptually. They serve as the first iteration of an idea and allow teams to think about the service in terms of how the experience unfolds over time. This saves an enormous amount of time and pain later.

Storyboards are also collaborative documents that anyone can contribute to. Their informal nature invites contributions from others, fostering teamwork and collective decision making.

FIGURE 8-2. A simple storyboard can be very effective, like this one created by UX designer Erik Hanson.

They become part of the common language of the team and function as a shared reference.

Figure 8-2 shows an example of a simple storyboard created in a workshop by UX designer Erik Hanson. It was used to demonstrate the essence of a new idea, which evolved and changed over the course of the ensuing discussion.

More formal storyboards take time. For instance, I helped create a storyboard of the intended experience on a recent project. The concept allowed people to take a picture of a technical problem and request help from a network of experts and friends.

First, I sketched a rough sequence of interactions using a drawing app on my iPad (see Figure 8-3). As a team, we iterated on this sequence several times. Then, we enlisted the help of Deb Aoki, a professional comic artist and graphic facilitator, to make the panels into a more presentable storyboard (see Figure 8-4).

The touchpoints and interactions are clearly depicted in this storyboard. But there is also a focus on the human experience: the initial problem is described, and the emotions of the resolution are represented. The storyboard helped form the idea and socialize the concept with others in the organization.

FIGURE 8-3. A draft storyboard shows an intended experience.

FIGURE 8-4. A revised version of the storyboard in Figure 8-3, created by expert illustrator Deb Aoki.

Comic strips are like storyboards and used to communicate a vision. Figure 8-5 shows an example from Kevin Cheng's book *See What I Mean* (Rosenfeld Media, 2012). Obviously Cheng is an expert illustrator. But don't be daunted: he breaks down the technique into its basic components to show that anyone can get started creating comic strips at some level.

Overall, storyboards are a type of visual storytelling. They depict the steps in an interaction and foster a shared understanding of a vision. You don't need to be an expert illustrator to create storyboards: sketching basic shapes and stick figures is all that's required to get started. Have an expert create a final version, if needed.

FIGURE 8-5. Comics are an effective way to envision future ideas, like this one by illustrator Kevin Cheng from his book *See What I Mean*.

Scenarios

Scenarios are detailed descriptions of an intended experience from the individual's perspective. They go hand-in-hand with storyboards, but are text-based rather than illustrated. Since no drawing is involved, the barrier to create them is even lower than with storyboards.

Consider this example of a scenario from the beginning of the landmark article "The Semantic Web" by Tim Berners-Lee, inventor of the World Wide Web, and his colleagues. These are the opening lines of his landmark article that set the stage for a broader, more technical discussion later on in the text:

The entertainment system was belting out the Beatles' "We Can Work It Out" when the phone rang. When Pete answered, his phone turned the sound down by sending a message to all the other local devices that had a volume control. His sister, Lucy, was on the line from the doctor's office: "Mom needs to see a specialist and then has to have a series of physical therapy sessions. Biweekly or something. I'm going to have my agent set up the appointments." Pete immediately agreed to share the chauffeuring.

At the doctor's office, Lucy instructed her Semantic Web agent through her handheld Web browser. The agent promptly retrieved information about Mom's prescribed treatment from the doctor's agent, looked up several lists of providers, and checked for the ones in-plan for Mom's insurance within a 20-mile radius of her home and with a rating of excellent or very

good on trusted rating services. It then began trying to find a match between available appointment times (supplied by the agents of individual providers through their websites) and Pete's and Lucy's busy schedules.

In a few minutes the agent presented them with a plan. Pete didn't like it—University Hospital was all the way across town from Mom's place, and he'd be driving back in the middle of rush hour. He set his own agent to redo the search with stricter preferences about location and time. Lucy's agent, having complete trust in Pete's agent in the context of the present task, automatically assisted by supplying access certificates and shortcuts to the data it had already sorted through.

Almost instantly the new plan was presented: a much closer clinic and earlier times—but there were two warning notes. First, Pete would have to reschedule a couple of his less important appointments. He checked what they were—not a problem. The other was something about the insurance company's list failing to include this provider under physical therapists: "Service type and insurance plan status securely verified by other means," the agent reassured him.

The words not in italics come from the original source of this scenario and indicate touchpoints with the Semantic Web. This example has many qualities of a well-written scenario. It's easy to understand, it's enjoyable to read, it describes an experience rather than technology, and it offers a clear vision.

Scenarios describe the ideal user experience. They give personas a voice and set them in motion. And as with storyboards, scenarios allow you to focus on edge cases. They let you explore specific experiences, including extreme situations.

Scenarios also help validate an idea. For instance, I once participated in an ideation workshop where we spent hours writing up our favorite ideas as scenarios. It was very telling: some of the most attractive ideas were difficult to describe in terms of the user experience. Based on these scenarios, we were better able to prioritize our ideas.

Rarely can you go from a rough idea on a sticky note directly to implementation. Steps are needed in between to expand on the features of a concept. Scenario writing is a quick way to involve everyone on the team and represent an intended experience in detail for evaluation and feedback.

Storylines

Storytelling is not only a means of communicating a vision, it helps make sense of complex problems. According to digital product strategist Donna Lichaw, author of *The User's Journey: Storymapping Products That People Love* (Rosenfeld Media, 2016), you can use the principles of storytelling to guide the design of products and services.

To do this, Lichaw relies on a structure common to most all stories, called *the narrative arc* (Figure 8-6).

This structure is not new. It can be traced all the way back to Aristotle. It is a timeless form used to tell stories over thousands of years and across cultures.

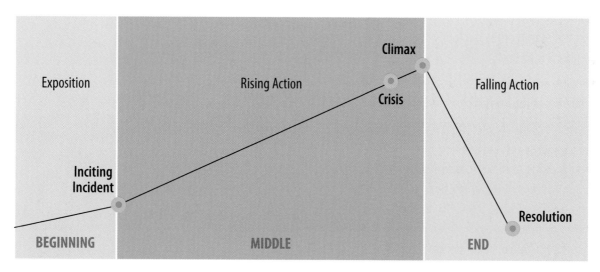

FIGURE 8-6. The archetypal narrative arc shows the rise in action before the resolution.

The elements of the narrative arc are:

- *Exposition:* Good stories establish the context and introduce the characters and situation at the beginning.

- *Inciting incident:* This is the point where something goes wrong or there is some change to the situation.

- *Rising action:* A good story builds over time. Intensity and action increase as the story unfolds.

- *Crisis:* The story culminates at the point of maximum friction. It's the point of no return.

- *Climax/resolution:* The climax is the most exciting part of the story and the point at which the audience realizes that all might be well again. This is when the problem that was surfaced at the inciting incident is resolved.

- *Falling action:* But wait, there's more. After the climax, the story comes back down in action and begins to end.

- *End:* This is the very end of the narrative. Typically, there is a return back to the original state.

The point of storylines is not storytelling, but rather building products and services *as if* you are crafting a story. In other words, apply the narrative arc to the design process itself. To do this, Lichaw recommends first mapping out an ideal journey against the narrative. Then design your product or service based on that flow.

Figure 8-7 shows an example of using a narrative arc to plan the content of a digital service. The intent is to make the user's journey into a dramatic, engaging story. The result is a strategy for content and features that meet audience needs in an engaging way.

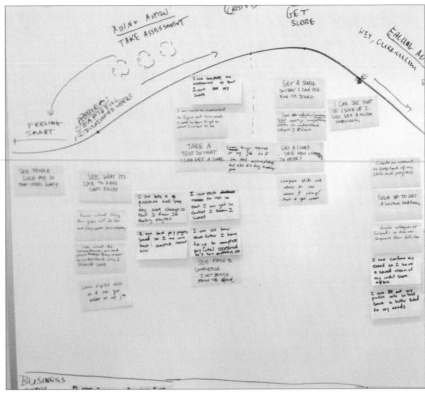

FIGURE 8-7. An example of a narrative arc and envisioned content from a workshop shows the rise of action and resolution.

Applying narrative arcs in design workshops is straightforward. Together with Lis Hubert, Lichaw describes the process in their article "Storymapping: A MacGyver Approach to Content Strategy" (*UX Matters*, 2014).

1. Hold a workshop with a broad set of stakeholders
2. Draw the user's journey as a narrative arc on a whiteboard
3. Map individual pieces of content users would need at each stage
4. Below that, record existing content
5. Identify gaps and weaknesses in the existing content
6. Prioritize and plan a broader content strategy

Following these steps results in a content strategy with focus and meaning. It aligns teams to a common purpose and yields more engaging services in general.

Design Maps

Design maps are simple diagrams of an ideal experience co-created by a team. The technique is described by Tamara Adlin and Holly Jamesen Carr in Chapter 10 of the book *The Persona Lifecycle*.

Creating a design map is a simple practice that requires only sticky notes and a whiteboard. The result is a map of an ideal experience. There are four basic elements in the map, each with a different color note:

- *Steps:* Blue notes denote the steps a given persona takes in a process.
- *Comments:* Green notes provide more details about each action, including thoughts, feelings, and pain points.
- *Questions:* Yellow notes capture questions a team has about the experience. They highlight their gaps in knowledge and assumptions about the proposed experience.
- *Ideas:* Pink notes are used to capture ideas how to provide a better service.

Figure 8-8 shows an example of a design map for a fictitious app. The steps, in blue, form the basis of the chronology across the top of the map. Comments, questions, and ideas appear below each step, forming an interlocking grid of sticky notes.

Interestingly, Adlin and Carr recommended using design maps asynchronously. The idea is to place a map in a common office area and invite colleagues to contribute to it individually. Over the course of days or weeks, team members can add questions and ideas as they come to light. With this, the map grows organically over time.

Otherwise, design maps can be used in workshops to envision a future experience. For instance, I once used design maps in an alignment workshop with three breakout groups. First, each group created an ideal *flow* for one of three experiences we were targeting. They also added *comments* to describe the steps in greater detail.

LUCAS DOWNLOADS THE APP	LUCAS CREATES AN ACCOUNT	LUCAS ALLOWS HIS CAMERA, EMAIL AND CONTACTS TO BE ACCESSED	LUCAS BUYS A NEW PRODUCT, E.G. ELCCTRONICS	LUCAS TAKES A PICTURE OF A BARCODE WITH THE APP	THE SYSTEM AUTOMATICALLY CONNECTS TO THE RIGHT USER MANUAL	(LATER) LUCAS HAS A PROBLEM WITH THE PRODUCT	LUCAS ACCESSES THE APP OR THE WEBSITE	LUCAS OPENS THE USER MANUAL	LUCAS AUTOMATCALLY CONTACTS CUSTOMER SUPPORT	LUCAS SPEAKS WITH AN AGENT	- OR - LUCAS CAN FIND A SERVICE PROVIDER IN HIS AREA
THE APP IS FREE	WE WILL OFFER SOCIAL SIGN IN	WILL PEOPLE ALLOW THEIR CONTACT INFORMATION FOR THIS APP?	OVER TIME, WE CAN MAKE RECOM-MENDATIONS FOR PRODUCTS AND STORES	THE SYSTEM NEEDS A DATABASE OF BARCODES	THE SYSTEM AUTOMATICALLY REGISTERS IT FOR WARRANTY	WE CAN OFFER A "PANIC BUTTON" IF LUCAS JUST WANTS HELP NOW	THE WEBSITE IS ALWAYS IN SYNC WITH THE APP	IF HE CAN'T FIX THE PROBLEM, HE CAN CONTACT CUSTOMER SUPPORT RIGHT AWAY	WITH ONE CLICK, THE APP FINDS THE SUPPLIERS CUSTOMER SUPPORT	THE PHONE TAKES OVER, BUT THE APP IS STILL RUNNING	WHAT ABOUT COST OF A SERVICE PROVIDER?
THERE IS A DIRECT LINK FROM OUR HOMEPAGE	WHICH SOCIAL NETWORKS SHOULD WE ALLOW?		CAN PEOPLE ALWAYS FIND THE PRODUCT BARCODE?				WILL HE REALLY REMEMBER THAT HE LISTED IT IN THE APP?	THE MANUALS CAN BE INTERACDTIVE		WE CAN PASS THE INFORMATION TO THE AGENT SO SHE ALREADY HAS A HISTORY	WILL PEOPLE TRUST THE SERVICE?
WHAT IS OUR REVENUE MODEL EXACTLY?			THE APP AUTOMATICALLY FOCUSES ON THE BARCODE - NO BUTTON REQUIRED				WE CAN PUSH NOTIFICATIONS IF A WARRANTY EXPIRES	THE APP REMINDS HIM IF THE WARRANTY IS GOOD OR NOT			WE TAKE A CUT OF THE COST AS A FINDERS FEE

FIGURE 8-8. An example of a design map, modeled after the technique outlined in *The Persona Lifecycle*.

Then, I rotated the groups so that they were now working with another group's design map. They read the steps and comments on the new design map and posed *questions* about each step on a different color sticky notes.

Finally, I rotated the groups once more. After we read all of the steps, comments, and questions of the preceding groups, the task was to *brainstorm* new ideas at the bottom of the map. We also sketched the best ones as wireframes. In total, each group engaged with all three diagrams and got to build on their colleague's thoughts.

Figure 8-9 shows part of one whiteboard used for this exercise. Note that the color coding of sticky notes varied from what Adlin and Carr set out. Instead, we used yellow notes for steps, blue for comments, pink for questions, and green for ideas. But the process for creating the design map was the same.

FIGURE 8-9. A section of a design map created in a workshop shows the various types of information on different-colored sticky notes.

Putting It All Together: Which Techniques Are Needed When?

This book is about possibilities. Throughout, I've highlighted many of the tools for mapping experiences, shown in Figure 8-10.

But with possibilities comes choice. To help you select the best approach, consider the types of models that describe an experience:

1. Models of individuals: who are you designing for? Personas, proto-personas, and consumer insight maps are examples.

2. Models of context and goals: maps of experiences describe the circumstances of interaction. What are the jobs to be done? What are their needs, feelings, and motivations?

3. Models of future experiences: finally, create models for the envisioned future state. What do solutions look like? How can we represent them for evaluation?

At a minimum, use one of each. More are possible, but be careful of model proliferation. Don't confuse your audience.

⚡ Alternatives for an informal diagramming might look like this:

- Proto-personas > Experience map > Storyboards
- Proto-personas > Design map

A more formal mapping process might include these models:

- Personas > Mental Model Diagram > Scenarios and storyboards > Value proposition canvas
- Consumer insight maps > Service blueprint > storylines > Business model canvas

Always keep the intent of mapping in mind: to tell the story of interactions (past and future) to align your team.

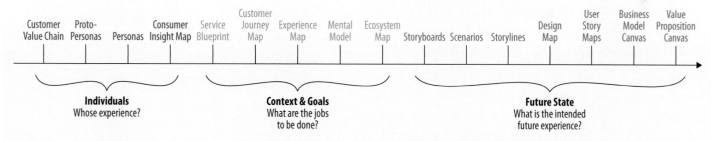

FIGURE 8-10. A sequence of techniques discussed in this book can be categorized into three groups: diagrams about individuals, context an goals, and future state diagrams.

User Story Mapping

My childhood neighbor had a Mr. Potato Head toy. If you're not familiar with this toy, it's a featureless plastic head to which you add various facial features. The resulting combinations can be humorous, e.g., Groucho Marx glasses with big red lips.

Producers of software typically want to avoid creating products that look like Mr. Potato Head. But without a common vision of what you are building, it's possible to unknowingly combine elements that don't go well together.

Agile development—the leading approach for software development—strives to break the product down into small chunks, called user stories. These are short descriptions of a feature told from the user's perspective. User stories typically have a common format:

As a <type of user>, I want <some goal> so that <some reason>

While utilizing user stories makes development more manageable, it can also cause teams to lose the big picture of what they are building. Focusing on individual features gives a team tunnel vision, losing the overall picture of what is being built.

To avoid the Mr. Potato Head effect in software development, Agile coach and expert Jeff Patton came up with a technique called user story mapping. He advises development teams to not assume everyone has the same view of the final product. In his book *User Story Mapping* (O'Reilly, 2014), Patton describes this phenomenon and how to overcome it:

If I have an idea in my head and I describe it in writing, when you read that document, you might quite possibly imagine something different…However, if we get together and talk, you can tell me what you think and I can ask questions. The talking goes better if we can externalize our thinking by drawing pictures or organizing our ideas using index cards or sticky notes. If we give each other time to explain our thoughts with words and pictures, we build shared understanding.

Don't assume that everyone has the same mental model of the outcome. More importantly, visualizations go a long way toward building a shared understanding (see Figure 8-11).

A strength of user story maps is that they are simple to comprehend. Figure 8-12 shows an example created by Steve Rogalsky, an expert agile coach with the company Protegra. You can see the alignment of user activities (in orange and blue sticky notes) to planned features (in yellow).

User story mapping has its roots in task modeling as pioneered by Larry and Lucy Constantine.[*] The technique is flexible, with different ways to approach creating a map. The main elements that most user story maps include are as follows:

---

[*] See, for example, Larry Constantine, "Essential Modeling: Use Cases for User Interfaces," *ACM Interactions* (Apr 1995). As well as other writings by Constantine and his wife, Lucy.

- *User types.* A brief description of the different roles the system is designed for. These are typically listed at the top or on the side (not shown in Figure 8-12).

- *Backbone.* This is a sequence of user activities listed across the top of the diagram. Frequently a more granular description of user tasks that form a flow across the phases accompanies them. These are listed horizontally just below the phases of the backbone.

- *User stories.* The body of the map contains stories needed to achieve the desired outcomes. These are typically prioritized and separated into releases.

FIGURE 8-11. Don't assume everyone has the same picture of the solution in their minds.

The backbone is similar to the chronology in an experience map. A user story map, however, tends to lack much of the detail and context of an experience map, such as thoughts and feelings. Instead, it focuses on software product development.

The process to user story mapping requires team participation from the very beginning. Follow these steps to involve everyone in the map's creation:

- *Frame the idea:* As a team, discuss *why* you are building the product. Identify and record the benefits and problems it solves. Also decide on *who* you are building the product for. Write your responses down at the top of the map.

- *Map the big picture:* Illustrate the flow of the solution chronologically, including details about specific actions. If possible, include the pains and joys users have today to inform your development decisions.

- *Explore:* Use the map to facilitate conversations about desired outcomes and the intended experience. Describe the features to support users and record them as stories on the map. Sketch solutions as needed, and go back and interview customers as well.

- *Create a release strategy:* Break the user stories into different releases, starting with the minimum that's necessary to reach the desired outcome.

- *Build, measure, learn:* As development progresses, track the team's learning against the user story map. Keep it in a visible place and refer back to it often.

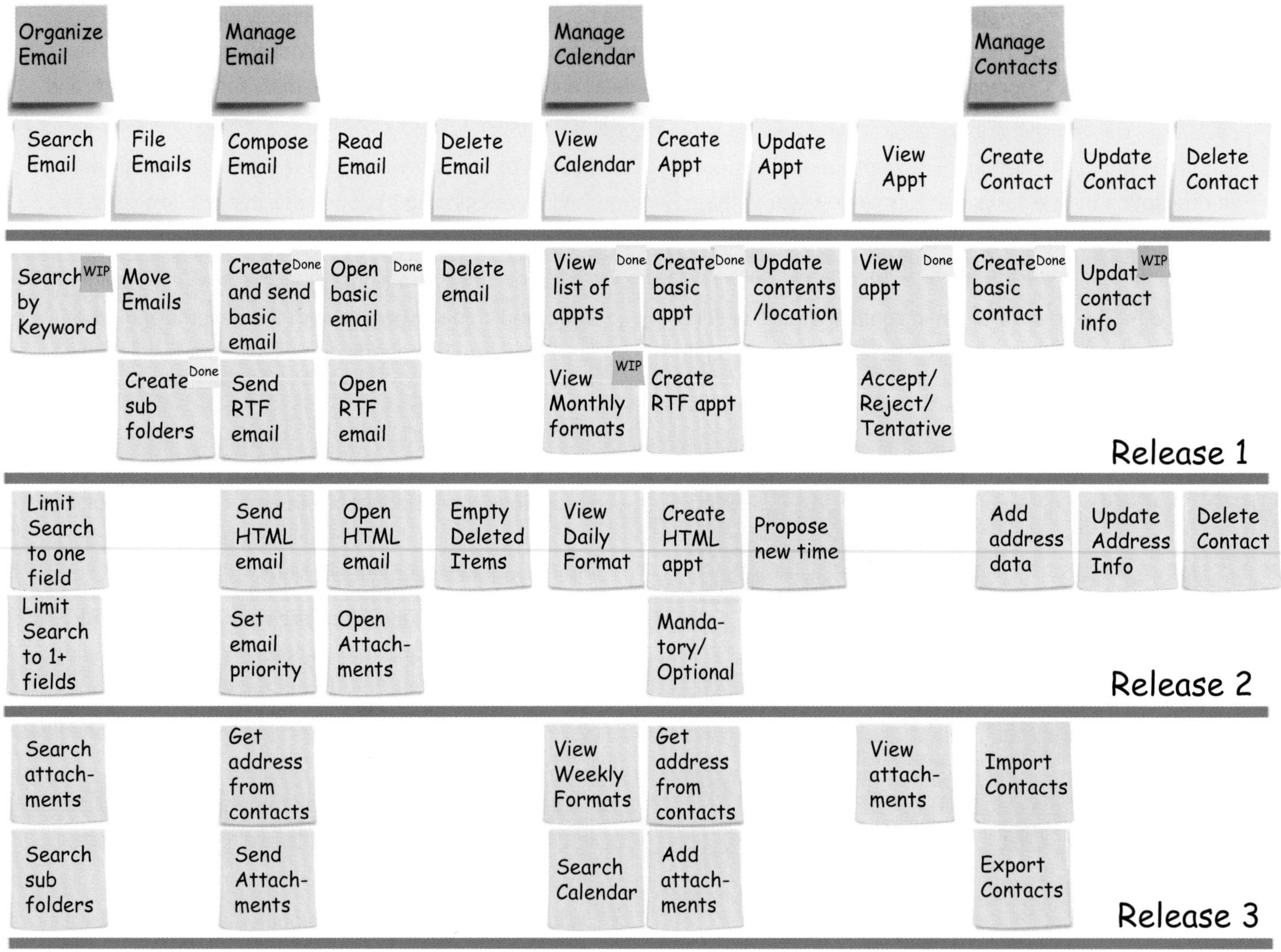

Organize Email

Search Email	File Emails

Manage Email

Compose Email	Read Email	Delete Email

Manage Calendar

View Calendar	Create Appt	Update Appt	View Appt

Manage Contacts

Create Contact	Update Contact	Delete Contact

Release 1

Search by Keyword [WIP]	Move Emails	Create and send basic email [Done]	Open basic email [Done]	Delete email	View list of appts [Done]	Create basic appt [Done]	Update contents /location	View appt [Done]	Create basic contact [Done]	Update contact info [WIP]
	Create sub folders [Done]	Send RTF email	Open RTF email		View Monthly formats [WIP]	Create RTF appt		Accept/ Reject/ Tentative		

Release 2

Limit Search to one field		Send HTML email	Open HTML email	Empty Deleted Items	View Daily Format	Create HTML appt	Propose new time		Add address data	Update Address Info	Delete Contact
Limit Search to 1+ fields		Set email priority	Open Attach- ments			Manda- tory/ Optional					

Release 3

Search attach- ments	Get address from contacts			View Weekly Formats	Get address from contacts		View attach- ments	Import Contacts
Search sub folders	Send Attach- ments			Search Calendar	Add attach- ments			Export Contacts

FIGURE 8-12. Story maps align development tasks with the intended user experience.

Typically, the exercise is done offline, utilizing sticky notes and a whiteboard. For instance, Figure 8-13 shows an example created in a team workshop. However, it's also possible to map stories visually online using software such as LucidCharts or MURAL (*http://mur.al*).

A user story map illustrates how user stories relate to one another in an overarching model. This allows teams to grasp the entirety of the system. More importantly, they align planning and development with actual user experiences. Ultimately, it's about a shared understanding of software a team intends to build to guide decisions, improve efficiency, and result in better outcomes.

FIGURE 8-13. This example of a user story map created by a team in a face-to-face workshop reveals prioritization of efforts into releases.

Further Reading

Donna Lichaw, *The User's Journey: Storymapping Products That People Love* (Rosenfeld Media, 2016)

> *Donna regularly writes and teaches about storylines. This is a complete volume on the techniques she's developed over the years. You can find more information online, including a pair of articles on UXMatters.com. Also see the book's page on the Rosenfeld Media website for updates and additional information:* http://rosenfeldmedia.com/books/storylines/.

Jeff Patton, *User Story Mapping* (O'Reilly, 2013)

> *Patton pioneered the technique of user story maps and details the approach in this book. It is well written and gets to key points quickly. Latter chapters include details on validation through lean processes.*

John Pruitt and Tamara Adlin, *The Persona Lifecycle: Keeping People in Mind Throughout Product Design* (Morgan Kaufmann, 2006)

> *This is one of the few full-length books on personas that is often cited as the key reference source on the topic. At nearly 700 pages it is thorough and comprehensive. Chapter 8 discusses design maps in detail.*

While utilizing user stories makes development more manageable, it can also cause teams to lose the big picture of what they are building.

Customer Journey Mapping Game

By Christophe Tallec

Working with multiple stakeholders is a challenge. They may have a different vision of the world driven by their individual goals and perspectives, whether coming from engineering, business, or public policy backgrounds.

We Design Services (WDS), a leading service innovation firm, developed the *customer journey mapping game* to facilitate communication in such complex environments. The game uses the customer journey as a catalyst for team interaction.

While several configurations of the game are possible, a typical process has the following steps:

1. Prepare the game: Before the game session, create a blank journey worksheet with swim lanes for relevant touchpoint and information types. Then furnish a set of cards representing possible touchpoints. These will vary depending on the domain and situation involved.

2. Select personas: Start the game by having the participants choose a persona. Ask, "Whose journey are you going to map?"

3. Set goals: Define a goal for this persona. What is the overall need and what are they trying to get done?

4. Add touchpoints: Then, for the selected persona, place the touchpoints in the order they might experience them. Do this step as a team.

1. Reflect: Find patterns in the experience across the different touchpoints. Where are there gaps and problems? Where are the emotional highs and lows? Where are there opportunities for the organization?

2. Repeat: Select a different persona or change the goals, and repeat the process. How do the journeys differ? What are common patterns across them? How would extreme users experience the touchpoints?

We piloted this technique for a major French city that wanted to gather stakeholders for a co-creation exercise. The goal was to reinvent urban transportation.

This project was a challenge because of the widely different perspectives of the different people around the table (Figure 8-14). The participants came from car manufacturing companies, large commercial firms, public transit companies, and labor unions, as well as users of the system.

Introducing this new methodology allowed us to develop a common language shared by everyone and dominated by no one. This language helped identify shared value between the different stakeholders.

FIGURE 8-14. Playing the journey mapping game engages everyone in the workshop.

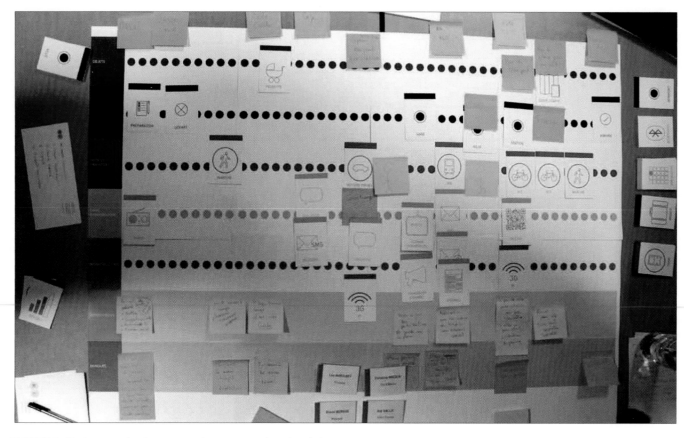

FIGURE 8-15. An example of a customer journey game board and elements.

This initial workshop confirmed that mapping the user journey as a group is an efficient way to visualize common touchpoints, interests, and ways to create value. It proved to be eye-opening for participants.

In this case, participants reported an increased sense of team alignment and cross-functional collaboration, in general, after our workshops. Unfortunately, it is rarely used by local governments looking to re-energize their local ecosystem.

The underlying problem is siloed thinking. The journey mapping game breaks down those departmental barriers and allows companies to think holistically and collaboratively.

We tested our approach with other companies and have invariably found that aligning disparate points of view allows them to uncover new business opportunities.

The customer journey mapping game was originally developed by Christophe Tallec and Paul Kahn. Figure 8-15 shows an example of what a completed game round looks like.

Tallec and Kahn also created an online version of the journey game. You can access this template online at: *http://prezi. com/1qu6lq4qucsm/customer-journey-mapping-game-transport/.*

About the Contributor

Christophe Tallec is the founder of We Design Services (WDS), a leading service innovation agency in France, advising organizations such as Airbus Group, SNCF, The National French Post Office Groupe La Poste, Qatar Foundation, World Bank, and other industries. WDS is committed to delivering cutting-edge experiences.

Diagram and Image Credits

Figure 8-2: Storyboard sketched by Erik Hanson, used with permission

Figure 8-3: Draft storyboard created by Jim Kalbach

Figure 8-4: Storyboard created by Deb Aoki (*http://www.debaoki.com*), used with permission

Figure 8-5: Comic created by Kevin Cheng from his book *See What I Mean* (Rosenfeld Media), used with permission

Figure 8-6: Narrative arch diagram created by Donna Lichaw, used with permission

Figure 8-7: Photo of storyline exercise by Donna Lichaw, used with permission

Figure 8-8: Example design map created by Jim Kalbach

Figure 8-9: Image of design map by Jim Kalbach

Figure 8-11: Illustration from Jeff Patton's book *User Story Mapping* (O'Reilly, 2014)

Figure 8-12: User story map created by Steve Rogalsky of Protegra *(http://www.protegra.com)*, used with permission

Figure 8-13: Image of user story map by Steve Rogalsky, used with permission

Figure 8-14: Image of workshop participants playing the journey game, by Christophe Tallec, used with permission

Figure 8-15: Photo of an example journey game board by Christophe Tallec taken from *http://servicedesigntools.org*, used with permission

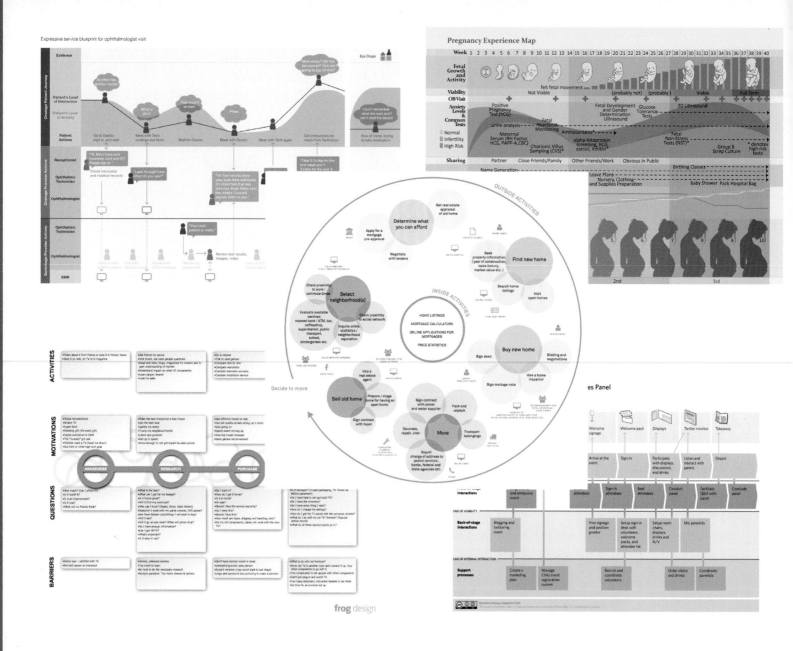

frog design

PART 3
Types of Diagrams in Detail

Part 3 discusses the key types of diagrams in more detail. Related techniques are introduced and discussed alongside these diagram archetypes to provide a broad context to mapping.

- *Service blueprints* are one of the oldest formal techniques and set the tone for other diagrams. Chapter 9 looks at service blueprints and ways they've been extended.

- *Customer journey maps* are perhaps the most popular type of diagram. Chapter 10 details the current practice of customer journey mapping and related techniques.

- *Experience maps* resemble service blueprints and customer journey maps closely, but with some important differences, discussed in Chapter 11.

- *Mental model diagramming* is a unique technique created by Indi Young. You are encouraged to get her book, *Mental Models*, but Chapter 12 summarizes key aspects of this method and related approaches.

- *Spatial maps and ecosystem models* are discussed in Chapter 13. These diagrams provide insight by relating parts of a system to each other spatially.

Keep in mind you'll find that terminology is used inconsistently in practice. It's a jungle of phrases that are seemingly interchangeable. What one person calls an experience map is another person's customer journey map.

But don't get stuck on the terminology. Instead, focus on how you'll tell the story of value alignment to your organization. You may even invent your own hybrid diagram or coin a new term in doing so.

This book is about possibilities, not a specific technique. My hope is that this provides some clarity, but more importantly, makes the mapping more approachable in general.

CHAPTER 9

Service Blueprints

We live in a service-based economy, yet most organizations fail to provide good services. For all of the money invested in technical R&D, organizations tend to overlook development of their service experience. This is changing. More and more, organizations realize that customer experience is a source of growth and competitive advantage.

But good service design remains elusive. Part of the challenge is that, unlike physical goods, the transitions between touchpoints in a service are intangible. They unfold in real time, and then those moments are gone.

Service design is a growing field that seeks to prevent unintentional service experiences. The objective of service design is to take deliberate actions that create, deliver, and sustain positive service experiences over time, consistently and repeatedly.

A focus of service has historically been face-to-face interactions. But as the digital and the physical worlds of service blend more and more, service design extends into the design of digital services as well. As a result, service design is interdisciplinary, drawing attention from people in sales, marketing, product management, product design, interaction design, and user experience.

This chapter provides an overview and historical background to service blueprints. It also touches on related and extended techniques, such as lean consumption and expressive service blueprinting.

Visualizing Services

Service design is not new. It can be traced back to the writings of G. Lynn Shostack in the early 80s. A cornerstone of service design is a map of the service process. Shostack refers to these as *service blueprints* in her original articles. Figure 9-1 shows an early example from Shostack's 1984 article "Designing Services That Deliver."

This blueprint is rather plain and resembles a flow diagram. Yet it yields valuable insight about the experience of dealing with a discount broker. For instance, there are about a dozen steps that are required to "prepare and mail statements."

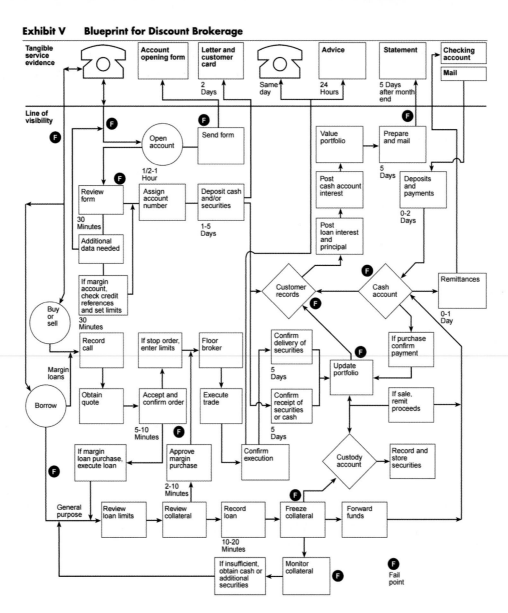

Exhibit V   Blueprint for Discount Brokerage

Tangible service evidence

Account opening form

Letter and customer card — 2 Days

Advice — 24 Hours

Statement — 5 Days after month end

Checking account

Mail

Same day

Line of visibility

Open account — 1/2-1 Hour

Send form

Value portfolio

Prepare and mail — 5 Days

Review form — 30 Minutes

Assign account number

Deposit cash and/or securities — 1-5 Days

Post cash account interest

Deposits and payments — 0-2 Days

Additional data needed

Post loan interest and principal

If margin account, check credit references and set limits — 30 Minutes

Buy or sell

Customer records

Cash account

Remittances — 0-1 Day

Margin loans

Record call

If stop order, enter limits

Floor broker

Confirm delivery of securities — 5 Days

Update portfolio

If purchase confirm payment

Borrow

Obtain quote

Accept and confirm order — 5-10 Minutes

Execute trade

Confirm receipt of securities or cash — 5 Days

If sale, remit proceeds

If margin loan purchase, execute loan

Approve margin purchase — 2-10 Minutes

Confirm execution

Custody account

Record and store securities

General purpose

Review loan limits

Review collateral

Record loan — 10-20 Minutes

Freeze collateral

Forward funds

If insufficient, obtain cash or additional securities

Monitor collateral

F Fail point

FIGURE 9-1. An early example of a service blueprint by G. Lynn Shostack shows the complexity of providing a service.

Shostack also includes an indication of potential fail points (noted with an "F" in a black circle). These are critical points where the service may show issues of inconsistency or break down completely.

Shostack stresses the overall importance of mapping activities in service design. She writes:

> The root of most service problems is, in fact, lack of systematic design and control. The use of a blueprint can help a service developer not only to identify problems ahead of time but also to see the potential for new market opportunities.
>
> …
>
> A blueprint encourages creativity, preemptive problem solving, and controlled implementation. It can reduce the potential for failure and enhance management's ability to think effectively about new services. The blueprint principle helps cut down the time and inefficiency of random service development and gives a higher level view of service management prerogatives.

Since then, service blueprints have become widely used. For instance, the British Standard Institution provides general guidelines for service design in BS 7000-3: 1994. This gives direction on the management of the design of service across industries from the customers' perspective. The intent of blueprinting is to isolate fail points—steps where the service may go awry—and address these accordingly.

Mary Jo Bitner and colleagues developed a more structured and normalized approach to service blueprinting. Figure 9-2 shows an example of a blueprint for a hotel, created by Bitner and her team.

The separate rows of information and color coding make this map easier to read than Shostack's example. It borrows from swim lane diagrams found in business process modeling. In doing so, this arrangement also makes both the service experience and the service provision more comprehensible. It better reveals the opportunities for improvement and growth.

More and more, organizations realize that customer experience is a source of growth and competitive advantage.

Specifically, this arrangement highlights the separation of *frontstage* interactions, which are what the individual experiences, and *backstage* interactions, the processes necessary to provide a service. The notion of frontstage and backstage is found throughout service design literature, and it reflects the basic principles of value alignment presented in this book. The metaphor recalls a theater, where the audience sees only what's on the stage. Everything backstage is invisible to them and goes into supporting the frontstage experience.

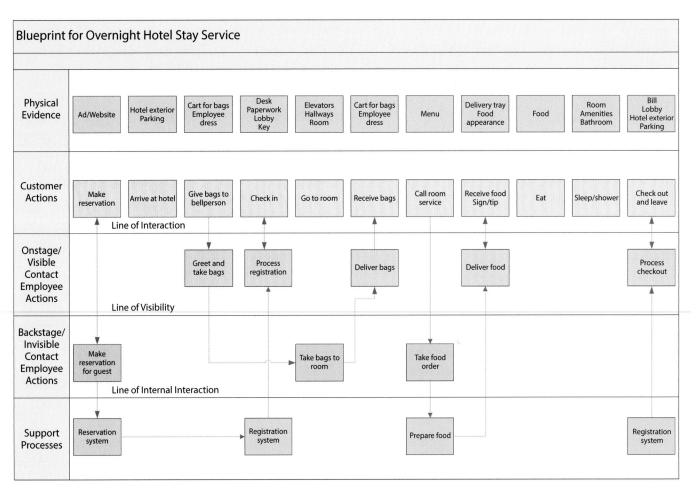

FIGURE 9-2. This service blueprint of a hotel service created by Bitner et al. represents a standard way of creating the diagrams.

Staying Lean

"Lean" is a broad topic that gets used in a variety of ways. All uses of the term, however, have one thing in common: the notion of reducing waste. James Womack and Daniel Jones, pioneers in the lean movement, outline fundamental principles in their landmark book *Lean Thinking*. The steps they recommend taking are:

1. *Specify the value.* State what value you are creating from the customer's perspective. Define this in terms of the whole experience, not just individual interactions.

2. *Identify the value chain.* The value chain is all of the actions and processes needed for an organization to deliver that value. In lean, the goal is to eliminate steps that do not add value.

3. *Optimize flow.* Lean is about increasing the efficiency of production. This means optimizing the backstage service processes.

4. *Create customer pull.* After flow is established, let the customer pull value upstream. Start with the customer demand or need, and align your offering to that.

Diagrams are an inherent part of lean practices. Value stream mapping is a specific technique for illustrating the value chain—see point #2. These graphs focus solely on the backstage processes needed to deliver value to the customer, as seen in Figure 9-3.

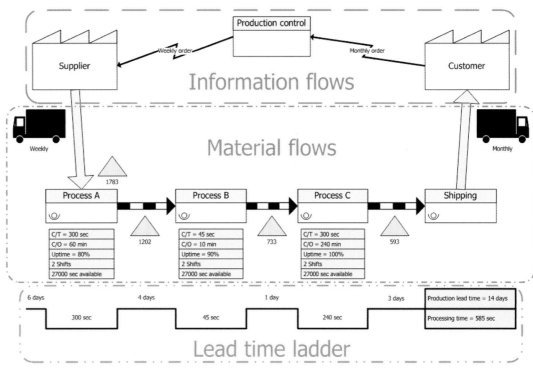

FIGURE 9-3. This example of a value stream map reveals a focus on time and efficiency.

This diagram resembles the bottom half of a typical service blueprint, for instance. And while it doesn't appear particularly customer-centric in nature, the intent of a value stream map is about delivering value. Authors Karen Martin and Mike Osterling explain its benefit in their book *Value Stream Mapping*:

> In most organizations, no one person can describe the complete series of events required to transform a customer request into a good or service...This gap in understanding is the kind of problem that leads to making improvements in one functional area only to create new problems in another area...It's the kind of problem that propels well-meaning companies to implement experience technology "solutions" that do little to address the true problem or improve the customer experience.

Being lean is being aligned. Alignment diagrams, then, not only fit into the lean canon, but they potentially extend it by including a rich description of customer experience.

Lean Consumption

One goal of value-centered design is reducing complexity on behalf of the customer. To illustrate this, Shostack examined the specific timings of each interaction in her original mapping studies in the 1980s.

Figure 9-4 shows precise timings for a service encounter Shostack offers as an example—in this case, getting a corner shoeshine. Since service encounters happen in real time, service designers should establish a standard and acceptable timeline, indicated directly on the blueprint.

James Womack and Daniel Jones coin the term "lean consumption" in their 2005 article of the same name. They describe the positive business returns and increased value creation for both sides of the equation. The authors write:

> Companies may think that they save time and money by off-loading work to customers, making it the customer's problem to get the computer up and running, and wasting the customer's time. In fact, however, the opposite is true. By streamlining the systems for providing goods and services, and making it easier for customers to buy and use them, a growing number of companies are actually lowering costs while saving everyone's time. In the process, these businesses are learning more about their customers, strengthening consumer loyalty, and attracting new customers who defect from less user-friendly competitors.

To visualize lean consumption, the authors recommend creating a map of the steps customers go through to consume products and services. They call these diagrams *lean consumption maps*.

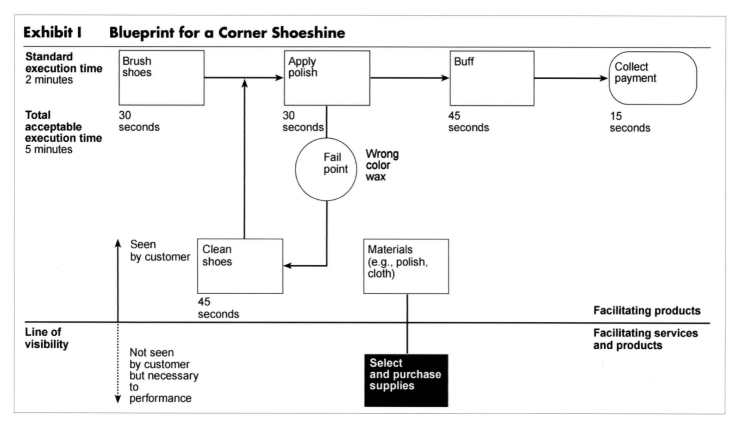

Exhibit I **Blueprint for a Corner Shoeshine**

Standard execution time 2 minutes

Brush shoes → Apply polish → Buff → Collect payment

Total acceptable execution time 5 minutes

| 30 seconds | 30 seconds | 45 seconds | 15 seconds |

Fail point — Wrong color wax

Seen by customer — Clean shoes — 45 seconds

Materials (e.g., polish, cloth)

Facilitating products

Line of visibility

Not seen by customer but necessary to performance

Select and purchase supplies

Facilitating services and products

FIGURE 9-4. This simple blueprint for a shoeshine includes timings down to the second.

Figures 9-5 and 9-6 show lean consumption maps created by Pete Abilla, a leading service designer expert. Compare the before (Figure 9-5) and after (Figure 9-6) states of a service encounter for a yearly car inspection and registration in the US.

The bar chart shows that the process takes the customer a total of 210 minutes, with touchpoints across two providers: the auto mechanic and the division of motor vehicles. After combining inspection and registration at Jiffy Lube, a national

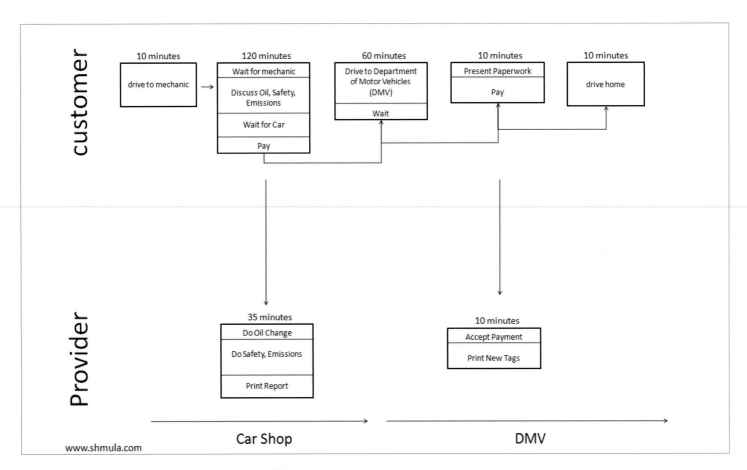

FIGURE 9-5. BEFORE—inspecting and registering a vehicle takes the customer 210 minutes across two service providers.

chain of service stations in the US, the process is reduced to just 65 minutes.

From the lean consumption perspective, the imperative for service providers is clear: don't waste the customer's time.

Making their experience as lean as possible improves satisfaction and loyalty. This ultimately gets reflected on the bottom line of the business.

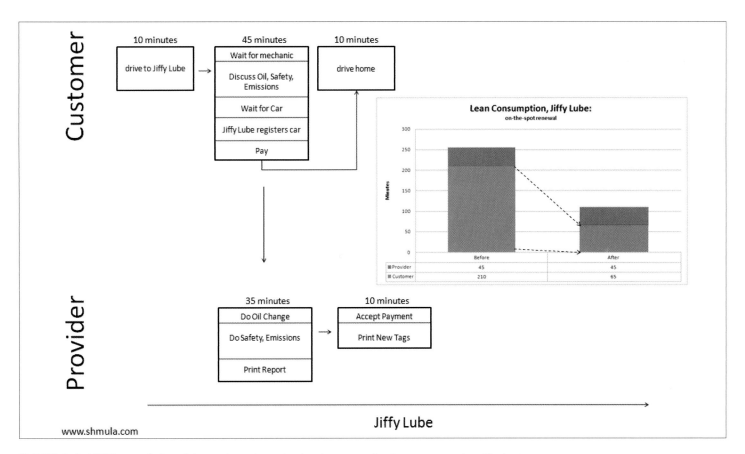

FIGURE 9-6. AFTER—a redesign of the service reduces the time investment for the customer to just 65 minutes.

Extending Service Blueprinting

Service blueprinting techniques continue to be extended. For instance, Wreiner and colleagues added multiple providers, as outlined in their 2009 article "Exploring Service Blueprints for Multiple Actors." Figure 9-7 shows interactions between three actors in a public parking lot: the motorist, the operator, and the owner of the lot.

A common criticism of service blueprints is that they don't explicitly include information about the individual's emotional state. To address this gap, Susan Spraragen and Carrie Chan added the dimension of feelings to service blueprints. "Expressive Service Blueprinting" looks at how the client's emotive state may vary during the service encounter. See the case study at the end of this chapter on "Expressive Service Blueprinting" for more details.

Andy Polaine, a leading service design expert, has also expanded on service blueprints by adding details about the emotional context. Inspired by Spraragen, he includes emotional information into his diagrams, reflected in Figure 9-8. Notice that Polaine maps multiple actors simultaneously as well. This adds a level of detail that makes the diagram more complex and may not be useful in all situations.

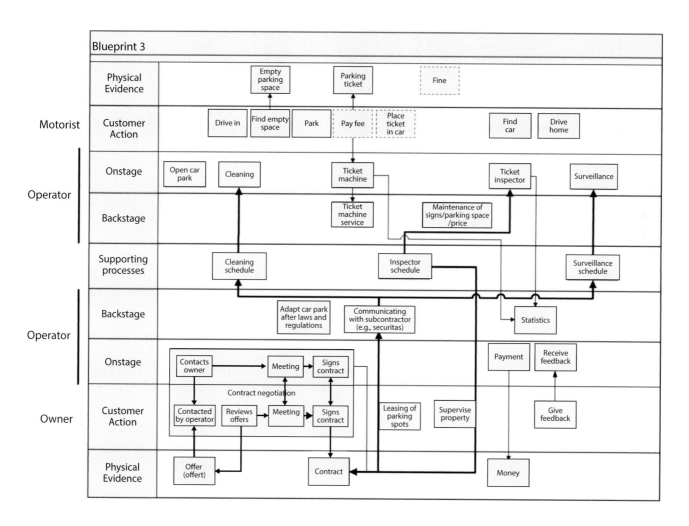

FIGURE 9-7. Wreiner and colleagues blueprinted three actors in a single map.

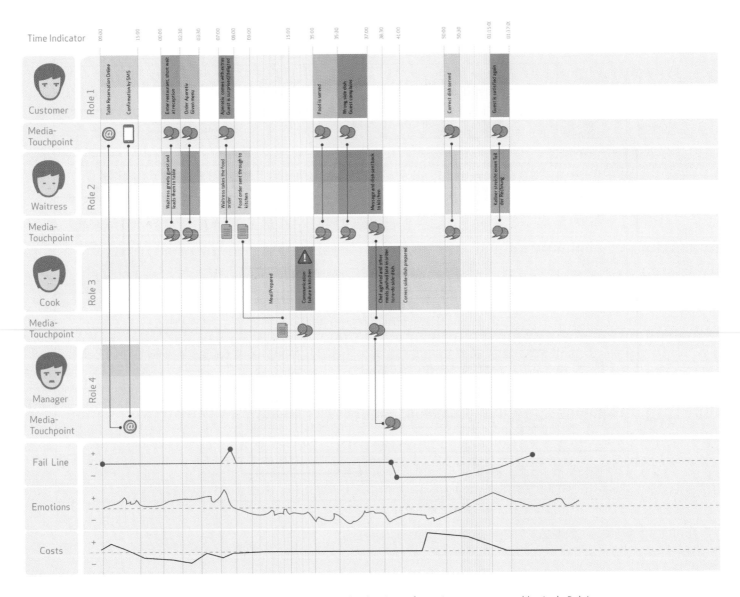

FIGURE 9-8. This expanded service blueprint includes multiple actors and indications of emotive states, created by Andy Polaine.

Elements of a Service Blueprint

Service blueprints consist of several layers of information. It's the interaction between these layers that provides a systems view of the service experience, as seen in Figure 9-9. Table 9-1 summarizes the main aspects that define service blueprints using the framework outlined in Chapter 2.

There are five key components of a service blueprint. The basic arrangement of these elements is illustrated in Figure 9-9.

- *Physical evidence.* The manifestation of the touchpoints that customers interact with are physical evidence. This can include physical devices, electronic software, and face-to-face interactions.

- *Customer actions.* These are the main steps a customer takes to interact with an organization's service.

- *Onstage touchpoints.* These are the actions of the provider that are visible to the customer. The line of visibility separates onstage touchpoints with backstage actions.

Point of view	Individual as the recipient of a service.
	Typically centered on a single actor, but may also include multiple actors when examining an entire service ecology.
Structure	Chronological.
Scope	Examples typically illustrate a discrete service encounter, but also include overviews of a whole service ecosystem.
Focus	Focus on service provision processes in a service encounter with emphasis on backstage action and touchpoints. Extensions of service blueprinting add emotive information.
Uses	Diagnosis, improvement, and management of existing service systems.
	Good for analyzing specific timings of service interactions, down to the minute in some cases.
Strengths	Simple, predefined structure with a clear focus of attention.
	Relatively light research and investigation needed.
	Suitable for co-creation with teams and stakeholders.
	Easy for others to understand from a single page.
Weaknesses	Lack many of the contextual, environmental cues of an experience (e.g., "noisy setting" or "great-tasting food").
	Metaphor of a *blueprint* is a misnomer: they are more like flow diagrams than an architectural blueprint.

TABLE 9-1. Defining aspects of service blueprints

- *Backstage actions*. These are the internal service provision mechanisms of the organization that are not visible to the customer, but that directly impact the customer experience.

- *Support processes*. These are internal processes that indirectly impact the customer experience. Support processes can include interactions between the organization and partners or third-party suppliers.

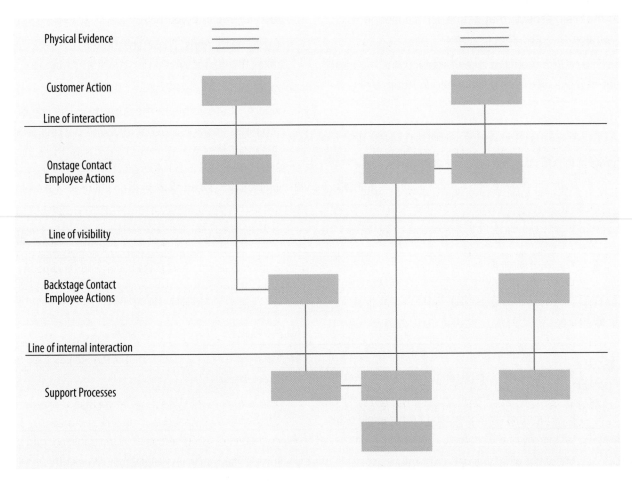

FIGURE 9-9. The basic elements and structure of a service blueprint align standard elements into rows.

Further Reading

Mary Jo Bitner, Amy L. Ostrom, and Felicia N. Morgan. "Service Blueprinting: A Practical Technique for Service Innovation," *Working Paper, Center for Leadership Services, Arizona State University* (2007)

> This is an academic article that has a wealth of practical information, including detailed instructions on creating a service blueprint. There are also numerous case studies in its use. This provides an excellent overview of service blueprinting in general.

Andy Polaine, Lavrans Løvlie, and Ben Reason. *Service Design* (Rosenfeld Media, 2013)

> This is one of the best resources available for a complete understanding of service design in general. The book is thorough and presents a cohesive argument for the growing field. Chapter 5 focuses specifically on diagrams as a part of the service design discipline.

G. Lynn Shostack. "How to Design a Service," *European Journal of Marketing 16/1* (1982) and G. Lynn Shostak. "Designing Services That Deliver," *Harvard Business Review* (1984)

> These two articles are frequently pointed out as the impetus for the service design movement. The latter of the two is available online from the Harvard Business Review *and is recommended reading. Although decades old, Shostak's observations and advice are wholly relevant today.*

James Womack and Daniel Jones. "Lean Consumption," *Harvard Business Review* (March 2005)

> Womack is an early pioneer in the lean movement. In this landmark article, he shifts attention from lean processes within an organization to the customer experience. He and Jones make a compelling case and present evidence for following the path of lean consumption.

Thomas Wreiner, Ingrid Mårtensson, Olof Arnell, Natalia Gonzalez, Stefan Holmlid, and Fabian Segelström. "Exploring Service Blueprints for Multiple Actors" (First Nordic Conference on Service Design and Service Innovation, 2009)

> This is a short case study of a project that resulted in a blueprint with several actors. Even with a simple example of a parking lot, the three-way relationship between actors reveals complexity in service provisions. The authors offer alternative ways to examine the service encounter.

Valarie Zeithaml, Mary Jo Bitner, and Dwayne Gremler. *Services Marketing-Integrating Customer Focus Across the Firm*, 6th ed. (McGraw-Hill, 2012)

> This is a main, early text in the service design literature. Though dry and academic at times, it provides a wealth of detail on service design. There is considerable attention to service blueprinting throughout the book, with an entire chapter on the subject.

Expressive Service Blueprint

By Susan Spraragen, with Carrie Chan

Evaluating and investigating service systems, consumer experiences, and service delivery outcomes is an ongoing task for service providers. Providers who view the service from the consumer's perspective may reveal opportunities for refining their offerings so they are differentiating and effective, and enable stronger customer relationships.

As I researched a human-centered approach to examining and illustrating a service system, I wondered what form or model would best represent and communicate this perspective. Business process modeling notations, data flow diagrams, and operational charts seem to put the consumer in a marginal role rather than an explicit one. They do not lend themselves to discussions about the human motivations, interactions, and emotive responses that all occur during a service encounter.

I then came across the work of Lynn Shostack and Mary Jo Bitner and saw how they employ a service blueprint, which is purposely drawn from the consumer's perspective. But these visualizations looked rather swim-lane-like in their format.

By expanding on their work and adding a dramatic shift in style, I hoped the service blueprint would enunciate with fervor: "Hey! There are humans in this picture—see how they respond and interact with your service!"

Most fortunately, I had an enlightening opportunity to work with Carrie Chan, a service designer who flourished with my challenge to: *Create a service blueprint with limited use of boxes and arrows. Create something that won't be brushed aside as yet another swim-lane or data flow diagram. I want to explicitly show the human emotions of a service encounter!* Together, we created a more organic look for describing a service episode—one that gave a personal voice to the service consumer and service provider.

Our approach uses graphic symbols, images, or plot lines to visualize the ebb and flow of the consumer's emotive response as they personally interact with the service provider. From our early designs, I coined the term *expressive service blueprinting*. The key components of an expressive service blueprint, which are distinct from a traditional service blueprint, are as follows:

- *Emotive responses.* Consumer emotions are clearly stated and graphically shown either through icons, photographs, graphs, or other elements. We chose elements that we can modulate in intensity, either through color or positioning, so that we can emulate the variability of a consumer's emotion during the service encounter. We embed those elements within the onstage journey area of the blueprint. In addition, we add the consumer's thoughts as they perform their service actions.

- *Layout.* More space is allocated to the onstage customer journey than the backstage area, as this stage of the blueprinting and design process emphasizes the consumer perspective. Moments of direct interaction with the provider are represented with vertical arrows indicating one-way or bidirectional conversations.

- *Provider identity.* The roles of the service participants are stated in terms of their function relative to the service domain. So rather than using generic terms like *provider* and *consumer*, we like to use terms that will resonate with actual team members in the provider organization.

Figure 9-10 shows an expressive service blueprint of a patient visit to an ophthalmologist. This is based upon interviews and observations with an ophthalmic technician who encounters a myriad of patients daily. A fundamental challenge illustrated here is one of prescription compliance.

In our example, the patient is left confused about their prescription and concerned about the cost of the medicine. The expressive blueprint illustrates the source of the confusion by tracking two emotive states: distraction and anxiety.

We delineate the fluctuation of these two emotions with graph-like elements embedded in the patient's onstage journey. For marking their distraction level we chose a line graph. The patient icon appears on the line at key moments of the service encounter.

When the patients are taking their eye exam and meeting with the ophthalmologist, they are not as distracted as they are during the key moment of information exchange about how to follow the prescribed regimen. The high level of distraction at this moment is further exacerbated by their growing level of anxiety about adding more medicine to their daily routine. The patient's varying anxiety levels are depicted with a wave form.

This expressive blueprint invites the viewer to determine when or how the prescription information might be more effectively administered, as the emotional state of the patient is clearly impacting the outcome of their visit.

This blueprint also suggests the complex backstage activities of the ophthalmologist. While the patient happens to be in the office, the doctor addresses a number of issues, only one of them concerning the care of this particular patient.

Expressive service blueprinting is a part of a larger effort for designing and prototyping services. It is a messy process that is best constructed collaboratively with key service providers and consumers. When building blueprints that explicitly note the consumer's varying emotive states, we add a unique descriptive layer to the investigation about the service encounter. This approach may give rise to truly understanding why and how service gaps emerge.

Expressive service blueprint for ophthalmologist visit

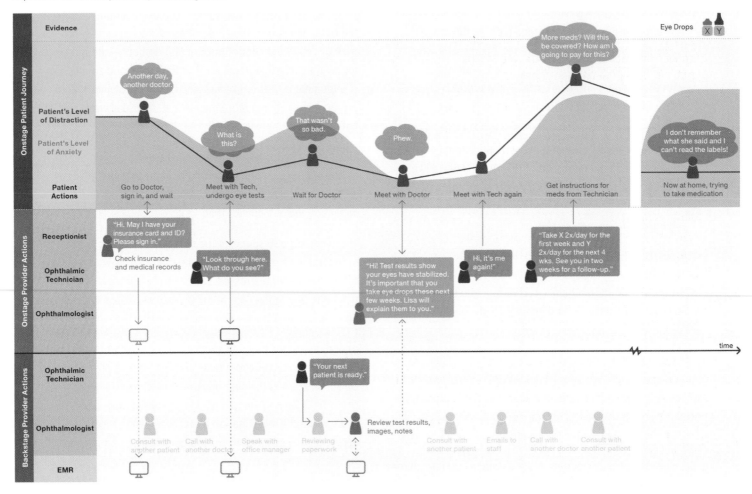

FIGURE 9-10. This example of an expressive service blueprint depicts an encounter with an ophthalmologist.

Further Reading

Susan Spraragen and Carrie Chan. "Service Blueprinting: When Customer Satisfaction Numbers Are Not Enough." (International DMI Education Conference, 2008).

Susan Spraragen. "Enabling Excellence in Service with Expressive Service Blueprinting," Case Study 9 in *Design for Services* by Anna Meroni and Daniela Sangiorgi (Gower, 2011).

About the Contributors

Susan Spraragen is a service design researcher, educator, and faculty member at Parsons School of Design Strategies. Susan lives in New York, where she enjoys hiking and taking photos along the Hudson River. She can be reached via LinkedIn at *https://www.linkedin.com/in/slspraragen*.

Carrie Chan is currently Strategy Director at Nurun San Francisco, where she works at the intersection of customer research, business, design, and technology to develop strategies for digital products and services across a variety of industries. She spends her free time on the opposite side of technology: dreaming of future travels, paper crafting, playing in a piano duo, and perfecting her marinara sauce recipe. She can be reached via LinkedIn at *linkedin.com/in/thinkcarrie*.

Diagram and Image Credits

Figure 9-1: Service blueprint by G. Lynn Shostack from her article "Designing Services That Deliver," *Harvard Business Review* (1984)

Figure 9-2: Service blueprint from Mary Jo Bitner, Amy L. Ostrom, and Felicia N. Morgan. "Service Blueprinting: A Practical Technique for Service Innovation," Working Paper, Center for Leadership Services, Arizona State University (2007)

Figure 9-3: Value stream map from Wikipedia, uploaded by Daniel Penfield, CC BY-SA 3.0

Figure 9-4: Blueprint for a corner shoeshine by G. Lynn Shostack from her article "Designing Services That Deliver," *Harvard Business Review* (1984)

Figures 9-5 and 9-6: Diagrams taken from a blogpost by Pete Abilla: "Lean Service: Customer Value and Don't Waste the Customer's Time" (*Schmula.com*, 2010), used with permission

Figure 9-7: Service blueprint from Thomas Wreiner, Ingrid Mårtensson, Olof Arnell, Natalia Gonzalez, Stefan Holmlid, and Fabian Segelström. "Exploring Service Blueprints for Multiple Actors" (First Nordic Conference on Service Design and Service Innovation, 2009)

Figure 9-8: Diagram taken from Andy Polaine. "Blueprint+: Developing a Tool for Service Design" (Service Design Network Conference, 2009), used with permission

Figure 9-10: Expressive service blueprint created by Susan Spraragen and Carrie Chan, used with permission

Part 3, bottom-left diagram: Customer journey map created by Adam Richardson, originally appearing in Adam Richardson. "Using Customer Journey Maps to Improve Customer Experience," *Harvard Business Blog* (Nov 2010)

CHAPTER 10

Customer Journey Maps

The exact origin of the term *customer journey map* (CJM) is unclear. The basic idea of looking across touchpoints seems to have its roots in Jan Carlzon's concept of moments of truth. (See Chapter 2 for more on moments of truth.) Carlzon advocated an ecological view of the customer experience, but he never explicitly talked about a map of the customer journey as such.

It wasn't until the field of customer experience management came into focus just before the turn of the century that journey mapping emerged. For instance, in a seminal article appearing in *Marketing Management* in 1994, authors Lewis Carbone and Stephan Haeckel speak of an *experience blueprint*, which they define as "a pictorial representation of the experience clues to be engineered, along with specification that describes them and their individual functions."

In 2002, customer experience expert Colin Shaw introduced the concept of what he calls *moment mapping*—recalling Carlzon. The resulting diagram (Figure 10-1) uses an arrow to map the phases of the customer experience.

From this, analysis opportunities for creating a positive customer experience can be derived, shown in Figure 10-2.

As a type of diagram, CJMs are derived from service blueprinting. For sure, the two types of diagrams are similar, particularly in structure (i.e., chronological). But there are also differences in point of view, scope, focus, and use.

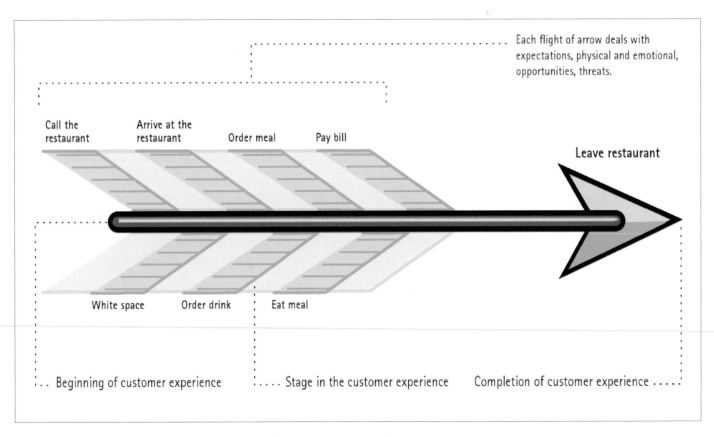

Each flight of arrow deals with expectations, physical and emotional, opportunities, threats.

Call the restaurant

Arrive at the restaurant

Order meal

Pay bill

Leave restaurant

White space

Order drink

Eat meal

Beginning of customer experience

Stage in the customer experience

Completion of customer experience

FIGURE 10-1. Colin Shaw's description of the elements of a moment map resembles contemporary CJMs.

Step	Booking	White space	Travel	Arrive at car park	Enter restaurant	Place order
Expectation	I'll get through quickly and they'll have availability	Nothing is going to happen until I get to the restaurant on the night	I am not going to be offered any form of directions	The parking will be easy	I will be greeted with a smile and they will be friendly —take me to my table	There will be sufficient choice—it will be presented in a friendly way
Threat	They are fully booked	Nothing does happen—lost opportunity	Customer doesn't know where it is	There are no parking spaces when customer arrives	Customer is ignored because all the staff are busy	There is nothing on the menu that the customer likes—restaurant runs out of an advertised choice
Opportunity to exceed physical expecations	Wow—when I made the booking they realised I had been before and what I had eaten!	Wow—I have just received a letter confirming my reservation together with a copy of the menu	Wow—the restaurant has sent me a map!	Wow—they have reserved me a space!	Wow—they were waiting to greet us as we walked through the door!	Wow—waiter gives you his personal recommendation about what is good
Opportunity to exceed emotional expecations	They recognise you and can remember when I dined last time	The letter is personalised to me and suggests some dishes I may like. This makes me happy	I'm reading the menu; it sounds great!	There is a sign outside the restaurant saying welcome to me!	We are greeted like long lost family	They remember what I had last time which shows they care
Emotion evoked	Surprise, anticipation	Surprise and anticipation	They care	I'm special	I'm with my friends	They care

FIGURE 10-2. A moment map table from Colin Shaw and John Ivens's book *Building Great Customer Experiences* (2002) includes emotional aspects of a customer journey.

The contemporary style of CJMs seems to have come about in the mid-2000s. Bruce Temkin, a leading customer experience expert, is one of the early advocates for CJMs and greatly promoted their use in the USA. In a Forrester report entitled "Mapping the Customer Journey," Temkin defines CJMs as "documents that visually illustrate customers' processes, needs, and perceptions throughout their relationships with a company."

Temkin points to the significance of CJMs in his later blog post "It's All About Your Customer's Journey":

> Companies need to use tools and processes that reinforce an understanding of actual customer needs. One of the key tools in this area is something called a customer journey map...Used appropriately, these maps can shift a company's perspective from inside-out to outside-in.

Figure 10-3 shows an example of a CJM created by Jamie Thomson of Mad*Pow. It visualizes a year of engagement in a high-level way that helped the product team see how game mechanics and coaching communications could work together. The aim was to support and nudge the player along a path toward his health goals.

Figure 10-4 shows another example, in this case for a broadband provider. This CJM was created by Effective UI, a leading digital experience consultancy. It includes a very prominent emotional curve in the center. This clearly suggests that many factors come into play, chief among these the emotional experience.

CJMs typically focus on the relationship of an individual as a customer of an organization. Frequently, they highlight some decision-making process. In Figure 10-4, the "Purchase" phase highlights the decision to buy.

But CJMs are versatile and have a range of uses. They are often used to better understand customer loyalty and how to improve existing customers' experiences. They help answer such questions as: How can an organization better engage customers? How can it provide value that keeps them coming back? How can it make services more relevant?

Creating great experiences is not about individual touchpoint optimization but rather how touchpoints come together into a unified whole. CJMs are a strategic tool to visualize touchpoints to manage them more effectively.

The *customer journey canvas* (Figure 10-5) is a variation of a CJM that is particularly good for getting input from the entire team. The open canvas arrangement invites others to contribute. The customer journey canvas was created by service design experts Marc Stickdorn and Jakob Schneider for their influential book *This Is Service Design Thinking*. The canvas-style template allows teams to audit their customer's journey together.

The basic format of the customer journey canvas reveals both frontstage and backstage components to the service experience. It aligns such things as pre-service actions of the provider to customer expectations, as well as how the provider will manage customer relationships over time after a service encounter.

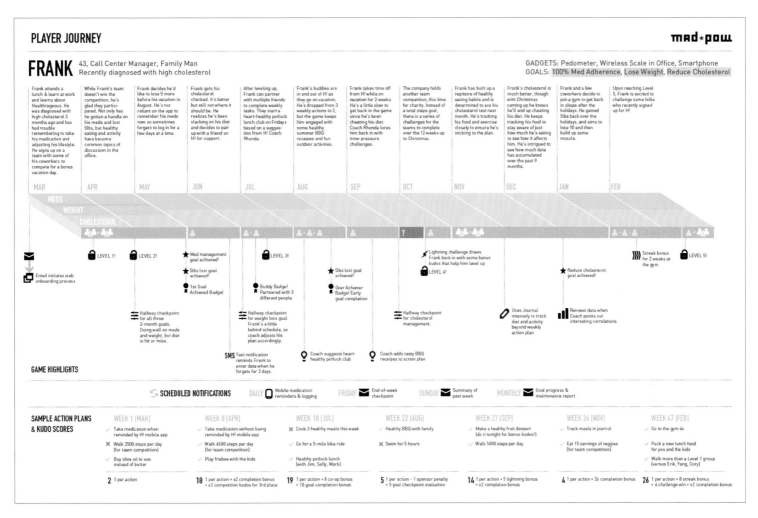

FIGURE 10-3. Customer journey map showing a one-year journey of a person playing a health behavior change game (created by Jamie Thomson).

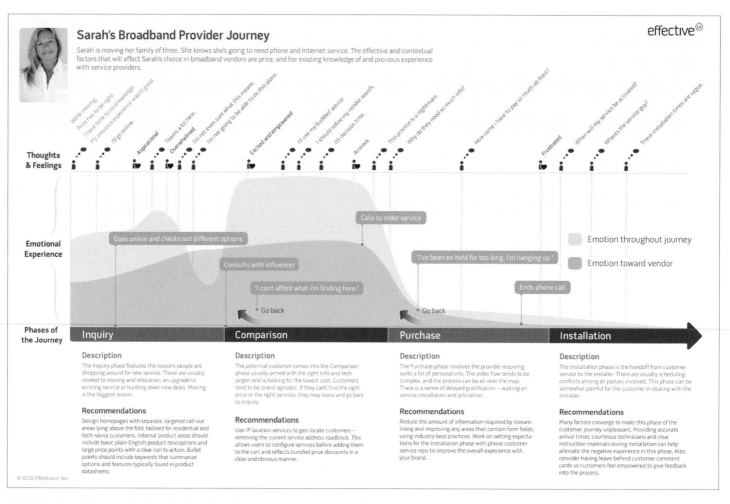

FIGURE 10-4. This example of a CJM for a broadband provider, created by Effective UI, focuses on emotional aspects of a journey.

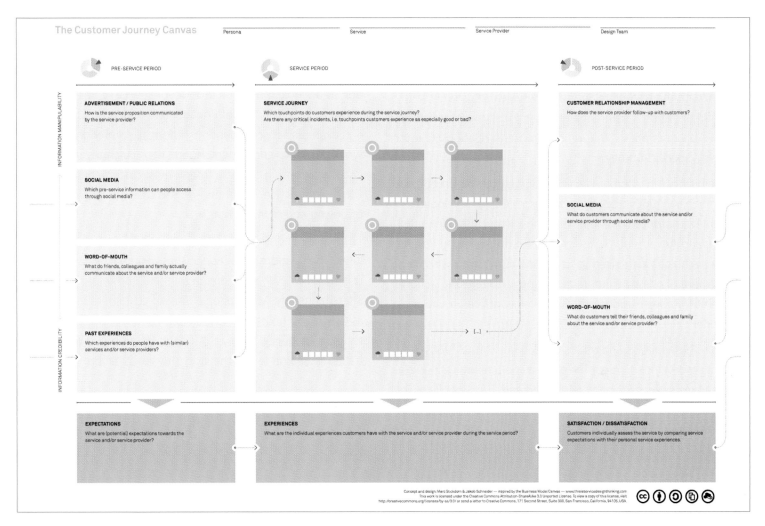

FIGURE 10-5. The customer journey canvas created by Marc Stickdorn and Jakob Schneider is a variation of the typical CJM.

Customer Lifecycle Maps

Some practitioners also make a distinction between CJMs and customer lifecycle maps.* The latter are broader yet and deal with the lifetime relationship between a customer and an organization. Customer lifecycles typically include slightly more abstract phases that reflect an overall relationship rather than a specific journey.

The history of customer lifecycle planning can be traced back to the early 1960s. For instance, Russell Colley developed a framework for evaluating advertising success in a book titled *Defining Advertising Goals for Measured Advertising Results*. The technique is referred to as DAGMAR for short. This model had several phases of interaction, from *awareness* to *action*. In 1961, Robert Lavidge and Gary Steiner offered a similar model.†

From these models and others formed during the 1960s, John Jenkins developed one of the earliest comprehensive lifecycle diagrams in his 1972 book *Marketing and Customer Behaviour*. Figure 10-6 shows his original model, which he calls the market continuum model.

From this perspective, a customer lifecycle map is about overall brand loyalty and the emotional connection to an organization as a whole, not just a product or service. CJMs are more about a particular type of engagement within that lifecycle, and example service blueprints historically center on specific types of service encounters. Figure 10-7 illustrates the approximate relationship of these three views: customer lifecycles, CJMs, and service blueprints—in this case, for the experience of buying and owning a car.

These distinctions are broad generalizations and not absolutes. The relationship between these approaches is not strictly hierarchical. What's more, in the field, these terms are used interchangeably. Many people refer to customer lifecycles as CJMs, and holistic service blueprints may show the end-to-end experience. In any case, don't get hung up on labels: focus instead on telling the story of value creation.

---

* See, for example, Lavrans Løvlie. "Customer Journeys and Customer Lifecycles," *Customer Blah* (Dec 2013).

† Robert Lavidge and Gary Steiner. "A Model for Predictive Measurements of Advertising Effectiveness," *Journal of Marketing* 25/4 (1961).

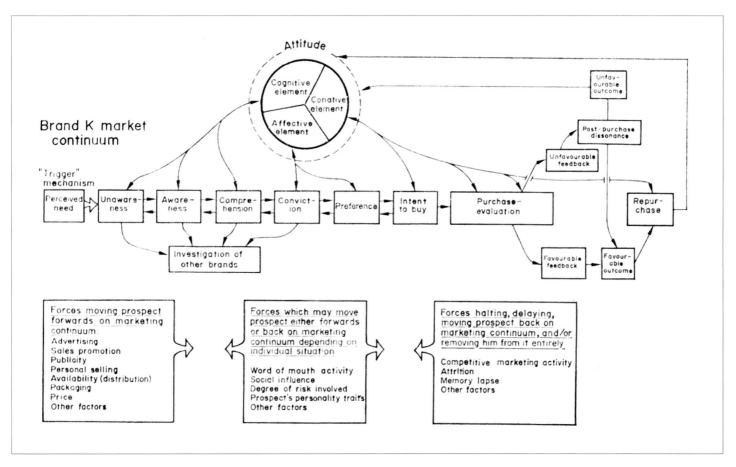

FIGURE 10-6. John Jenkins's model of the customer lifecycle (1972) represents perhaps the earliest example of a journey map.

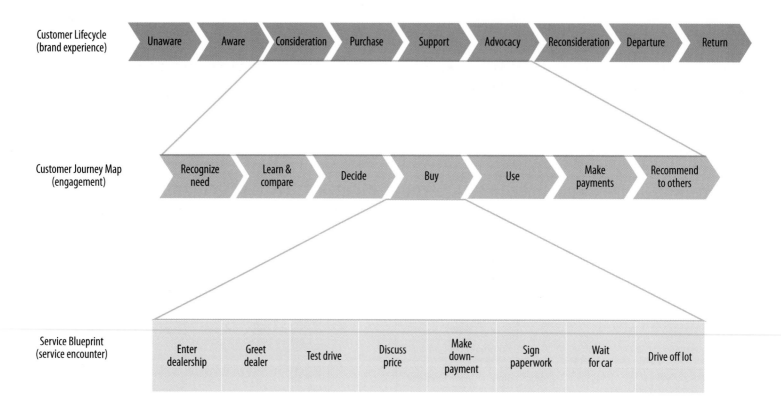

FIGURE 10-7. Customer lifecycles look at the overall relationship to a brand. Customer journey maps look at a particular type of engagement. Service blueprints typically analyze specific types of service encounters.

Related Models

Outside of commercial settings, Everett Rogers uncovered the complexity of adoption of new products. In his landmark book *Diffusion of Innovations*, Rogers outlines his *innovation-decision process* based on decades of research (Figure 10-8).

Though dating back to the 1960s, this process resembles typical phases of modern CJMs. In fact, John Jenkins cites Rogers's model as a direct influence on the early map shown in Figure 10-6.

The attitude of the individual during the *persuasion* phase, in particular, is critical. Rogers was able to narrow down predictors of decision-making in this phase to a set of five basic principles. These are the questions decision makers ultimately ask before adopting a new product or service:

- Relative advantage. Is it better than existing alternatives?
- Compatibility. Is it appropriate? Does it fit into my beliefs and values?
- Complexity. Is it easy to comprehend and use?
- Trialability. Can it be tested without penalty?
- Observability. Can it be observed and understood?

If most are answered affirmatively, the chance of adoption is higher. In other words, these are the key factors that influence the decision-making process.

Keep in mind that these are *perceived* characteristics. That is, the perception of value is in the mind of the customer, not an absolute property of a product or service. Similarly, CJMs seek to understand how an offering is actually perceived by customers, from their vantage point.

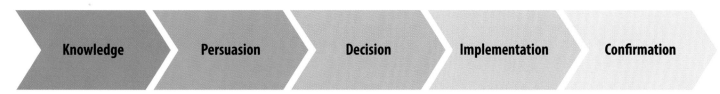

Knowledge → Persuasion → Decision → Implementation → Confirmation

FIGURE 10-8. The innovation-decision process, first described by Everett Rogers.

The Conversion Funnel

The decision to make a purchase is typically seen as a funnel (Figure 10-9). The exact phases or steps along the way can vary, depending on how the funnel is conceived.

FIGURE 10-9. Typical marketing funnel showing progression through the customer journey.

The metaphor suggests that people enter into a wide opening and get funneled into making a purchase. But at various points, there are decisions to leave the process, thereby reducing the number of people that continue all the way to conversion.

Market researchers at McKinsey and Company suggest a new model, which they call the *consumer decision journey.** They believe consumers are increasingly changing the way they research and buy products and services. They do much more upfront research and comparison than ever before, particularly online. (See the sidebar, "Zero Moment of Truth" in Chapter 2 for more on these shifts.)

Figure 10-10 reflects their updated decision-making model.

The circular arrangement of this model reflects a need to reevaluate how consumers go through their decision-making process. In this age of empowered consumers, the process is more circular. One person's experiences after purchase become the next person's evaluation criteria. With this model, there is no more "top of the funnel" where consumers enter en masse.

---

* See David Court et al. "The Consumer Decision Journey," *McKinsey Quarterly* (Jun 2009) and David C. Edelman. "Branding in the Digital Age: You're Spending Your Money in All the Wrong Places," *Harvard Business Review* (Dec 2010).

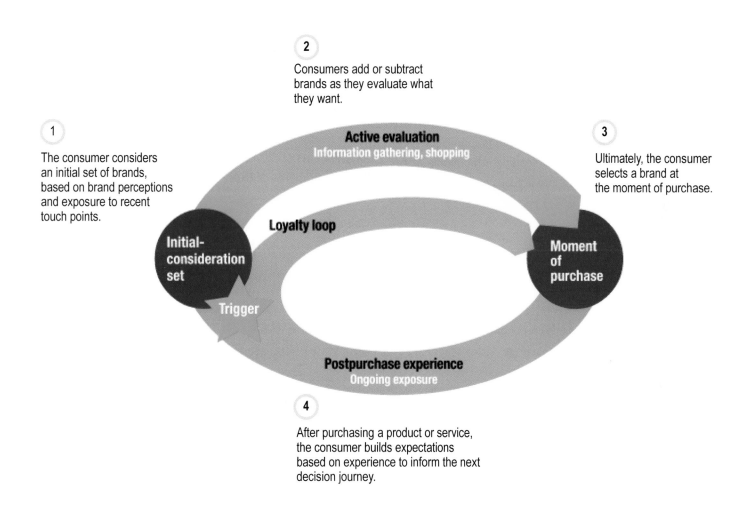

2

Consumers add or subtract brands as they evaluate what they want.

1

The consumer considers an initial set of brands, based on brand perceptions and exposure to recent touch points.

Active evaluation
Information gathering, shopping

3

Ultimately, the consumer selects a brand at the moment of purchase.

Loyalty loop

Initial-consideration set

Trigger

Moment of purchase

Postpurchase experience
Ongoing exposure

4

After purchasing a product or service, the consumer builds expectations based on experience to inform the next decision journey.

FIGURE 10-10. The consumer decision journey, as visualized by consultants at McKinsey, changes the basic notion of a funnel.

Elements of CJMs

CJMs aren't mere inventories of touchpoints. They include deeper insight into the motivations and attitudes of customers. What makes them purchase? What keeps them satisfied? These are the types of questions a CJM needs to address.

Consider the elements and structure of the map in Figure 10-11. Each touchpoint is clearly indicated in the middle across different channels. Below those are actual satisfaction scores from quantitative sources.

CJMs are decidedly less formulaic than service blueprints. They can include a number of different elements and information types, such as pain points, moments of truth, brand perception, and more. The creator of a CJM should include aspects appropriate to an organization's needs. Some typical elements of CJMs include actions, goals, emotions, pain points, moments of truth, touchpoints, satisfaction, and opportunities.

Table 10-1 summarizes the main aspects that define customer journey maps using the framework outlined in Chapter 2.

Point of view	Individual as a consumer
Structure	Chronological
Scope	End-to-end experience, from recognizing a need to ending the relationship
	Often centered on a single person's journey, but can also show a holistic, aggregate map across personas and touchpoints.
Focus	Focus primarily on the consumer experience, with very little on backstage processes
Uses	Used for touchpoint analysis and optimization
	Strategic planning for customer experience management, marketing, and branding initiatives
Strengths	Simple to understand
	Widespread use
	Suitable for co-creation with teams and stakeholders
Weaknesses	Typically view individuals as consumers
	Often leave out internal processes and actors

TABLE 10-1. Defining aspects of customer journey maps

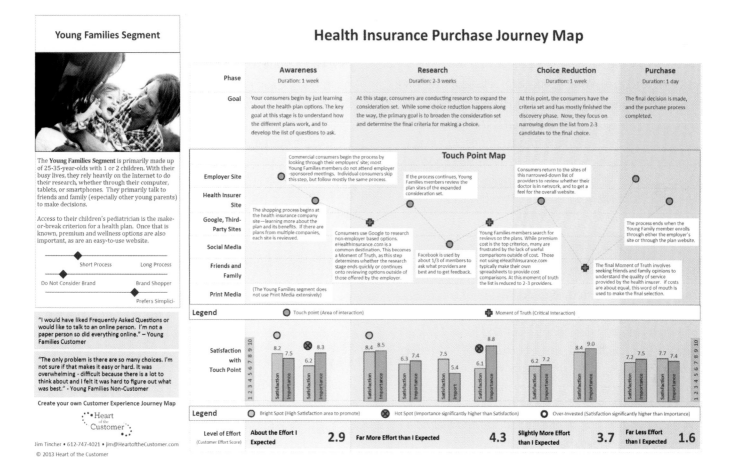

FIGURE 10-11. A CJM for purchasing health insurance, created by Jim Tincher at Heart of the Customer, shows the typical elements.

Further Reading

David Court et al. "The Consumer Decision Journey," *McKinsey Quarterly* (Jun 2009)

> *Consultants at McKinsey did extensive research around the world to arrive at a new model for consumer purchasing decisions. This supersedes the traditional funnel model, with a circular model of decision making. See also an in-depth article by McKinsey principal David Edelman: "Branding in the Digital Age: You're Spending Your Money in All the Wrong Places," Harvard Business Review (Dec 2010).*

Joel Flom. "The Value of Customer Journey Maps: A UX Designer's Personal Journey," *UX Matters* (Sept 2011)

> *This is a good case study around the use of customer journey maps at Boeing, including a good illustration of a map with an interesting layout and form. Look at this article if you need some arguments for convincing others. The author was first skeptical of their use, but concludes: "By producing journey maps that illustrate an optimal customer experience, we enable stakeholders and executives to identify, prioritize, and maintain focus on the changes that matter."*

Megan Grocki, "How to Create a Customer Journey Map" *UX Mastery* (Sep 2014)

> *This is a short but very informative article on the overall process of journey mapping. Grocki breaks it down into nine steps. This article includes a short video explaining the approach very well.*

Tim Ogilvie and Jeanne Liedtka. "Journey Mapping," Chapter 4 in *Designing for Growth* (Columbia Business School Publishing, 2011)

> *This book is fundamentally about design thinking and its relevance to business. The authors outline an end-to-end process for customer-centered design with many methods, the first of which is customer journey mapping. Chapter 4 deals exclusively with mapping and includes a step-by-step methods of creating them.*

Arne van Oosteroom. "Mapping Out Customer Experience Excellence: 10 Steps to Customer Journey Mapping," *MyCustomer.com* (2010)

> *Van Oosteroom is a leading service design expert in Europe and well versed in customer journey mapping. This is a short article that makes some important points about CJMs, including how they build empathy, understanding, and trust within teams. There is a quick guide to creating a CJM at the end of the article.*

Everett Rogers. *Diffusion of Innovations*, 5th ed. (Free House, 2003)

> *Considered the bible of innovation adoption, this lengthy book is based on decades of research in a variety of fields. Though the book first appeared in 1962, the 5th edition was written in 2003 and includes a section on the Internet. Still, the principles and discussions in this landmark book are wholly relevant to discussions of decision-making processes and innovation adoption today. Rogers is perhaps better known for his model of innovation adopter types, including coining terms such as "early adopters."*

Adam Richardson. *"Using Customer Journey Maps to Improve Customer Experience,"* Harvard Business Blog (Nov 2010) and *"Touchpoints Bring the Customer Experience to Life,"* Harvard Business Blog (Dec 2010).

> *This pair of articles from expert Adam Richardson of frog design covers some basics of CJMs. The second one dives deeper into touchpoint analysis and provides some good tips and examples of what to look for and map. The important thing about these articles is that they appear in a leading business venue. Pointing to these can help get the attention of stakeholders at different levels.*

Bruce Temkin. "Mapping the Customer Journey," *Forrester Reports* (Feb 2010)

> *Bruce Temkin was an early advocate of customer journey maps and did a great deal to increase their use and profile. Writing for Forrester, he produced several key reports on the topic that were influential. This report is one of his first with Forrester; see other writings from Temkin on the subject.*

Customer Journey Mapping in Practice

by Jim Tincher, Mapper-In-Chief, Heart of the Customer

Seeking to identify specific ways to boost loyalty and referrals among its radiology patients, Meridian Health reached out to the customer journey map experts at Heart of the Customer (HotC).

HotC's Mapper-in-Chief, Jim Tincher, and his team worked with Meridian's Vice President of Marketing, Chrisie Scott, and Director of Experience Marketing, Tria Deibert, to identify several key customer segments (personas) to focus on in creating their customer journey maps, to shed light on the differing needs of each type of patient, and to explore what they were thinking and feeling during each step of their healthcare experience.

They began with a hypothesis based on input from internal staff: that scheduling difficulties were the primary source of customer frustration. But as is often the case in journey mapping, it soon became apparent that the touchpoints employees believed to be problematic were not actually causing friction for customers.

Data gathered from dozens of patients through journaling exercises and more than half a dozen focus groups during the early stages of the mapping process revealed that patients found Meridian's scheduling and registration procedures to be straightforward and smooth, with particularly high marks given to their caring and competent staff. Patients were also quite satisfied with other touchpoints that were identified during the

mapping process, including the actual treatment they received.

At the same time, highlighted moments of truth revealed an issue that did need to be addressed: many patients didn't know what to expect at different stages of their journey, and weren't initially offered guidance to navigate from step to step.

Focusing on two of the journey maps HotC created for Meridian—those representing patients on either end of the experience spectrum—illustrates the unique value of customer journey mapping.

On one end, there's Seen-it-all Stanley (Figure 10-12), a heavy healthcare user whose familiarity with "the system" tempers both his expectations and his anxiety level. He knows to leave a little extra time for parking, he can relax and enjoy watching TV in the waiting room until he's called in, and he knows when he can expect his test results.

Minor inconveniences or delays don't faze Stanley because he knows he's in good hands. Meridian has already earned his loyalty, and needs only to maintain the high level of service it already provides in order to keep it.

On the other end of the spectrum is Newbie Natalie (Figure 10-13), who is "learning the ropes" as she navigates Meridian's radiology services for the first time. Understandably, Newbie

Natalie is more nervous, which magnifies the negative impact of friction during any touchpoint in her journey.

Parking difficulties get Natalie's visit off to a bad start, and not knowing when to expect her test results unnecessarily adds to her already elevated anxiety level. As a result, even though she is satisfied with the treatment she receives, and even though those kinds of problems are unlikely to recur on subsequent visits, they negatively impact her overall experience.

That finding was key to determining where to focus future customer engagement efforts, because Natalie won't be a Newbie for long. If her first experience is peppered with uncertainty and inconvenience, regardless of how minor, she will have little incentive to choose Meridian next time around.

So therein lay Meridian's greatest opportunity: meet Natalie's needs today, so that she can transition into a loyal, satisfied Seen-it-all Stanley tomorrow.

With that information and completed customer journey maps in hand, HotC moved on to the action component of the customer journey mapping process by leading workshops to brainstorm and prioritize ways to improve Newbie Natalie's experience.

Once it was determined that better communication was key, Meridian was able to devise ways to provide clearer, more specific guidance for each step of her journey. In doing so, Meridian keeps her anxiety to a minimum, helps her avoid unnecessary inconvenience, and provides the information that allows her to frame realistic expectations.

Had Meridian not engaged HotC to create customer journey maps and instead—per staffers' initial perceptions of what the priority should be—focused on "improving" their scheduling and registration processes, not only would their efforts have been fruitless, they might even have decreased customer satisfaction by tampering with a system with which patients were happy. Instead, customer journey mapping illuminated simple, effective steps Meridian could take to turn anxious new patients into loyal and satisfied healthcare users.

About the Contributor

Heart of the Customer Mapper-in-Chief Jim Tincher sees the world in a special way: through the eyes of customers.

With a lifelong passion for customer experience, Jim founded HotC to help companies of all sizes increase customer engagement. Before launching the company, Jim led customer engagement initiatives at Best Buy and UnitedHealth Group. In the process, he became an expert in using Voice of the Customer research to identify unmet needs, develop new products, and improve customer service. His *HotC Journey Maps* are a powerful tool designed with one simple goal: customer loyalty.

Jim's fascination with customer experience also led him to become a *Certified Customer Experience* Professional. He is also an active member of the *Customer Experience Professionals Association (CXPA)*, serving as one of their CX Experts and providing advice to members worldwide.

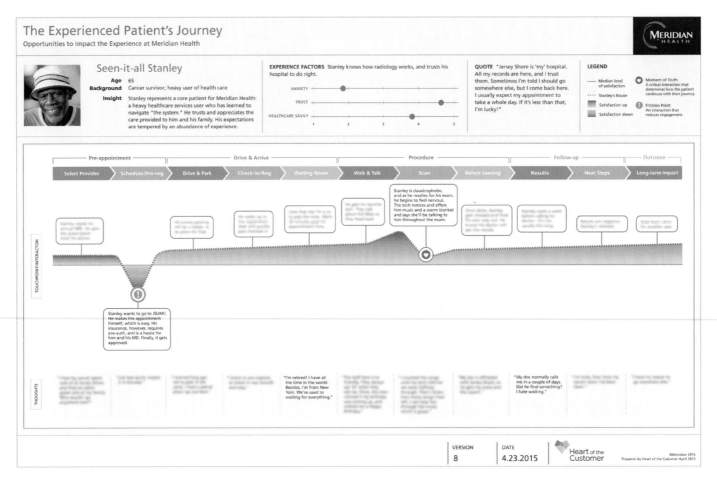

FIGURE 10-12. Customer journey map for Seen-it-all Stanley, created by Heart of the Customer for Meridian (journey map design by Design Ahead).

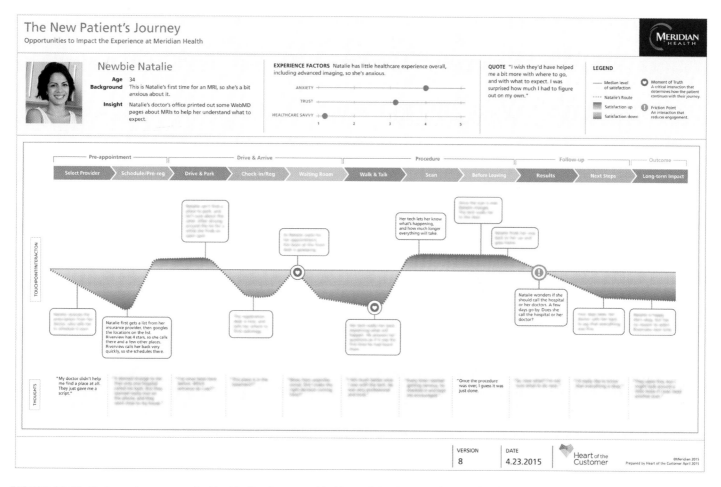

FIGURE 10-13. Customer journey map for Newbie Natalie, created by Heart of the Customer for Meridian (journey map design by Design Ahead).

Diagram and Image Credits

Figures 10-1 and 10-2: Moment map diagram and table from Colin Shaw and John Ivens. *Building Great Customer Experiences* (Palgrave Macmillan, 2002)

Figure 10-3: Customer journey map created by Jamie Thomson (Mad*Pow), originally appearing in Megan Grocki, "How to Create a Customer Journey Map" *UX Mastery* (Sep 2014), used by permission.

Figure 10-4: An example of a CJM for a broadband provider, created by Effective UI, used with permission

Figure 10-5: The customer journey canvas created by Mark Stickdorn and Jakob Schneider, from *This Is Service Design Thinking*, CC BY-SA 3.0

Figure 10-6: Model of the customer lifecycle by John Jenkins from his book *Marketing and Customer Behaviour* (Pergamon Press, 1972)

Figure 10-10: David Court et al. "The Consumer Decision Journey," *McKinsey Quarterly* (Jun 2009)

Figure 10-11: CJM by Jim Tincher, used with permission. *http://www.heartofthe-customer.com/customer-experience-journey-map-the-top-10-requirements/*

Figure 10-12: Map created by Jim Tincher, Heart of the Customer, designed by Design Ahead (*http://www.designahead.com*), used by permission from HotC and Meridian

CHAPTER 11

Experience Maps

As the Internet continues to grow and evolve, service ecosystems become more complex. Products are connected. The idea of a standalone offering is already something of the past. Building the proverbial better mousetrap does not necessarily win anymore.

Instead, thinking in terms of ecosystems is the new competitive advantage. Steve Denning, a popular business writer with *Forbes* magazine, puts it this way.

> Even better products can disappear with alarming rapidity. By contrast, ecosystems that delight customers are difficult to build, but once built, are difficult to compete against.*

Successful organizations will be determined by how well their services fit with each other and, more importantly, how well they fit into people's lives.

Ecosystem design doesn't apply only to large organizations. GOQii, for example, is a small company that makes a wearable fitness band. But unlike other bands, this one is connected to a trainer, who provides personalized health feedback. Meeting daily goals set by the trainer earns Karma points, which users can then donate to good causes.

By connecting activities around the field of fitness, GOQii created an ecosystem of experiences. This is an implicit part of the GOQii value proposition, reflected in their customer-facing diagrams, as seen in Figure 11-1.

Systems are now multifaceted and bring complexity with them. Hugh Dubberly, renowned designer and business consultant, believes models are an antidote. In an interview, Dubberly states:[†]

> We need models for planning systems, for thinking about the elements and the rules together, for thinking about how systems integrate with other systems embedded in systems of yet more systems. We need

---

* See the full article at: Steve Denning. "Why Building a Better Mousetrap Doesn't Work Anymore," *Forbes* (Feb 2014).

† From an interview with Hugh Dubberly conducted by David Brown. See "Hugh Dubberly. Supermodeler." *GAIN : AIGA Journal of Design for the Network Economy* (2000).

models not just of what appears on computer screens, not just of pathways, not just of interactions. We now also need models of goals and contexts. We need models of abstract ideas.

Alignment diagrams represent these types of models. Experience maps, in particular—the topic of this chapter—look at the broader context of human activity, beyond the offerings of just one organization. They show the connections between people, places, and things, and they aid in the design of ecosystems.

Maps of Experiences

By some definitions and uses, *experience maps* overlap completely with *customer journey maps*. For sure, the two terms are used interchangeably in practice. You may even find a mashup of terminology as well, with phrases such as "customer experience maps" and "experience journeys." Don't worry about the semantic differences of these labels. Instead, focus on the story you need to tell in your organization.

That said, there are general differences between experience maps and customer journey maps we can point to. Customer journey maps tend to view the individual as a consumer of the products and services. As the name implies, they are about the relationship of an individual as a *customer* of a specific service.

Experience maps, on the other hand, typically focus on a general human activity within a given domain. The company or organization may not even be explicitly stated, or there may be many organizations involved.

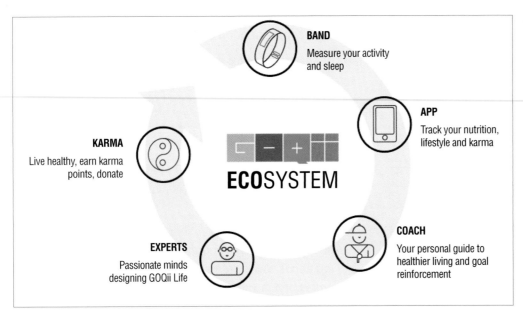

FIGURE 11-1. The GOQii.com ecosystem includes a fitness band, an app, coaches and experts, and donations of Karma points earned.

From this standpoint, experience maps separate experiences from solutions. They help shift an organization's collective thought from features or internal processes toward the desired outcomes people seek.

One of the earliest examples of an experience map comes from Gene Smith and Trevor von Gorp of nForm, a leading experience design agency in Canada. Figure 11-2 shows their map for a video game enthusiast.

Although this map includes a purchase phase, that is not the focus of the diagram. Smith describes how their motivation was to understand the context of gaming in greater depth in his blog post entitled "Experience Maps: Understanding Cross-Channel Experiences for Gamers." He writes:

> The solution we came up with was an experience map—a diagram that combines a persona with an abstracted story about the gamer's journey from researching games to purchasing, playing to sharing experiences about that game. The story includes the details on the different channels where gamers get their information along with supporting quotes from our research.

Successful organizations will be determined by how well their services fit with each other and, more importantly, how well they fit into people's lives.

Experience maps fundamentally recognize that people interact with many products and services from a multitude of providers in many situations. These experiences shape their behaviors and their relationship with any one organization. Examining this broader context will become increasingly crucial as products and service become connected with each other.

Consider the map shown in Figure 11-3, created by Diego S. Bernardo, a design strategist in Pittsburgh, Pennsylvania. His aim was to illustrate the ups and downs of growing food in the city. Negative experiences (in red) indicate reasons why someone might stop the activity. Dropout points are indicated with red lines pointing down.

The positive experiences (in blue) show the feelings on growing food in the city. This diagram reminds us to look not only for pain points, struggles, and fears in an experience, but also aspects that motivate and encourage. The loops in the diagram indicate positive feedback loops and increased engagement throughout the experience.

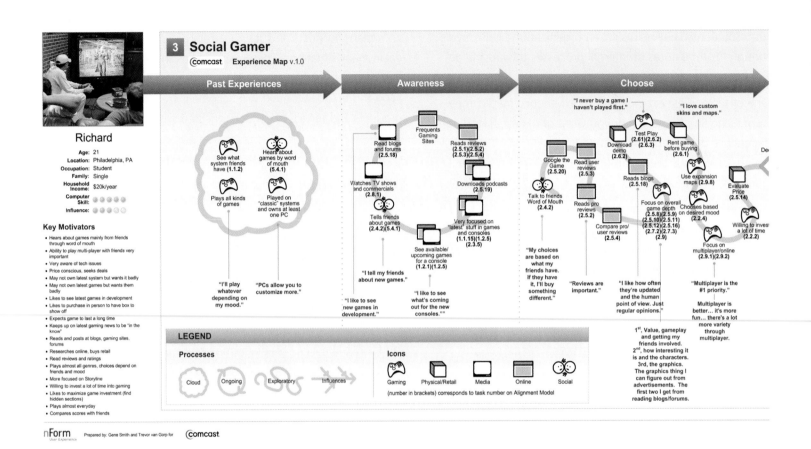

FIGURE 11-2. This experience map for social gamers shows a clear chronology from left to right.

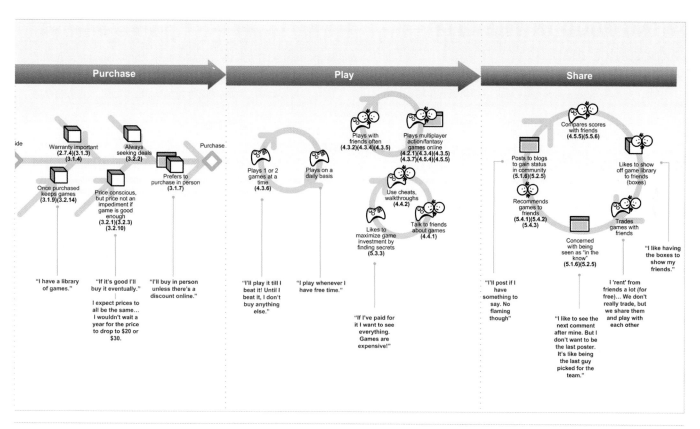

Purchase

Warranty important
(2.7.4)(3.1.3)
(3.1.4)

Always
seeking deals
(3.2.2)

Once purchased
keeps games
(3.1.9)(3.2.14)

Price conscious,
but price not an
impediment if
game is good
enough
(3.2.1)(3.2.3)
(3.2.10)

Prefers to
purchase in person
(3.1.7)

Purchase

"I have a library
of games."

"If it's good I'll
buy it eventually."

I expect prices to
all be the same...
I wouldn't wait a
year for the price
to drop to $20 or
$30.

"I'll buy in person
unless there's a
discount online."

Play

Plays 1 or 2
games at a
time
(4.3.6)

Plays on a
daily basis

Plays with
friends often
(4.3.2)(4.3.4)(4.3.5)

Plays multiplayer
action/fantasy
games online
(4.2.1)(4.3.4)(4.3.5)
(4.3.7)(4.5.4)(4.5.5)

Use cheats,
walkthroughs
(4.4.2)

Likes to
maximize game
investment by
finding secrets
(5.3.3)

Talk to friends
about games
(4.4.1)

"I'll play it till I
beat it! Until I
beat it, I don't
buy anything
else."

"I play whenever I
have free time."

"If I've paid for
it I want to see
everything.
Games are
expensive!"

Share

Compares scores
with friends
(4.5.5)(5.5.6)

Posts to blogs
to gain status
in community
(5.1.6)(5.2.5)

Likes to show
off game library
to friends
(boxes)

Recommends
games to
friends
(5.4.1)(5.4.2)
(5.4.3)

Concerned
with being
seen as "in the
know"
(5.1.6)(5.2.5)

Trades
games with
friends

"I like having
the boxes to
show my
friends."

"I'll post if I
have
something to
say. No
flaming
though"

"I like to see the
next comment
after mine. But I
don't want to be
the last poster.
It's like being
the last guy
picked for the
team."

I 'rent' from
friends a lot (for
free)... We don't
really trade, but
we share them
and play with
each other

GROWING FOOD IN THE CITY
User experience map

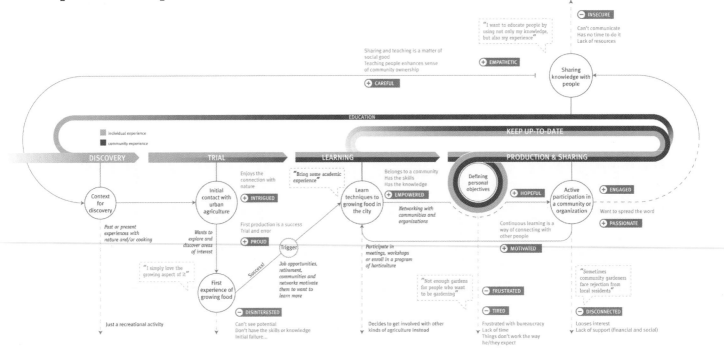

FIGURE 11-3. An experience map for growing food in Chicago focuses on positive and negative factors.

Notice also that no organization is explicitly named in this diagram. Still, providers of related services or city officials could use this map to help understand and plan better food growing programs.

Figure 11-4 shows another example of an experience map—in this case, visiting a museum called the Exploratorium—created by Brandon Schauer and designers at Adaptive Path. There is no purchase decision in this diagram. Rather, it seeks to illustrate

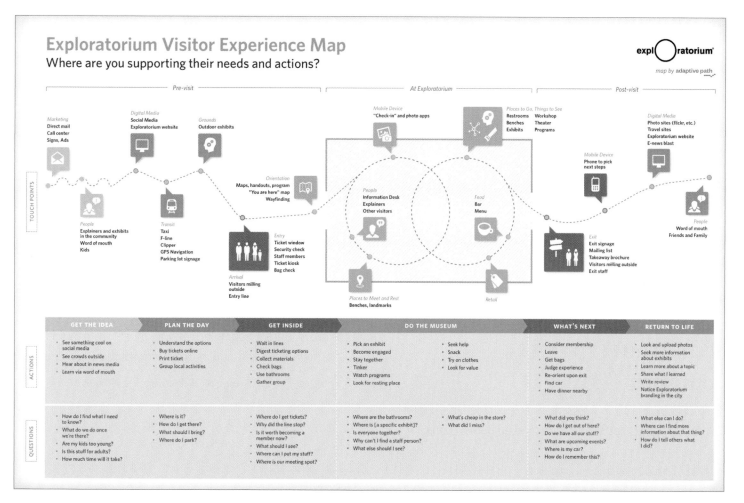

FIGURE 11-4. Visitors' experiences visiting the Exploratorium captured in a single overview.

the actions and thoughts of museum goers, both inside and outside of the museum. For instance, touchpoints at the top of the diagram include things like "Taxis" and "GPS."

More importantly, working through the diagramming process had a positive impact on the Exploratorium team. In a blog post, Schauer indicates the effect of the mapping effort:

> *What we found impressive was how quickly this diverse group aligned by using the maps on a small set of opportunities that could yield the most impact on the visitor experience.**

With maps as a centerpiece for the conversation, the team was able to find consensus and alignment.

Related Models

Experience maps are concerned with how the provider's offering fits into a person's experience, not the other way around. They provide a view of a given domain from the user's point of view.

Related types of diagrams also take this perspective, including jobs maps and workflow diagrams.

Jobs Maps

The concept of *jobs to be done*, briefly outlined in Chapter 2, provides a rich basis for understanding human behavior and motivations. From this perspective, people are seen as goal-driven individuals seeking to achieve some desired outcome. Supporting those outcomes is ultimately the value that organizations create.

Tony Ulwick has done some of the most advanced work in applying "jobs to be done" theory in practice. His company, Strategyn, bases its consulting offering on jobs to be done. Together with his colleague Lance Bettencourt, Ulwick proposes a model for understanding jobs to be done as a sequence of steps. They call these *job maps.*[†]

All jobs are processes that have a universal structure, the authors believe. Figure 11-5 shows the steps in the normalized process they propose.

The goal of creating a job map is to uncover what a person is trying to get done and to examine specific points in the flow by breaking them down. According to Ulwick and Bettencourt, the universal steps in completing a job are:

1. *Define:* This step includes determining objectives and planning the approach to getting the job done.

2. *Locate:* Before beginning, people must locate inputs, gather items, and find information needed to do the job.

3. *Prepare:* In this step, people set up the environment and organize materials.

---

* Brandon Schauer. "Exploratorium: Mapping the Experience of Experiments," *Adaptive Path Blog* (Apr 2013), *http://adaptivepath.org/ideas/exploratorium-mapping-the-experience-of-experiments*.

---

† Lance Bettencourt and Anthony Ulwick. "The Customer-Centered Innovation Map," *Harvard Business Review* (May 2008).

4. *Confirm:* Here, individuals make sure the materials and the environment are properly prepared.

5. *Execute:* In this step, individuals perform the job as planned. From their perspective this is the most critical step in the job map.

6. *Monitor:* People evaluate success of the job as it is being executed.

7. *Modify:* Modifications, alterations, and iterations may be necessary to complete a job.

8. *Conclude:* This step refers to all of the actions taken to complete and wrap up the job.

The divisions of this sequence, however, may not be how a person experiences the world. Instead, a job map is a model that helps us understand human activity with a consistent framework. You may find yourself modifying this framework in practice to fit your situation.

With a job map in hand, organizations can better create products and services that people actually need. Bettencourt and Ulwick urge teams to use job maps collaboratively to identify opportunities:

> With a job map in hand, you can begin to look systematically for opportunities to create value...A great way to begin is to consider the biggest drawbacks of current solutions at each step in the map—in particular, drawbacks related to speed of execution, variability, and the quality of output. To increase the effectiveness of this approach, invite a diverse team of experts—marketing, design, engineering, and even some lead customers—to participate in this discussion.

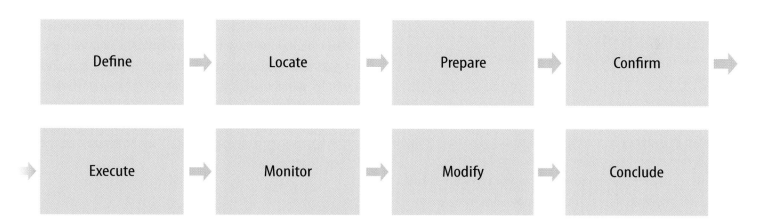

FIGURE 11-5. The job map, as proposed by Bettencourt and Ulwick, has eight phases.

Innovation opportunities can come at any step in the job map. Consider these examples:

- Weight Watchers streamlines the "Define" stage with a system that does not require calorie counting.

- To gather items during the "Locate" step while moving house, U-Haul provides customers with kits that include different types of boxes needed.

- Nike helps joggers evaluate success of the job in the "Monitor" step with a sensor in the running shoe that provides feedback about time, distance, pace, and calories burned via a connection to an iPod.

- Browser-based SaaS software updates automatically so users don't have to install new versions, thereby reducing complexity in the "Modify" step.

Note that job maps are typically narrower in scope than experience maps. As a result, the two can work hand-in-hand. You can use an experience map to show the high-level view of an ecosystem, and drill down on specific areas with job maps to detail specific steps.

Workflow Diagrams

Related to experience maps and job maps, workflow diagrams break down the steps taken to achieve a goal. These diagrams focus on how a sequence of tasks fits together, often between multiple actors. They are more akin to a service blueprint.

A swim lane diagram is a specific type of document that is widely used to show workflow. Typically these diagrams show the steps of an interaction between a user and different parts of a system in a very mechanical way. The columns or rows of the diagram—depending on its orientation—make up the "swim lanes." This aids in seeing different actors and components in an interaction.

Figure 11-6 shows a typical swim lane diagram with parallel actions with a system—in this case, for the workflow of placing a purchase order with a sales agent.

It's clear that this diagram does not explicitly include contextual information or details about customer emotions. Instead, swim lane diagrams focus on the flow of tasks, materials, and information chronologically. Often, a workflow diagram may accompany an experience map to show detailed interactions of a specific phase within a broader context.

Swim lane diagrams can be expanded to include information about an individual's experience. Figure 11-7 shows an example diagram created by Yvonne Shek of nForm that includes a graphic storyboard and details about the person involved in the interaction.

This approach extends the swim lane technique by adding experiential context.

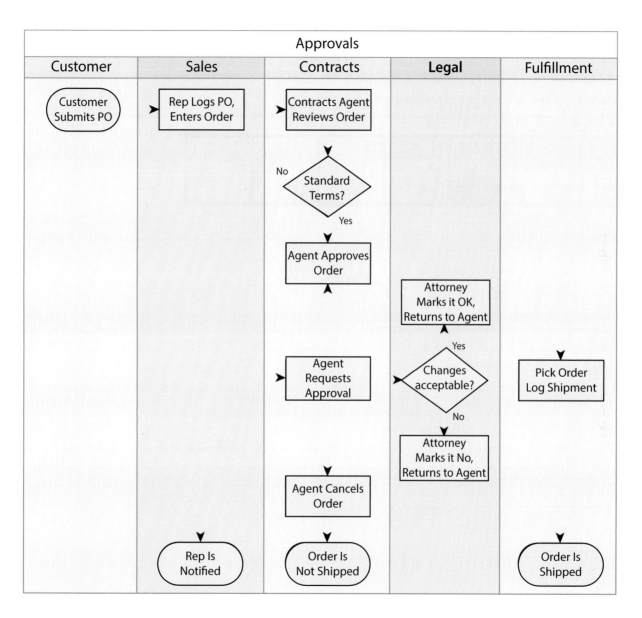

FIGURE 11-6. An example of a typical swim lane diagram separates activities into discrete columns.

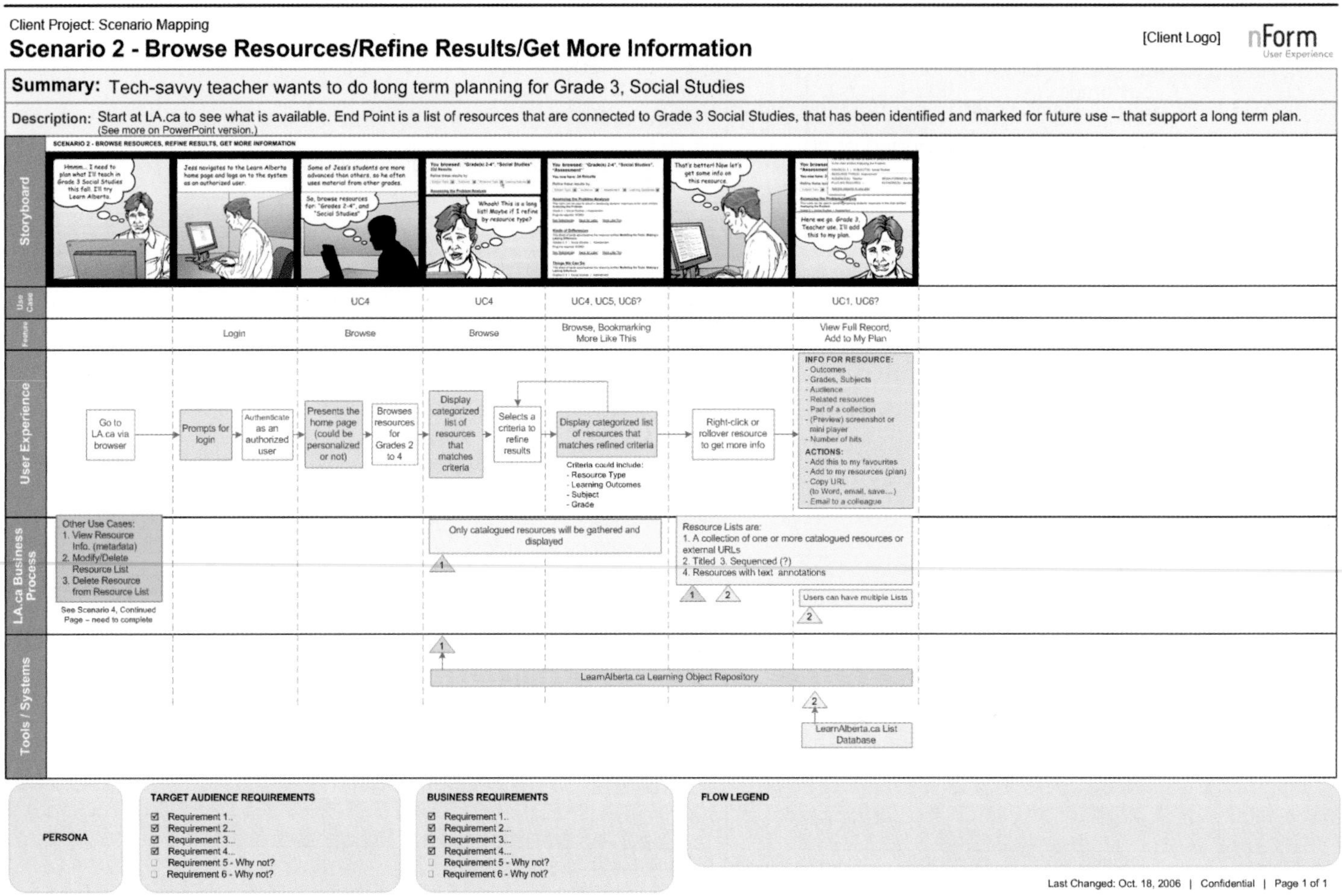

Scenario 2 - Browse Resources/Refine Results/Get More Information

[Client Logo] nForm
User Experience

Summary: Tech-savvy teacher wants to do long term planning for Grade 3, Social Studies

Description: Start at LA.ca to see what is available. End Point is a list of resources that are connected to Grade 3 Social Studies, that has been identified and marked for future use – that support a long term plan.
(See more on PowerPoint version.)

SCENARIO 2 - BROWSE RESOURCES, REFINE RESULTS, GET MORE INFORMATION

Storyboard

Use Case

| | UC4 | UC4 | UC4, UC5, UC6? | UC1, UC6? |

Feature

| Login | Browse | Browse | Browse, Bookmarking More Like This | View Full Record, Add to My Plan |

User Experience

Go to LA.ca via browser → Prompts for login → Authenticate as an authorized user → Presents the home page (could be personalized or not) → Browses resources for Grades 2 to 4 → Display categorized list of resources that matches criteria → Selects a criteria to refine results → Display categorized list of resources that matches refined criteria → Right-click or rollover resource to get more info

Criteria could include:
- Resource Type
- Learning Outcomes
- Subject
- Grade

INFO FOR RESOURCE:
- Outcomes
- Grades, Subjects
- Audience
- Related resources
- Part of a collection
- (Preview) screenshot or mini player
- Number of hits

ACTIONS:
- Add this to my favourites
- Add to my resources (plan)
- Copy URL (to Word, email, save....)
- Email to a colleague

LA.ca Business Process

Other Use Cases:
1. View Resource Info. (metadata)
2. Modify/Delete Resource List
3. Delete Resource from Resource List

See Scenario 4, Continued Page – need to complete

Only catalogued resources will be gathered and displayed ①

Resource Lists are:
1. A collection of one or more catalogued resources or external URLs
2. Titled 3. Sequenced (?)
4. Resources with text annotations
① ②

Users can have multiple Lists ②

Tools / Systems

①

LearnAlberta.ca Learning Object Repository

②

LearnAlberta.ca List Database

TARGET AUDIENCE REQUIREMENTS	**BUSINESS REQUIREMENTS**	**FLOW LEGEND**
☑ Requirement 1...	☑ Requirement 1...	
☑ Requirement 2...	☑ Requirement 2...	
☑ Requirement 3...	☑ Requirement 3...	
☑ Requirement 4...	☑ Requirement 4...	
☐ Requirement 5 - Why not?	☐ Requirement 5 - Why not?	
☐ Requirement 6 - Why not?	☐ Requirement 6 - Why not?	

PERSONA

Last Changed: Oct. 18, 2006 | Confidential | Page 1 of 1

FIGURE 11-7. Swim lane diagrams can be expanded to be rich in context of the user experience.

Elements of Experience Maps

The elements of experience maps are very similar to a customer journey map. But experience maps tend to be even more freeform, with facets of information included or not depending on the story being told. Conventions are emerging, however. Typical elements of experience maps include some or all of the following:

- Phases of behavior
- Actions and steps taken
- Jobs to be done, goals, or needs
- Thoughts and questions
- Emotions and state of mind
- Pain points
- Physical artifacts and devices
- Opportunities

Experience maps tend to break away from a focus on the purchasing decision—a key distinguishing factor to customer journey maps. Although a purchase may be part of the experience, the focus on the map is not necessarily making a decision.

Table 11-1 summarizes the main aspects that define experience maps using the framework outlined in Chapter 2.

Perspective	Individual as goal-driven, operating within a broad system or domain and interacting potentially many services.
Organization	Chronological.
Scope	Holistic process of a defined experience, from end-to-end, including actions, thoughts, and feelings.
	May be limited to a single individual or aggregate behavior across actors.
Focus	Focus primarily on the human experience, with often little or no explicit backstage processes.
Uses	Used for analysis of ecosystem relationships and the design of solutions.
	Inform strategic planning and innovation.
Strengths	Offer a fresh, outward perspective that helps build empathy.
	Provide insight beyond the relationship with a single organization or brand.
Weaknesses	Can be viewed as too abstract by some stakeholders.
	Detailed diagrams can lead to overanalysis and "mapping overload."

TABLE 11-1. Defining aspects of experience maps

Further Reading

"Adaptive Path's Guide to Experience Mapping" (2013), *http://mappingexperiences.com*

> The folks at Adaptive Path put together an excellent guide on experience mapping. This is a short, free PDF that covers the process from beginning to end. It is a great resource for people new to the technique or those who just need a solid overview.

Lance Bettencourt and Anthony W. Ulwick. "The Customer-Centered Innovation Map," *Harvard Business Review* (May 2008)

> Bettencourt and Ulwick deepen techniques involving jobs to be done with a practical way of mapping out jobs. It's a simple and efficient system for use in innovation efforts. They conclude: "When companies understand that customers hire products, services, software, and ideas to get jobs done, they can dissect those jobs to discover the innovation opportunities that are the key to growth."

Chris Risdon. "The Anatomy of an Experience Map," *Adaptive Path Blog* (Nov 2011)

> This excellent article breaks down the technique of experience mapping into its constituent components. Chris Risdon is a leader in experience mapping and has done some of the most extensive work outlining methods for the technique.

Gene Smith. "Experience Maps: Understanding Cross-Channel Experiences for Gamers," *nForm Blog* (February 2010)

> This is a short blog post by Gene Smith, who graciously shares several experience maps. These are some of the first examples in the category and have served as a model for subsequent experience mapping.

Workflow Diagrams at LexisNexis

by Jim Kalbach

LexisNexis is a worldwide provider of legal and professional information. While employed there, I led an effort to map the workflow of lawyers in four international markets—France, Australia and New Zealand, Germany, and Austria.

To secure funding I pitched the idea to senior leaders, who agreed to support the research. We decided to start with mid-sized law firms in France as the pilot project. After that, I mapped the workflow of barristers in Australia and New Zealand, and then of lawyers in small firms in Germany and in Austria.

The approach in each country was to follow the lifecycle of a client matter from the perspective of the lawyer. We wanted to understand the complex series of actions lawyers take to complete a client matter, from beginning to end. This was strategically relevant for the business at the time.

Investigation

In each country, I first collected existing research and looked for patterns. For instance, in France some recent segmentation work had recently been completed. From this, I was able to get an initial understanding of the market and the types of law firms that existed.

I also spoke with internal stakeholders in each country. This helped build an initial picture of an approximate lawyer's workflow, which in turn guided subsequent research.

Of course, there was significant field contact with actual customers. We conducted between 10 and 20 on-site interviews in each country. The audio of each session was recorded and transcribed, so the full text was available for analysis. Photographs provided additional context.

Illustration

After investigation, I then created workflow diagrams from all of the data collected—both internal and external. I kept the orientation of the diagrams horizontal so they could be viewed at eye level during the workshops. When printed, each workflow diagram was 10–15 feet long.

First, I modeled a high-level map of phases of a client matter. This was similar, but not exactly the same, in each country. As an example, Figure 11-8 shows a simplified version of the main phases for legal cases in Germany.

The diagrams included three different types of actors simultaneously: lawyers, secretaries, and all other actors in the workflow. As a result, they consisted of many rows of information, seen labeled on the left side of Figure 11-9.

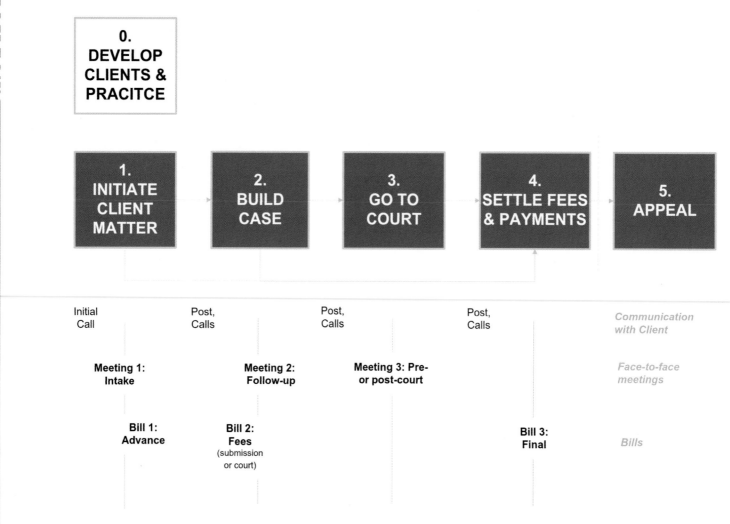

FIGURE 11-8. The top-level phases for a lawyer's workflow with a client matter in Germany reflects an end-to-end experience.

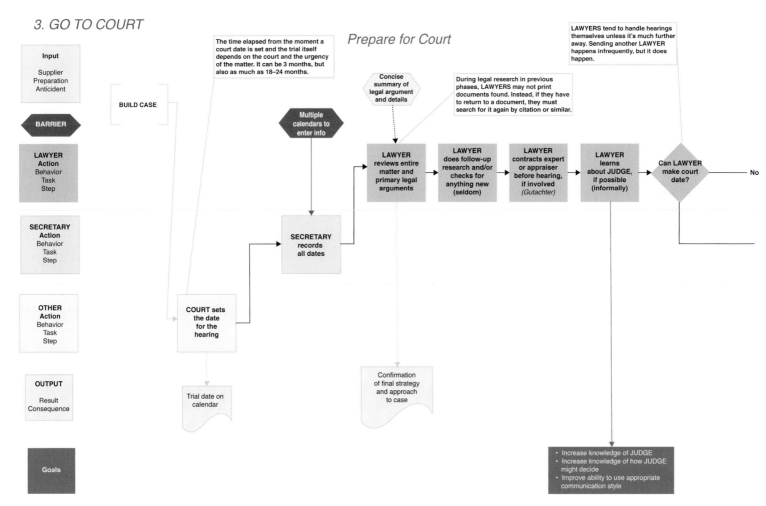

3. GO TO COURT

Prepare for Court

Input
Supplier
Preparation
Anticident

BUILD CASE

BARRIER

LAWYER
Action
Behavior
Task
Step

SECRETARY
Action
Behavior
Task
Step

OTHER
Action
Behavior
Task
Step

OUTPUT
Result
Consequence

Goals

The time elapsed from the moment a court date is set and the trial itself depends on the court and the urgency of the matter. It can be 3 months, but also as much as 18–24 months.

Multiple calendars to enter info

Concise summary of legal argument and details

During legal research in previous phases, LAWYERS may not print documents found. Instead, if they have to return to a document, they must search for it again by citation or similar.

LAWYERS tend to handle hearings themselves unless it's much further away. Sending another LAWYER happens infrequently, but it does happen.

LAWYER reviews entire matter and primary legal arguments

LAWYER does follow-up research and/or checks for anything new (seldom)

LAWYER contracts expert or appraiser before hearing, if involved *(Gutachter)*

LAWYER learns about JUDGE, if possible (informally)

Can LAWYER make court date? — No

SECRETARY records all dates

COURT sets the date for the hearing

Trial date on calendar

Confirmation of final strategy and approach to case

- Increase knowledge of JUDGE
- Increase knowledge of how JUDGE might decide
- Improve ability to use appropriate communication style

FIGURE 11-9. One page from a 20-page workflow diagram illustrates a detailed experience.

Pain points and goals are also included, as well as notes on state of mind and emotion. Personas, typical workweek charts, and org charts accompanied the diagrams for a complete description of the lawyer's experience.

Alignment

A highlight of each effort was the alignment workshop. In each country, this allowed stakeholders to understand the workflows and arrive at their own conclusions about the experience. These were day-long sessions with three sections:

- *Understanding the lawyer's experience:* Each breakout group focused on a section of the workflow and read through all of the steps. Through dot voting, the teams were tasked with identifying critical moments. Where are the stakes highest? What moments are emotionally charged for users? Figure 11-10 reflects a diagram from this step during a workshop in France.

- *Brainstorming:* After understanding the experience and where the biggest pain points were, the groups came up with new ways to support customers in their work. Figure 11-11 shows brainstorming in a group of people with mixed roles during a workshop in France.

- *Group presentations:* Each team selected their leading ideas from the brainstorming session and described them in greater detail, including sketches of the proposed solutions. These were then presented to everyone else in the workshop for feedback and questions.

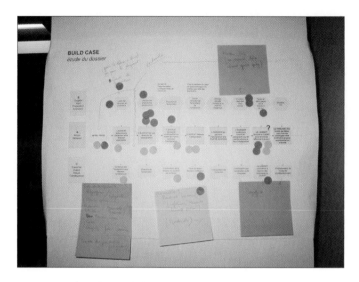

FIGURE 11-10. The workshop teams engaged with the workflow diagrams to identify pain points, moments of truth, and business opportunities, among other things.

After the workflow mapping projects were completed in the different countries, we presented the workflow diagrams at the yearly senior staff meeting. Upper managers from all international business units flew to Montreux for a series of meetings across three days.

I helped facilitate further workflow alignment exercises, which culminated in a mock trial. Leaders volunteered to play different roles in a fake court case.

FIGURE 11-11. Brainstorming during an alignment workshop involved stakeholders across functions and departments.

Outcomes

Internally, the alignment exercises helped gain empathy for our customers and build a common understanding of their work. For instance, in Australia, one stakeholder commented: "These workflow diagrams should be used to onboard new employees." He felt they were foundational in understanding our customers.

Since the diagrams for each country followed a similar format, we could compare the practice of law in different markets to see where the differences lie.

Concrete offerings also emerged. For example, we launched a new format for easily scannable legal news. This came out of a realization that lawyers spend a significant amount of time waiting at court and could use that time to keep up on news.

In another market, we launched a new solution targeting legal assistants—a previously unaddressed market segment. The workflow exercises informed this new offering.

Overall, the workflow mapping efforts in each country provided a deep view into the daily experience of lawyers. To this day, the work is considered a key resource for customer understanding within the company.

Diagram and Image Credits

Figure 11-2: Experience map created by Gene Smith and Trevor von Gorp of nForm, taken from "Experience Maps: Understanding Cross-Channel Experiences for Gamers," *nForm Blog* (Feb 2010), used with permission

Figure 11-3: Experience map created by Diego S. Bernardo (*www.diegobernardo.com*), taken from his blog post "Agitation and elation [in the user experience]" (*http://diegobernardo.com/2013/01/05/agitation-elation-in-the-user-experience/*) used with permission

Figure 11-4: Experience map for the Exploratorium from a case study by Brandon Schauer: "Exploratorium: Mapping the Experience of Experiments," *Adaptive Path Blog* (Apr 2013), *http://adaptivepath.org/ideas/exploratorium-mapping-the-experience-of-experiments*, used with permission

Figure 11-6: Swim lane diagram from Wikipedia, public domain

Figure 11-7: Swim lane diagram with storyboard by Yvonne Shek of nForm, used with permission

Figures 11-8 through 11-11: Diagrams and photos by Jim Kalbach, used with permission from LexisNexis

CHAPTER 12

Mental Model Diagrams

The term *mental model* has its roots in psychology. It refers to someone's thought process about how the world works—their frame of reality.

Mental models allow us to predict how things work. They are cognitive constructs built on beliefs, assumptions, and past experiences. But a person's mental model is a *perception* of a how a system functions, not necessarily how it actually may work.

For instance, say you come into your house on a cold day. To get warmed up quickly, you turn the thermostat way up. Your assumption is that the higher thermostat setting, the more heat will come out.

But a thermostat does not work like a faucet valve. It's more like a switch: the heat goes on or off depending on set temperature (see Figure 12-1). In this scenario, you'd have a wrong mental model of how the system actually works. The room won't get warmer faster. Instead, the heater will simply stay on longer to reach a higher temperature.

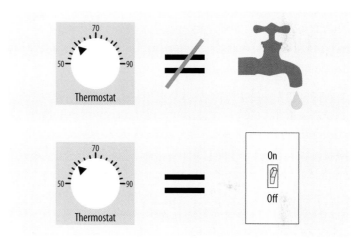

FIGURE 12-1. Thermostats are more like switches, not faucets.

The lesson for providers of products or services is profound: your understanding of the systems you create differs from the user's understanding. You have far more knowledge about how the system actually works than others do.

The difference in mental models is a key point Don Norman makes in his landmark book *The Design of Everyday Things* (1988). Figure 12-2 shows his now-iconic graphic of three different models at play: the model the designer has of the system, the actual system model, and the mental model the user has of the system.

The goal of design is to understand the mental model of the people you are designing for. To do this, you need a feedback loop, indicated by the two arrows on the right side of Figure 12-2. It requires the ability to put your own perspective to the side and to view the system as a user might. In a word, designing requires empathy.

The diagrams explored in this book help you understand the feedback loop between the user and the system. But there is something broader. The mental model the user has of the system is framed by that system. If you explore the mental model of a person, rather than a user, who is trying to achieve a purpose, then you can break out of the system frame. You can discover aspects of how a person thinks that have nothing to do with the system, but everything to do with how that person accomplishes their intent.

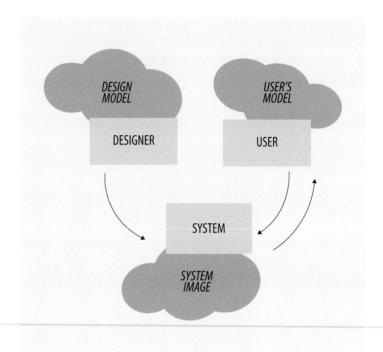

FIGURE 12-2. Don Norman's well-known diagram illustrates that the designer's model is not the same as user's mental model.

Mapping is a key way to understand mental models and make them visible to your organization. In practice, mapping experiences is effectively mapping someone's mental model. The approach discussed in this chapter focuses on a specific technique developed by Indi Young simply called *mental models diagrams*.

Mental Model Diagrams

In 2008 Indi Young published a formal method for visualizing mental models in her book of the same title. Figure 12-3 shows an early example of a mental model used in the book. This instance examines "movie going."

Mental model diagrams are typically very long documents and can extend 10–15 feet across a wall when printed. The diagram in Figure 12-3 has been broken into two parts to fit on the page.

The top half of the diagram describes the mental model patterns across a set of people. There are three basic levels of information in this portion of the diagram (Figure 12-4):

Boxes

These are the basic building blocks, shown as small squares. The boxes contain a person's thoughts, reactions, and guiding principles. (Originally, Young refers to these as "tasks" but has since moved away from that language to avoid confusion with physical actions only.)

Towers

Boxes form groups based on affinity, called towers. These are the areas with colored backgrounds on a diagram.

Mental spaces

Towers, in turn, form affinity clusters called mental spaces. The mental spaces are labeled above towers, between the dark vertical lines.

A dark line in the center separates the mental model from "support"—all of the products and services that address the thought process within a tower. From this arrangement, we see the basic principles of alignment at work.

Overall, this approach of describing mental models focuses on people, not tools. For instance, instead of writing "Filter image colors in Photoshop," focus on the root task and record "Alter image colors" or perhaps, "Improve image color."

The diagrams also don't reflect personal preference or opinion. Instead, strive to focus on what goes through a person's mind—their internal voice—and capture that in the diagram.

As a result, of all the diagrams covered in this book, the top half of mental model diagrams are the most person-focused in nature. This provides an advantage in flexibility: they can be applied to any domain or situation. Mental model diagrams also enjoy longevity: once completed, a mental model will change only slowly, often remaining relevant for years.

However, mental model diagrams may also overwhelm others with detail. I have seen business leaders ask for a simpler model. But that detail is also a strength for those looking to deeply understand people's state of mind.

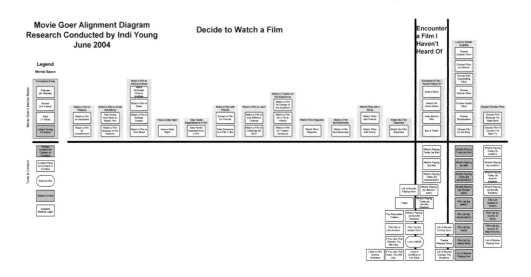

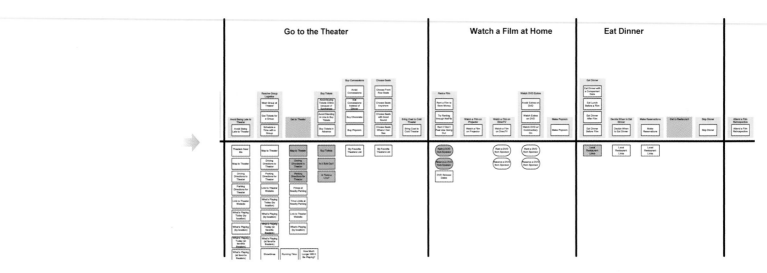

FIGURE 12-3. An example of a mental model diagram shows the overall experience of movie going.

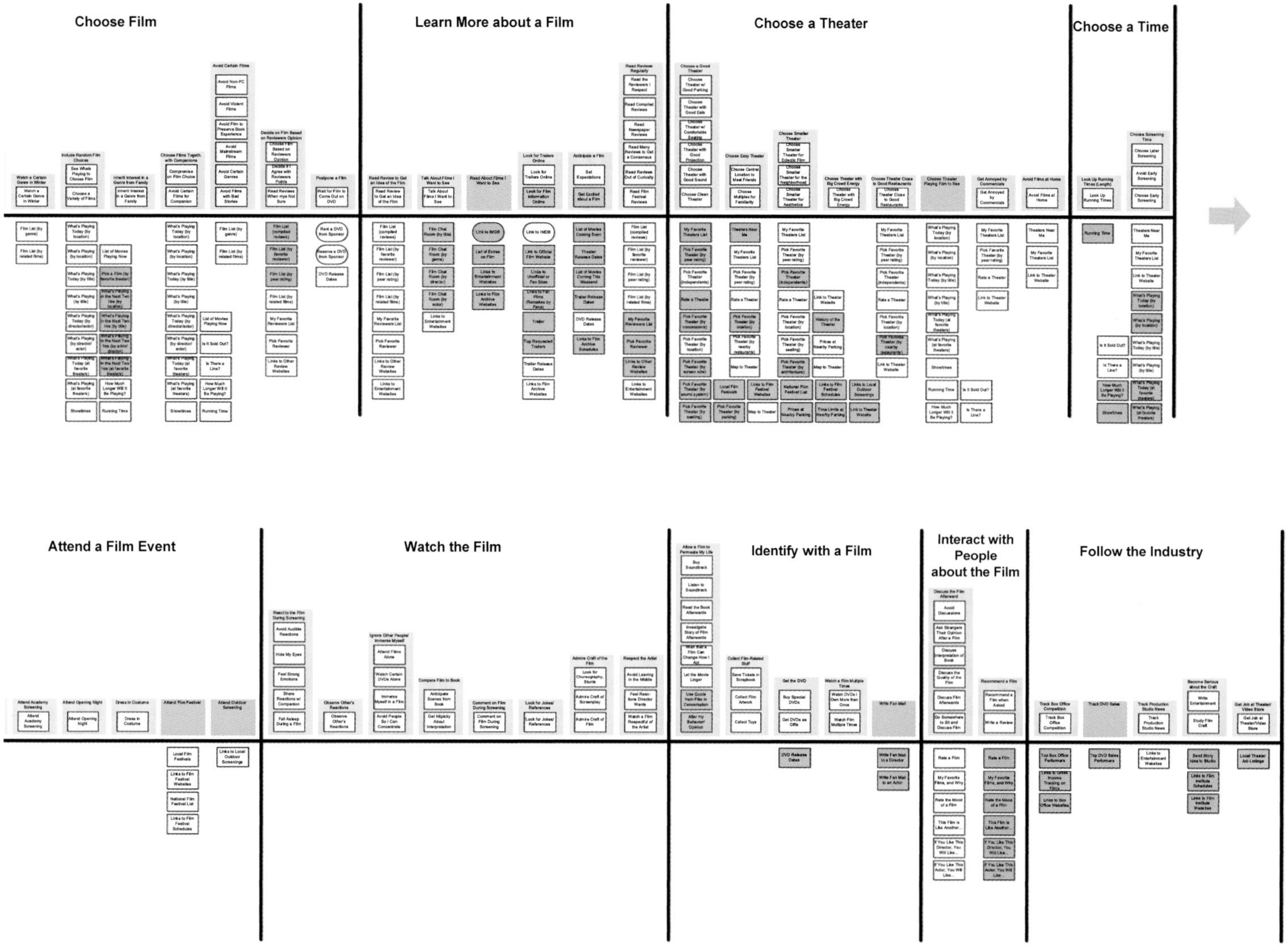

Choose Film

Learn More about a Film

Choose a Theater

Choose a Time

Attend a Film Event

Watch the Film

Identify with a Film

Interact with People about the Film

Follow the Industry

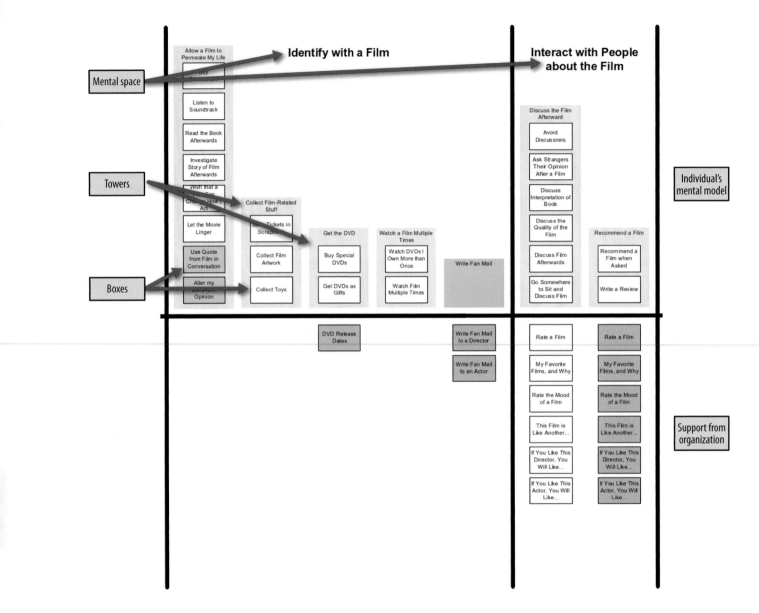

FIGURE 12-4. The three basic elements in a mental model diagram are boxes, towers, and mental spaces.

Combing the Transcripts

The process for creating mental model diagrams is similar to the steps outlined in Chapters 4–7 of this book. One main difference is the normalization of research findings into standard format. This normalization makes the process of finding affinities between items much easier.

You begin analysis by combing interview transcripts for relevant information. The time spent combing gives the research a much stronger understanding of what each participant meant as they repeat and re-explain their thinking to others. This process stands at the heart of the mental model technique. Every element on the diagram follows a similar format:

1. Start with a verb, to focus on the thinking, rather than the goal.

2. Use the first person to put the researcher in the participant's shoes.

3. Add one idea per box, for simplicity and clarity.

Each element comes from the thinking you hear from participants. If you record the listening session and get a transcript, you can draw each element from the transcript as a quote. To make it easier to find affinities between the elements, write a summary of each quote using this form:

[I (optional)] [verb] [noun] [qualifiers]

This strict uniformity allows for the arrangement of elements hierarchically: boxes are grouped into towers, towers are grouped into mental spaces. The process begins with distilling elements from the transcripts. The aim is to get the essence of people's mental models into the prescribed format.

Formatting tasks takes practice. It's not merely a process of copying phrases from the raw texts gathered during research. To illustrate, Table 12-1 shows some hypothetical quotes about drinking coffee. On the right are example summaries in the prescribed format you might derive from this data.

DIRECT QUOTE FROM RESEARCH	SUMMARIES
"When I get up, my body is just saying 'get some coffee!' It's like I can't function without it. So the first thing I do pretty much every morning is make coffee—it's almost automatic. I think I can almost do that in my sleep. I'll then enjoy a cup with breakfast or while reading the newspaper."	Feel nonfunctional until I get coffee
	Feel compelled to make coffee in the morning
	Enjoy a cup of coffee in the morning
"My wife and I both really like drinking coffee in the morning. It's a good way to wake up—it gets you going. Actually, I don't quite feel right until I've had my first cup."	Enjoy a cup of coffee in the morning
	Crave coffee in the morning
	Feel not-quite-right until after my first cup of coffee

TABLE 12-1. Example of summaries (right) in a normalized format derived from raw research texts (left).

Rapid Mental Model Method

⚡ Creating a mental model diagram can take a lot of effort. Formal projects with 20–30 participants take weeks or months to complete. It's a valuable upfront investment, but some organizations don't want to take the time.

After *Mental Models* was published, Young developed a method for creating diagrams quickly—within days. She describes this approach in a post entitled "Lightning Quick Method." It centers on a single workshop with stakeholders.

Here is a summary of Young's rapid approach to gathering data and finding affinities:

1. Solicit stories in advance

Collect short stories about a particular topic from your target audience a week in advance. This can be done through email, short listening sessions, as well as via social media and other online sources. The stories are accounts of how people reason their way toward a purpose captured on 1-2 pages. If you need to, rewrite these stories using the first person so all of the texts have a similar perspective.

2. Comb and summarize

Read through the stories aloud in the workshop. With either large sticky notes or in a shared document, different team members record summaries as you read. Within a few hours, you should be able to produce 100 discrete summaries.

3. Group by patterns

Once the summaries begin to accumulate, start grouping them by the intent of the storywriter. Many of these first groups will change as you add summaries. As you get further, you can begin to organize the towers into mental spaces. You should be able to create a provisional structure within an afternoon.

4. Brainstorm

Use the remainder of the workshop to brainstorm solutions. Where are the gaps between how people are reasoning and how your organization supports that reasoning? What opportunities do you see?

The rapid method is ideal for teams that need to act on results quickly. The result is a first-generation diagram that reflects what you have collected at this point. It may need further validation. But since people's stories are collected up front, this diagram is nonetheless grounded in reality.

From Construct to Structure

The hierarchical nature of mental model diagrams makes them particularly relevant for the practice of information architecture. The process can be described as *grounded*: a bottom-up approach starting with summaries of how people describe their reasoning, reactions, and guiding principles as they accomplish a purpose larger than your offering. Then, it's a matter of successively grouping information into higher-level categories (Figure 12-5).

The result is a categorization that matches the actual mental model of the people you serve and reflects vocabulary that people have used in interviews. App and web designers, for example, can then use this scheme as the basis for navigation. This greatly improves usability of the navigation and ensures its longevity as well.

Young describes the process of deriving structure and mapping it to navigation in detail. Figure 12-6 is an example of the process outlined in her book. It shows how mental spaces can be grouped into categories that then serve as the main navigation for a website.

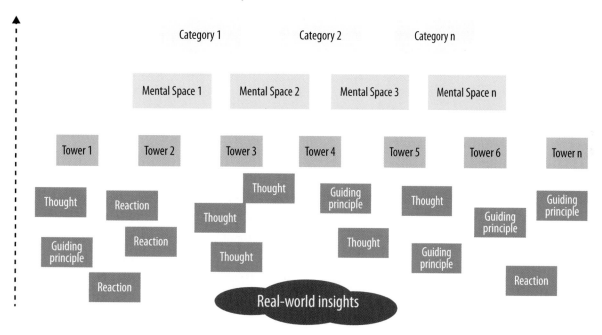

FIGURE 12-5. Deriving structure from mental model diagrams is a bottom-up process grounded in a real-world insights.

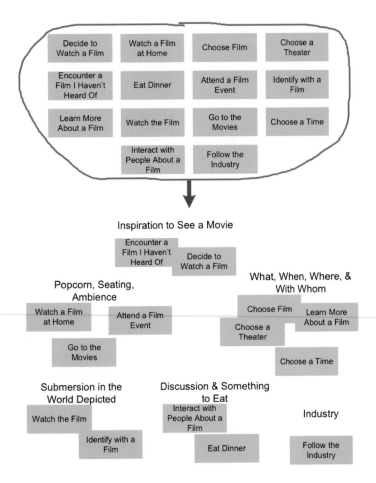

FIGURE 12-6. Cluster mental spaces to come up with top-level categories that can be used for website navigation, for instance.

Related Approaches

The origins of investigation into mental models goes back to the work of Kenneth Craik in his 1943 book *The Nature of Explanation*. He offers a concise, simple-to-understand definition of mental models:

> The mind constructs small-scale models of reality to anticipate events, to reason, and to underlie explanation.

Later, Philip Johnson-Laird did some of the most significant research on the subject, resulting in a full-length book entitled *Mental Models* (1983). Early attempts at representing mental models visually reflect a hierarchical arrangement of information.

For instance, Johnson-Laird's approach looked at how a meaningful story builds up across events and episodes. His was grounded in textual analysis, which he then visualized (Figure 12-7).

Broadly speaking, this represents the technique of *laddering*: showing layers of causality from granular evidence to high-level conclusions. Mental model diagrams are also based on a type of laddering.

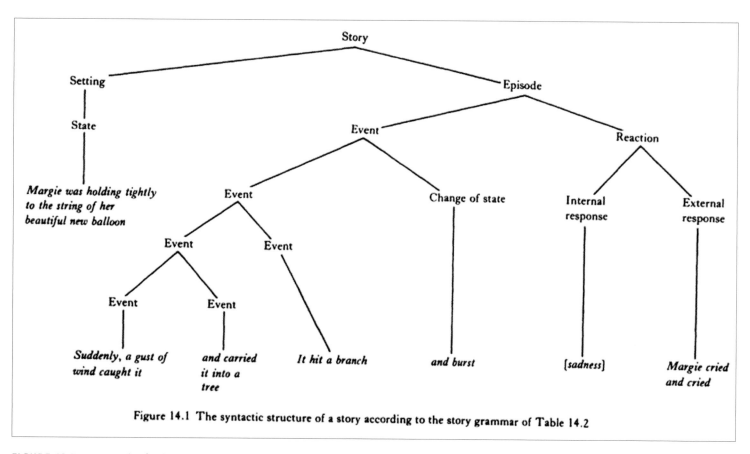

Figure 14.1 The syntactic structure of a story according to the story grammar of Table 14.2

FIGURE 12-7. An example of a diagram by Philip Johnson-Laird reflects the hierarchical nature of mental model analysis.

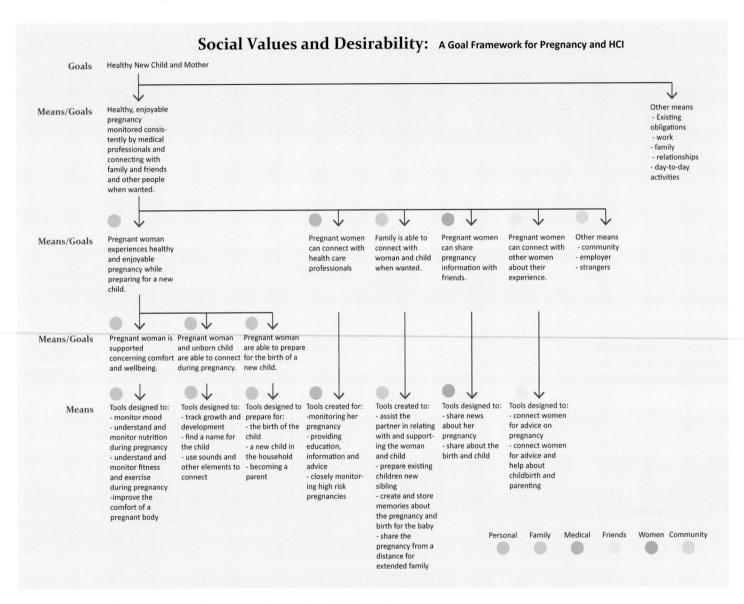

FIGURE 12-8. A goals-means framework connects solutions with underlying goals.

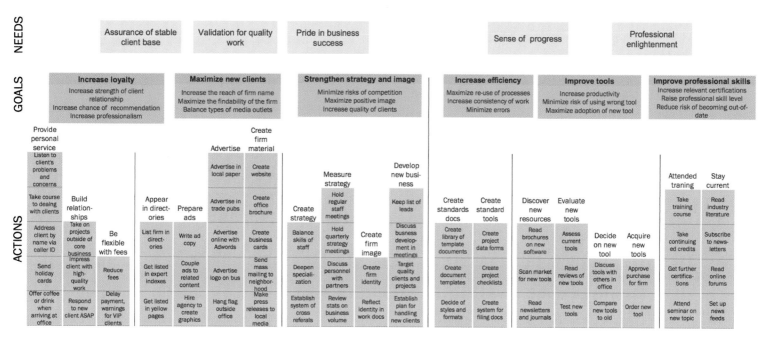

FIGURE 12-9. A hierarchical map reflects the business development activities for an architecture firm.

Consider the laddering in the goals-means framework, shown in Figure 12-8. This shows a hierarchy of goals and means for pregnancy, created by designer Beth Kyle. At the top is primary goal of having a healthy child and mother. The means of achieving that are listed on the next level. The process iterates until specific solutions and features are determined at the lowest level.

In another example, Figure 12-9 shows the new business activities of an architectural firm. This is a diagram I created on a previous project, modified to conceal both the firm and my client.

Because new business activities can happen in any order, using a hierarchical representation made sense in this case. It allowed me to show relationships between actions without putting them on a timeline. Through laddering, higher-level goals and needs can then be identified.

Elements of Mental Model Diagrams

Of the types presented in Part 3 of this book, mental model diagrams represent an archetype for hierarchical illustrations. Indi Young's seminal book, Mental Models, provides a step-by-step guide to creating these diagrams, as well as ways to use them in practice.

Broadly speaking, mental model diagrams reflect the concept of laddering—a grounded, bottom-up approach to creating models of human experiences based on observations.

Table 12-2 summarizes the main aspects that define mental model diagrams using the framework outlined in Chapter 2.

Point of view	Thoughts, emotions, and guiding principles that go through a person's mind in a given context as they achieve a purpose
Structure	Hierarchical
Scope	Very broad and inclusive of multiple perspectives across individuals
Focus	Behavior, reasoning, beliefs, and philosophies of individuals
	The support organizations offer
Uses	To develop empathy by understanding what goes through people's minds
	To find opportunities for innovation based on deep understanding of human behavior
	To derive navigation and high-level information architecture
	To guide the flow of your offering so that it supports the thinking captured in the diagram
Strengths	Normalized formats provide consistent results
	Deep insight into human thinking with respect to the scope of the purpose the person is trying to achieve
Weaknesses	Final diagrams can be overwhelming in detail
	Lack of chronological flow

TABLE 12-2. Defining aspects of mental model diagrams

Further Reading

Thomas Reynolds and Jonathan Gutman. "Laddering theory, Method, Analysis, and Interpretation," *Journal of Advertising Research* (1988)

> *This is an older article from two of the primary originators of the laddering approach, based on Gutman's means-end approach outlined a few years earlier. This is a detailed description of the technique with many examples. In general, laddering grounds conclusions you make in evidence.*

Indi Young. *Mental Models* (Rosenfeld Media, 2008)

> *Indi pioneered a specific technique for illustrating mental models in the early 2000s. This is a meticulously detailed book with step-by-step instructions. This book is essential for anyone interested in completing a mental model diagramming project.*

Indi Young. "Try the 'Lightning Quick' Mental Model Method," Indi Young blog (March 2010)

> *In this blog post, Young describes a modified process to creating and using mental model diagrams that can be done in a matter of days. It offers a quick alternative to the full-blown method outlined in her book.*

A Forward-Thinking Insurance Company: Mental Model

By Indi Young

This particular case study represents a common scenario where a product or service already exists, and the organization is seeking a way to make incremental improvements.

The example organization is an insurance company.[*] The company offers auto insurance and home insurance. There is a group within the company, separate from any of these businesses, tasked with strategic direction and new products. The group has existed for two years, created by a few of the executives in response to discussions in the boardroom about competition and innovation. The executives wanted to experiment with something beyond traditional industrial methods. Recently, this group has conducted a few person-focused studies, one of which was about what goes through people's minds during and immediately after an auto accident. Because of what they discovered, the group suspects there might be something related to learn from thinking patterns during near-misses.

They want to conduct another study as a twin to the accident study, so they have a stronger foundation from which to create their potential ideas for new directions. The group hopes to use

the discoveries to guide the way they provide services to the individuals they insure.

The scope of their subsequent study is: "*What was on your mind during and after a memorable near-miss accident?*" This scope is not restricted by type or location of the incident. The team will hear stories from people who have nearly had accidents in the kitchen or on the road, by themselves or in a crowd, where someone is at fault or no one is at fault. Because this is person-focused research, the accident does not have to relate to the product—auto insurance—that the company provides. The team is after the styles of thinking and manners of decision making during a near-miss, whether or not it has to do with autos. The patterns of thinking can then be used as a framework for new ideas about auto insurance.

Near-Miss Accidents

The team began by conducting listening sessions with 24 people. They began each session with the question, "*What was on your mind during and after a memorable near-miss accident?*" Then they let the participant take the conversation wherever, within that scope.

Here is the first part of one of the stories. The Listener digs into various things that were mentioned so that she can better

---

* Because it's difficult to get legal permission to use genuine studies and transcripts, the insurance company case study is fake. The 24 participant stories that were collected are true, but the ideas that emerged from the findings are invented from a foundation of two decades' experience.

understand the reasoning and reactions that went through the participant's mind at the time.

17: Bracket Fell Off the Work Truck—Transcript

Listener: I'm looking for stories that will help me understand what goes through people's minds in near-accidents or injuries. Do you have any near-accidents or near-injuries that you remember?

Speaker: I guess this counts as a near-accident, because it was an actual accident, but it could have been much worse. So I think it counts as both. It wasn't recent—it must have been when my daughter was 4 or 5. These don't have to be car things, right?

Listener: Right.

Speaker: This is one of those things when you're driving on the freeway, and you're going 65 miles per hour. I was right behind a fencing company truck. An aluminum bracket tumbled off the little storage cabinet above the truck. I wasn't even that close behind it—just a normal distance. I was driving my Honda Odyssey, and the bracket struck the windshield right in front of my face. Instant spider web! It was one of those things that happens in a flash. I had all this adrenaline. So, I'm going to pull up to this other car and tell them to pull over. So I get in the other lane and I pull up next to them. I look over and it is four men, and three of them are asleep! I've got to stop them to get their

insurance. I was gesticulating at them. There was another some sort of a service car, or some sort of county-related government car. I tried to flag them down, and they just looked confused. Finally I drove home and looked at it. Boy, am I glad for tempered glass. If this had happened 50 years ago, I would be dead. And my daughter was in the car seat in the back going, "What's going on, mom?"

Listener: Wow! Yes, thank goodness for tempered glass. That's so scary to think about! You said the word "adrenaline." What do you mean?

Speaker: That's the part where you kind of panic a little bit. Everything's happening fast but sort of slow at the same time. Your heart's beating fast, and you're not quite sure what the right thing to do is, but you have to do *something*. You have a smidgeon of common sense to not veer off the road. But this sort of thing has never happened before, so some of the adrenaline is from being in unfamiliar water. I wasn't sure what to do next. Maybe I should get the name of the company. I tried to get the license plate. I remember looking them up on the Internet when I got home. I was thinking, *"Can I just call them and tell them, 'you guys did this to my car.'"* I was upset.

Listener: You were upset?

Speaker: It's a good $500 when something happens to your car! But the adrenaline was also knowing it could have been worse. You just get scared. Everything on that truck should have been packed up and strapped down. This stuff happens all the time, though, which is what's scary. In a perfect world, nothing would ever happen like this. So it was adrenaline to do something: fight or flee. Or a little of both. [laughs]

Listener: You say you looked them up on the Internet when you got home?

Speaker: I looked them up to make sure it was a company. I thought about calling them, but what would I have said? How can I prove that anything happened? It happened on a freeway going 65 miles per hour. There were no witnesses. All I have is a car that needs a new windshield and is undrivable. I decided I guess there's nothing I can do about this, except chalk it up to one of life's experiences. Try to learn from it. Never drive behind a work truck like that. Tell my teenagers never to drive behind a truck. There are all sorts of scary scenarios; you can drive yourself crazy with it. When my husband got home he said I got lucky. He said, "That was in a really bad spot. You could have really gotten hurt."

Listener: What was going through your mind when he told you that?

Speaker: That I completely agree, "Yeah, you're right." "Oh yeah, it wasn't just my imagination." It was a validation. I *am* as lucky as I think I am.

Writing Summaries

After collecting stories, the team sat down to go over the details in the written transcripts. Making sense of what a person said from the transcript provided them double the depth of understanding rather than simply listening. It involved corralling messy, meandering dialog, picking out certain quotes to put with other parts of this person's dialog, and forging a better idea of what he really meant to convey. This work allowed the team to absorb participants' thoughts, reactions, and philosophies. The team developed deep cognitive empathy with the participants.

Here are some example quotes the team worked through. They strung together several quotes from one transcript that represented the same concept, jotted down whether it was reasoning/thinking, a reaction, or a guiding principle, tried out a few verbs that could possibly star as the first scintillating word of the summary, then wrote the summary for that concept.

Maybe I should get the name of the company. ... get the license plate. ... if that happened to someone else, and they were telling me about it, I'd ask, "Who did it?" ... to get information about them ... I remember looking them up on the Internet when I got home. ... I looked them up to make sure it was a company.

(thinking)

Verbs: Get, Find, Look, Identify ...

Summary: Identify who made this accident happen, by the name of the company or the license place, because I want to know who did it.

Finally I drove home ... I decided I guess there's nothing I can do about this, except chalk it up to one of life's experiences.

(thinking)

Verbs: Drive, Decide, Think, Chalk, Realize, Conclude ...

Summary: Decide to drive home because there was nothing I could do

Finding Patterns

After summarizing all the concepts in all 24 transcripts, the team looked for patterns across the summaries. As patterns started to form, they found surprises, as well as things they expected. Both the surprises and the nonsurprises became extremely useful later for reframing their thinking.

When the team was finished, they went through all the piles a second time to see if the piles themselves formed into bigger groups. Here is a list of all the piles they labeled (the indented *a, b, c* level) and the groups that formed based on these piles (the *1, 2, 3* level).

Patterns Found in Transcript Summaries for Near-Miss Accidents

1. Recognize I am in a dangerous situation
   a. Feel shocked to suddenly be in a situation that could be dangerous
   b. Feel terrified that I'm about to have an accident (or get hurt)
   c. Figure out if this is a dangerous situation

2. Get safe again
   a. Behave in a smart way so I can get out of this dangerous situation safely, despite the adrenaline
   b. Reach out mentally to others for help to get out of the situation

3. Find out if anyone was hurt
   a. Worry I might have hurt someone
   b. Feel relieved I was/others were not hurt
   c. Reassure people I am not hurt

4. Feel relieved it's over
   a. Feel grateful to the person who helped me get out of the dangerous situation
   b. Feel relieved the danger is over
   c. Spend some time getting the adrenaline out of my system
   d. Feel surprised I reacted this way

5. Feel angry at the other person involved.

   a. Feel angry at the person who could have avoided causing this

   b. Confront the other person (or not) so he knows he put me out

   c. Confront the person so he won't do it again to anyone else

   d. Try to defuse the tension between me and the other person involved

   e. Wonder what the other person involved was thinking

   f. Feel upset that the person who did this probably wasn't paying attention, doesn't care

6. Feel upset with myself

   a. Feel upset with myself about my role in the incident (being partially to blame)

   b. Feel embarrassed at my reaction, lack of skill

7. Return home/to what I was doing

   a. Carry on with what I was doing (or not)

   b. Get back home

8. Follow the insurance process

   a. Exchange insurance information with the other person because there was some minor damage

   b. Feel compelled to do things I don't think need to be done because of the insurance process

9. Spend time thinking about what happened

   a. Try to figure out what just happened/how

   b. Think about what would have happened if

   c. Feel amazed how such a minor thing caused such big repercussions

   d. Feel grateful for emotional support from people after the incident

   e. Figure the accident could have been worse, which qualifies it as a near-miss

10. Try to prevent this from happening again/to others

   a. Report the incident (or not) to authorities so they know what happened

   b. Convince someone in charge to do something to prevent this from happening again

   c. Change my actions so this doesn't happen again

   d. Prevent an accident by following safe habit

The Mental Model Diagram

The labels from the piles the team put together are the titles of the towers in the mental model diagram. The boxes within each tower are each of the summaries, themselves. The affinity groups that formed are the mental spaces for the diagram (Figure 12-10).

Zero In on Current Business Goals

There are quite a few patterns the team found in the summaries. Their next step was to bring attention to some of the behaviors related to priorities articulated in this year's business goals. These are the business goals:

- Increase membership—attract more insurance customers (a perennial goal)

- Reduce claims (a perennial goal)

- Leverage the company's social capital (has been a goal for four years)

- Offer more services via mobile apps, phone or tablet—to help people "on the scene" (has been a goal for the past two years)

- Increase employee pride in what the company does (new this year)

With these organization-wide goals in mind, the team went through the list of patterns and chose those of interest. These are patterns that the team thinks might be able to affect some of the goals.

Patterns that seem associated with yearly goals

- Reassure people I am not hurt

- Confront the person so he won't do it again to anyone else

- Try to defuse the tension between me and the other person involved

- Feel upset with myself about my role in the incident (being partially to blame)

- Feel embarrassed at my reaction, lack of skill

- Spend some time getting the adrenaline out of my system

- Report the incident (or not) to authorities so they know what happened

- Convince someone in charge to do something to prevent this from happening again

- Change my actions so this doesn't happen again

- Feel compelled to do things I don't think need to be done because of the insurance process

- Prevent an accident by following safe habits

- Figure the accident could have been worse, which qualifies it as a near-miss

Get Started Inspiring Ideas

Finally, during some working sessions with key stakeholders, the team used these patterns to touch off some ideation. Using the actual stories they heard in the listening sessions, the team helped the group cycle through extensions that might end in various ways for the organization. They guided the working session so that the ideas were not limited to an existing product or a service.

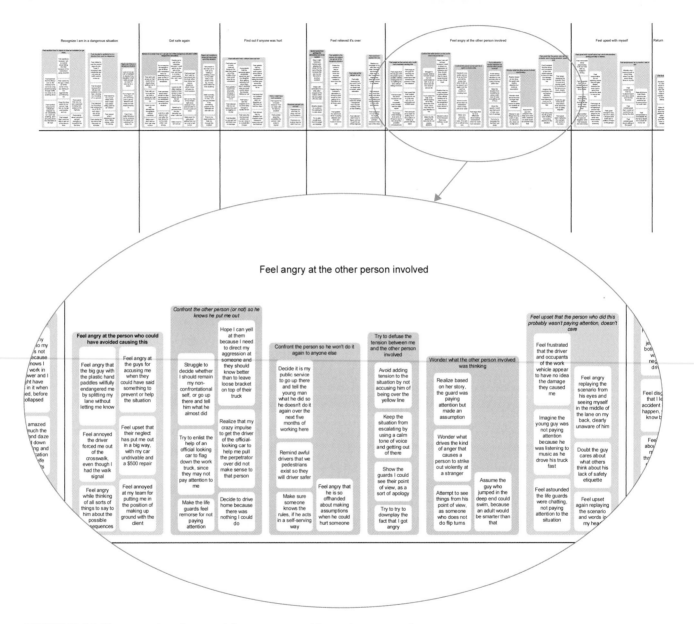

FIGURE 12-10. The top portion of a mental diagram generated from primary research.

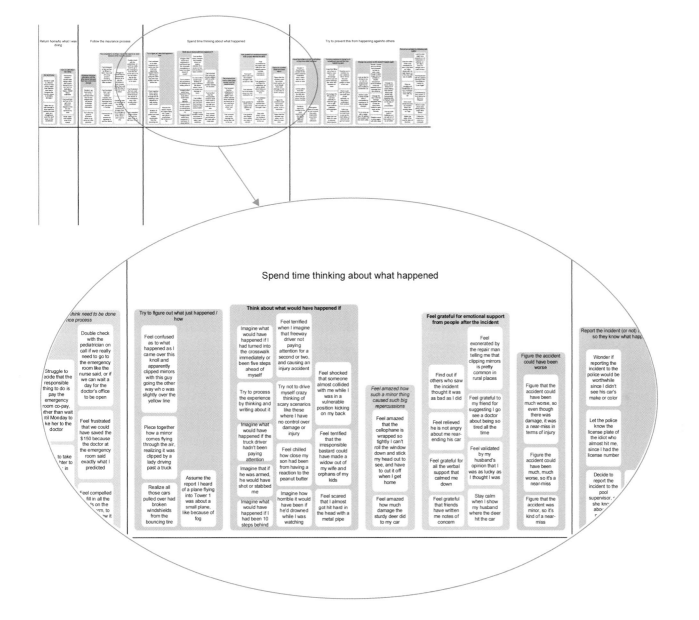

Spend time thinking about what happened

Try to figure out what just happened / how

Feel confused as to what happened as I came over this knoll and apparently clipped mirrors with this guy going the other way who was slightly over the yellow line

Try to process the experience by thinking and writing about it

Piece together how a mirror comes flying through the air, realizing it was clipped by a lady driving past a truck

Realize all those cars pulled over had broken windshields from the bouncing tire

Assume the report I heard of a plane flying into Tower 1 was about a small plane, like because of fog

Think about what would have happened if

Imagine what would have happened if I had turned into the crosswalk immediately or been five steps ahead of myself

Feel terrified when I imagine that freeway driver not paying attention for a second or two, and causing an injury accident

Try not to drive myself crazy thinking of scary scenarios like these where I have no control over damage or injury

Imagine what would have happened if the truck driver hadn't been paying attention

Imagine what if he was armed, he would have shot or stabbed me

Imagine what would have happened if I had been 10 steps behind

Imagine how horrible it would have been if he'd drowned while I was watching

Feel shocked that someone almost collided with me while I was in a vulnerable position kicking on my back

Feel chilled how close my son had been from having a reaction to the peanut butter

Feel terrified that the irresponsible bastard could have made a widow out of my wife and orphans of my kids

Feel scared that I almost got hit hard in the head with a metal pipe

Feel grateful for emotional support from people after the incident

Feel amazed how such a minor thing caused such big repercussions

Feel amazed that the cellophane is wrapped so tightly I can't roll the window down and stick my head out to see, and have to cut it off when I get home

Feel amazed how much damage the sturdy deer did to my car

Find out if others who saw the incident thought it was as bad as I did

Feel relieved he is not angry about me rear-ending his car

Feel grateful for all the verbal support that calmed me down

Feel exonerated by the repair man telling me that clipping mirrors is pretty common in rural places

Feel grateful to my friend for suggesting I go see a doctor about being so tired all the time

Feel validated by my husband's opinion that I was as lucky as I thought I was

Stay calm when I show my husband where the deer hit the car

Figure the accident could have been worse

Figure that the accident could have been much worse, so even though there was damage, it was a near-miss in terms of injury

Figure the accident could have been much, much worse, so it's a near-miss

Figure that the accident was minor, so it's kind of a near-miss

Report the incident (or not) so they know what happ...

Wonder if reporting the incident to the police would be worthwhile since I didn't see his car's make or color

Let the police know the license plate of the idiot who almost hit me, since I had the license number

Decide to report the incident to the pool supervisor, ... she kno... abou...

...think need to be done ...nce process

Double check with the pediatrician on call if we really need to go to the emergency room like the nurse said, or if we can wait a day for the doctor's office to be open

Struggle to ...acide that the responsible thing to do is pay the emergency room co-pay, ...ther than wait ...til Monday to ...ke her to the doctor

Feel frustrated that we could have saved the $150 because the doctor at the emergency room said exactly what I predicted

...to take ...hter to ...in

Feel compelled ...fill in all the ...'s on the ...rm, to ...w it

Here are a few of the ideas the group came up with, along with notes about feasibility and questions to further explore before deciding whether to pursue an idea.

Idea: Warn Others of This Hazard or Error

Pattern: Some customers want to report the incident so that authorities know what happened, so they are aware of a hazard or of the process not working right.

Idea: Choose a few details to describe the hazard or error. If these details don't cover it, type in a description. We'll get the information to people who can warn others.

Goals Met:

Reduce Future Claims: Getting the message out to the channels that customers already use, such as traffic reports or Google maps, will help them become aware of a road hazard. They can drive a safer route.

Build Social Capital: If we can get the message out that the customers are supplying these valuable hazard reports, and we're getting it to the right people, that would certainly build our reputation.

Increase Membership: Customers will feel satisfaction helping others avoid what they experienced. They may pass the word to others.

Idea: Claim-Lite

Pattern: Several of the near-misses are actually minor accidents. People are thinking "it could have been so much worse." The subsequent interaction with the insurance process become too entangling, when people think of their incident as a near-miss.

Idea: Create a new kind of claim for when the people involved consider it minor, and they don't want the process to become too involved.

Goals Met:

Increase Membership: If it is a positive experience, customers will talk about this kind of claim. After the new process seems to be working and stable, we can use it in our marketing.

Reduce Future Claims: This should actually read, "reduce claims," since we'll replace a certain percentage of claims with the "lite" version.

This insurance company example demonstrates the way person-focused research can reframe the way an internal group approaches improvements to their offerings and to their internal processes. Not every idea should be pursued. The team will want to test them. Some of the ideas will wait until later; others will never see any more attention. It's even possible that none of the ideas from an interval make sense for the organization. Try not to become too attached. What's key is to use your empathic understanding of people that the idea supports to clearly judge whether to invest more resources in it, or let it wither. Successful organizations know the difference.

Diagram and Image Credits

Figure 12-2: Diagram by Don Norman from his book *The Design of Everyday Things* (1988)

Figure 12-3: Diagram by Indi Young from her book *Mental Models* (Rosenfeld Media 2008), used with permission

Figure 12-6: Image from Indi Young's book *Mental Models* (Rosenfeld Media, 2008), used with permission

Figure 12-7: Diagram by Philip Johnson-Laird from his book *Mental Models* (Harvard Business Press, 1983)

Figure 12-8: Goals-means framework by Beth Kyle from "With Child: Personal Informative and Pregnancy." *http://www.bethkyle.com/EKyle_Workbook3_Final.pdf*

Figure 12-9: Diagram by Jim Kalbach

Figure 12-10: Diagram by Indi Young, used with permission

IN THIS CHAPTER

- Introduction to spatial maps
- Isometric projections and ecosystem models
- Case Study: Gigamapping: Canadian Governance in the Digital Era

CHAPTER 13

Spatial Maps and Ecosystem Models

The cause of the great cholera outbreak in London in 1854 was initially unclear. Prior to Louis Pasteur's germ theory, many thought the disease was in the air. John Snow, a London physician, had a different explanation. He believed cholera was in the water. After microscopic examinations were inconclusive, Snow instead analyzed the spread of cholera to prove his hunch.

To do this, Snow mapped cholera cases in Soho, London (Figure 13-1). The resulting patterns demonstrated causality: proximity to a certain water pump correlated to cholera cases with high predictability. The decline of cholera is credited to Snow's recommendation to shut down that pump.

Snow's map contains multiple layers of information—streets, houses with cholera cases, and water pumps—just enough to reveal previously undetected evidence (in this case, the cause of a disease). The approach is simple but effective: Snow was able to generate a hypothesis based on his simple map: *if the*

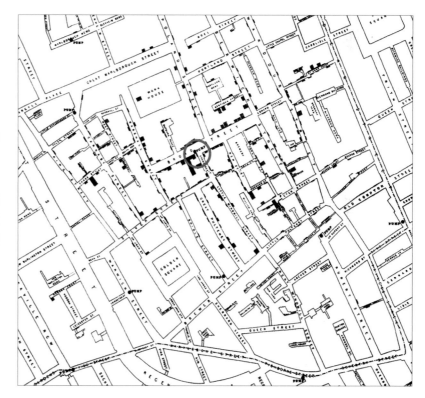

FIGURE 13-1. John Snow's map of London during the great cholera outbreak of 1854. The red circle highlights the water pump that was the source of the disease.

city shuts down a specific pump, *then* cases of cholera would decline.

Visualizations offer an immediacy of comprehension and help us arrive at such conclusions. Maps show interrelationships in an ecosystem.

It may not be immediately apparent, but I would argue that there is alignment in Snow's example: water (a service provided by the waterworks department), water pumps (the touchpoints to that system), and households with cholera in Soho (individuals). What Snow showed was that the means of treating and storing water miles away affected people in central London. This conclusion is generally credited with the start of public health practices around the world.

This is why I love maps of all kinds: they provide an overview and, with some creative imagination, show new relationships leading to new insight. Armed with only a map and a few data points, John Snow was able to see what the best microscopes of the time couldn't. That's powerful.

Similarly, this is what mapping offers: new insight. It starts with an investigation and illustration of the human condition and then works out ways to support people's needs.

This chapter deals with two types of diagrams: spatial maps and ecosystem models. Neither is chronological or hierarchical in organization. Instead, the location of the information on the page is important to the diagram's meaning and interpretation. Both seek to portray an ecological view of people's experiences and to show a broad system of interaction.

Each type is discussed below separately. By the end of the chapter, you should grasp similarities and differences between them, as well as have an understanding of approaches other than chronological and hierarchical diagrams.

Spatial Maps

By definition, models tend toward abstraction and simplification. This helps teams distill and communicate insights, and allows others in the organization to benefit from that insight.

Too much simplification results in a loss of richness and full context of the actual human experience. On the other hand, too much detail can overwhelm. There is always a struggle between detail and comprehensibility with diagrams.

Kim Erwin, associate professor at the Illinois Institute of Technology, Institute of Design, focused on making complex information easier to understand without losing the detail. She developed an information-dense format called *consumer insight maps*, which she describes as follows:

Consumer Insight Maps promote emotional contact with research, showcase important complexity in consumers' lives and support persistence of the consumer voice throughout (and often beyond) a design process… Consumer Insight Maps are designed to take the complexity of consumers' lives—the dense, messy, interconnected ambitions, activities, anxieties that thread throughout their days—and flatten them out so that we might examine them more systematically.

Figure 13-2 shows an example of a consumer insight map.

According to Erwin, the key to their effectiveness is the manner in which the information is arranged. The technique relies on principles from cartographic maps by showing relationships between information types.

For instance, Erwin defines different *zones* of information, seen in Figure 13-3—mindset, activities, anxieties, attitudes, and product opportunities. Within each zone, subgroups of information provide refinement and depth to the overall story told by the map.

The result is an easy-to-understand overview that exposes the diversity of aspects of an experience without an oversimplified portrayal. Borrowing from principles of cartography, consumer insight maps present information in context, allowing the reader to orient to the territory, and consume the information at micro and macro levels as desired.

Consider another example in Figure 13-4, created by UX designer Patrick Kovacich while working at Citrix. *Collaboratonia* is a hypothetical "place" that visualizes various jobs to be done while collaborating with others. These were derived from extensive user research efforts by the Citrix UX team.

This is actually more of an affinity diagram than a map. However, the physical placement of the information shows interrelationships between the different themes, reinforced by color coding.

With spatial maps, *layering* is the primary means to show alignment. Just as John Snow overlaid various facets of information on his map of London to gain insight, Figure 13-5 shows current organizational capabilities on top of the basic spatial map.

Each color represents a different way to support customer needs. From this layering, the team can see the gaps and redundancies in their offerings. New insights emerge from the ensuing discussions.

Visualizations offer an immediacy of comprehension and help us arrive at such conclusions. Maps show interrelationships in an ecosystem.

FIGURE 13-2. An example of a consumer insight map, created by Kim Erwin.

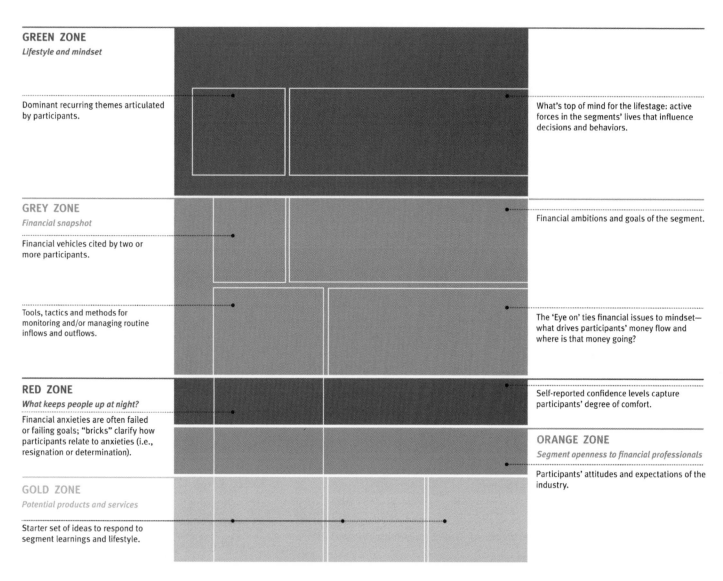

GREEN ZONE
Lifestyle and mindset

Dominant recurring themes articulated by participants.

What's top of mind for the lifestage: active forces in the segments' lives that influence decisions and behaviors.

GREY ZONE
Financial snapshot

Financial vehicles cited by two or more participants.

Financial ambitions and goals of the segment.

Tools, tactics and methods for monitoring and/or managing routine inflows and outflows.

The 'Eye on' ties financial issues to mindset— what drives participants' money flow and where is that money going?

RED ZONE
What keeps people up at night?

Financial anxieties are often failed or failing goals; "bricks" clarify how participants relate to anxieties (i.e., resignation or determination).

Self-reported confidence levels capture participants' degree of comfort.

ORANGE ZONE
Segment openness to financial professionals

Participants' attitudes and expectations of the industry.

GOLD ZONE
Potential products and services

Starter set of ideas to respond to segment learnings and lifestyle.

FIGURE 13-3. The structure of a consumer insight map results in a high density of contextual information.

FIGURE 13-4. Collaboratonia is a spatial map showing needs and goals in collaborating at work.

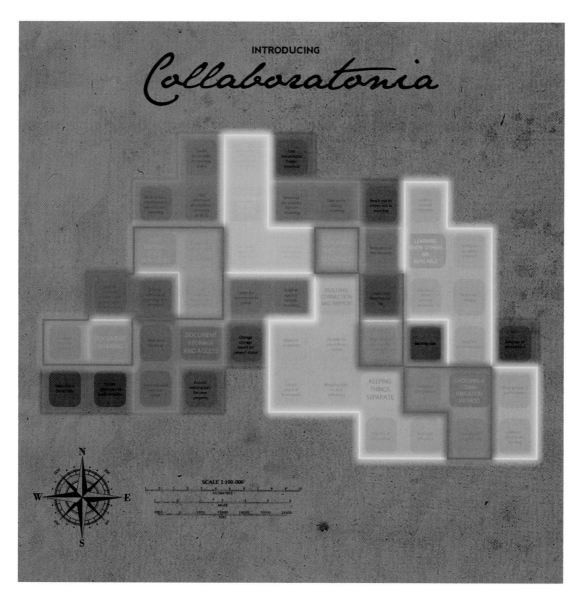

FIGURE 13-5. Layers of information on top of Collaboratonia, showing various current capabilities.

Isometric Projections

An *isometric projection* is a specific type of spatial map. It's a method of illustrating three-dimensional objects in two dimensions. Isometry is achieved with rotated angles of objects on the diagram. When all line angles are kept the same, a sense of a plane is created.

A simple example of an isometric projection appears in Figure 13-6. This was created by Chiara Diana and Roberta Tassi while at the Domus Academy of Research & Consulting. The project's intent was to improve the experience of tourists visiting Rome. In particular, they sought to attract people to lesser-known sites of the city.

In this example, the plane on which the elements sit isn't explicitly represented, for instance, with a shape or border. Instead, the parallel angles of all of the elements creates a consistent 3D effect. Light shadows amplify the illusion of a spatial model.

In another example of isometric maps, Figures 13-7a–d show a series of diagrams created by Paul Kahn, Julia Moisand Egea, and Laurent Kling, one of which is shown in Chapter 1 (see Figure 1-7). These illustrate the ecosystem of content production at the Institut National de Recherche et de Sécurité (INRS), a large French government organization.

In Figure 13-7a, the plane of the isometric projection is represented with colored areas, which the designers call *carpets*. Each of these represents a different department within the organization. Content formats and systems are overlaid on the carpets for a base diagram of the organization.

Figures 13-7b–d show variations of the base diagram with additional layers and types of information. Figure 13-7b shows the flow of content between departments, in particular the duplication of content from one to another. Figure 13-7c uses the same model to look at research activities across the organization, using a different color scheme across the diagram. Figure 13-7d shows access to the websites, also using a different color scheme.

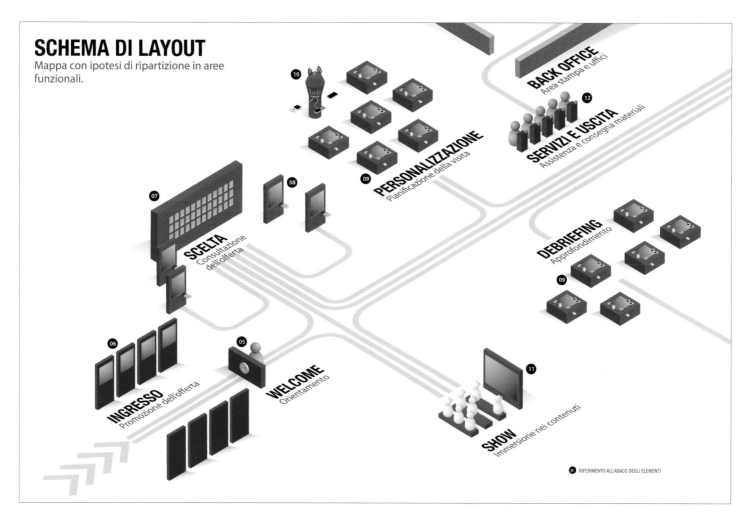

SCHEMA DI LAYOUT
Mappa con ipotesi di ripartizione in aree funzionali.

BACK OFFICE
Area stampa e uffici

SERVIZI E USCITA
Assistenza e consegna materiali

PERSONALIZZAZIONE
Pianificazione della visita

SCELTA
Consultazione dell'offerta

DEBRIEFING
Approfondimento

INGRESSO
Promozione dell'offerta

WELCOME
Orientamento

SHOW
Immersione nei contenuti

🔵 n RIFERIMENTO ALL'ABACO DEGLI ELEMENTI

FIGURE 13-6. An isometric map of a service experience for tourists to Rome represents touchpoints spatially.

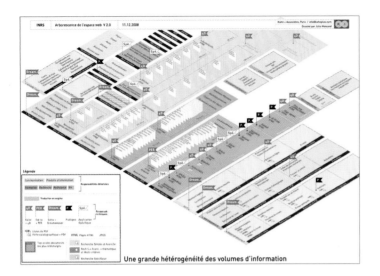

FIGURE 13-7a. The base map of content production within the organization.

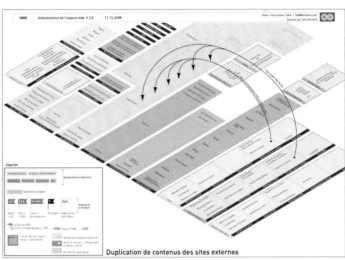

FIGURE 13-7b. Overlays showing the duplication of content on external sites.

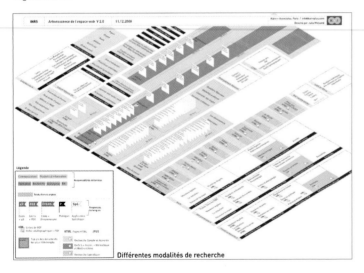

FIGURE 13-7c. Extending the base map to show various search engines and indexes.

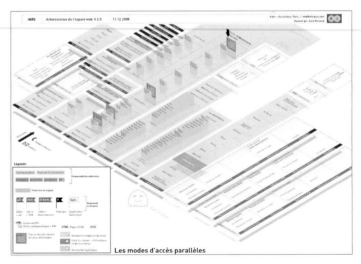

FIGURE 13-7d. This version shows that a portion of the website was duplicated to make it available to Google for search indexing.

Figure 13-8 shows an interesting example that combines two different diagram structures. This diagram was created by Mark Simmons, along with Aaron Lewis, as part of their master's work for the Sustainable Product-Service System Innovation program at Blekinge Tekniska Högskolan in Karlskronn, Sweden.

The top part of the diagram shows a *spatial* map of the dynamics of peer-to-peer car sharing. The bottom half takes touchpoints from the spatial map and arranges them in a *chronological* customer journey.

Both are generalized depictions that highlight critical questions within the service ecosystem. From the spatial map on the top, for instance, it becomes apparent that getting the borrower to and from the owner's car is a logistical hurdle.

From the chronological map on the bottom there is a better sense of the interaction between the borrower, the owner, and the car sharing service. It shows how most of the interaction happens between the borrower and the owner, and the platform makes that match. Each of the two representations brings unique insight.

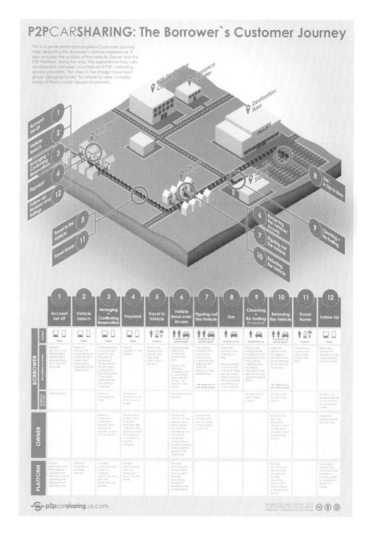

FIGURE 13-8. A combination of a spatial map (top half) and a chronological diagram (bottom half) for person-to-person car sharing.

Ecosystem Models

Cloudwash is an experimental prototype of a reimagined washing machine created by Berg, a cloud services integrator (a now defunct firm). The system integrates a variety of services involved in washing clothes, such as contacting a plumber, scheduling use of the washing machines, and ordering detergent (Figures 13-9).

Berg has no direct stake in those services, yet the envisioned system combines them seamlessly. This type of ecosystem thinking looks at the jobs to be done and brings the pertinent services together in a single experience.

Ecosystem models provide a holistic view of an individual's experience, helping conceive systems such as Cloud Wash. The visualizations expose otherwise invisible aspects of an experience, leading to opportunities for innovation.

Figure 13-10 shows an example of an ecosystem map appearing in the book *Service Design*, by Andy Polaine, Lavrans Løvlie, and Ben Reason (Rosenfeld Media, 2013). This is a visualization of a car sharing service created for FIAT.

The center of the diagram illustrates the relationship of the driver to the car. Moving outward, the relationships start including passengers, other cars, other services, communities, society, and the Earth. The concentric circles are then divided into slices for the categories who, when, where, what, why, and how. Touchpoints are added to represent different interactions in the ecosystem. Such diagrams allow teams to see and discuss the various relationships in a tangible way.

FIGURE 13-9. Cloudwash integrates a range of services from multiple providers. (Photos by Timo Arnall, copyright Berg.)

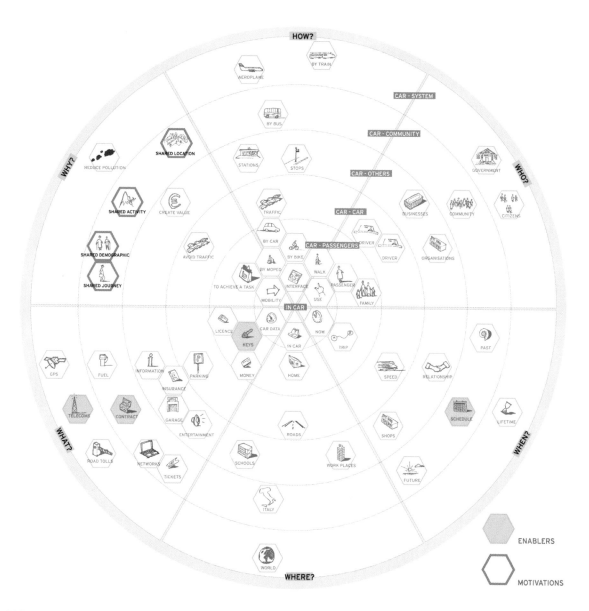

FIGURE 13-10. An ecosystem map for a car sharing service.

Elements of Spatial Maps and Ecosystem Models

The final type of diagram in Part 3, spatial maps, contrast both chronological and hierarchical models. They show relationship and insights through a physical layout of information.

Spatial arrangements of information provide a broad overview of an ecosystem. Taking a step back, viewers can get the big picture quickly; or, they can zoom in to a section for more detail. Frequently, overlays or variations of the diagram provide different snapshots of insight that tell multiple stories of value creation.

Table 13-1 summarizes the main aspects that define spatial maps using the framework outlined in Chapter 2.

Point of view	Include perspectives of multiple actors and multiple interaction types with the organization
Structure	Spatial
Scope	Holistic, capturing elements of experiences across many levels of interaction
Focus	Focus on actor relationships, tasks, goals, and interaction types
	Range from specific to very broad, may include considerations of community and society
Uses	Gaining a broad understanding of existing experiences across actors and touchpoints
	Highlighting gaps and inefficiencies in a system with overlays of information
	Building and understanding strategy
	Innovating new, meaningful experiences
Strengths	Rely on a metaphor people can relate to
	Provide a holistic overview
	Compact format that stakeholders can easily grasp
	Engaging and suitable for workshops
Weaknesses	Lack sequence or chronology of information
	Can take a long time to create
	Hard to create together as a group
	Lack detail, omit indication of emotions and feelings

TABLE 13-1. A summary of the main dimensions of spatial maps.

Further Reading

Kim Erwin. "Consumer Insight Maps: The Map as Story Platform in the Design Process," *Parsons Journal for Information Mapping* (Winter 2011)

> *Professor Erwin presents a technique that directly draws on the predictable structure of geographic maps, called consumer insight maps. This framework helps teams make sense of experiences in a direct and immediate way. She focuses on four aspects of cartographic maps to incorporate in her visualizations: zones, elevations, topographies, and blueprints. The spatial combination of information results in a platform for delivering powerful, visual stories that speak to diverse stakeholders.*

Isabel Meirelles. *Design for Information* (Rockport, 2013)

> *This is an excellent book on information design in general. The author offers very detailed discussions of spatial maps and isometric projections. This book contains a wealth of illustrations and case studies.*

Kerry Bodine. "How to Map Your Customer Experience Ecosystem," *Forrester Reports* (May, 2013)

> *This is a brief report from Forrester that defines what a customer experience ecosystem map is, how it is used, and what the benefits are. Only a few limited examples are included, however.*

Sofia Hussain. "Designing Digital Strategies, Part 1: Cartography," *UX Booth* (Feb 2014) and "Designing Digital Strategies, Part 2: Connected User Experiences," *UX Booth* (Jan 2015)

> *In this pair of articles, design expert Sofia Hussain discusses approaches to mapping ecosystems. She favors circular diagrams that get away from a linear, left-to-right depiction of chronology. The focus on behaviors and motivations recalls Young's mental model diagrams. Hussein's maps are very compact and present a clear overview at a glance.*

Gigamapping: Canadian Governance in the Digital Era

By Peter Jones

A *Gigamap* is a large-scale visualization of the systemic relationships within a complex domain. Gigamaps can appear like infographics at first, but in fact they are time-intensive team constructs based on qualitative research. It takes time to learn the system methods, which is why Gigamaps are taught as a studio practice and are developed through iterative research.

For the Governance case, a team of faculty and grad students working with Greg van Alstyone of OCADU's *Strategic Innovation Lab* (sLab) facilitated a series of civic and expert engagements. This was part of ongoing research on future governance, led by PI Evert Lindquist of University of Victoria.

One of our contributions was to iteratively develop a Gigamap over the series of workshops, a later version of which is shown in Figure 13-11.

The diagram has three primary zones of information.

At the top are inset *systemigrams* representing key citizen issues: access, privacy, and open data.

In the middle we see a spatial metaphor for the current government ecosystem, the challenges it faces in the future, and a vision for transformed societal governance on the right.

The bottom of the Gigamap shows "waves of change," or the forces future decision makers must contend with over the next two decades. This reflects the Three Horizons model of foresight and captures the progression from today's tensions toward a long view of a preferred future.

Compelling maps of social systems require a project team to conduct a deep dive of research in the domain, engage stakeholders and experts to understand the salient drivers, and critique the developing artifact in iterative studio sessions to evolve the underlying system theory that best explains the observations.

For this project, we held several workshops from 2014 to 2015 that contributed narratives and "subsystems" to the map, developed in-studio with a graduate student team. Sessions included:

- A Canadian-wide stakeholder workshop in December 2014, with "lightning talks" by experts on Open Space, and small group workshops.

- In January we engaged 35 civic innovators in small group sessions to elicit influence maps on the important systemic relations (*designwithdialogue.com*).

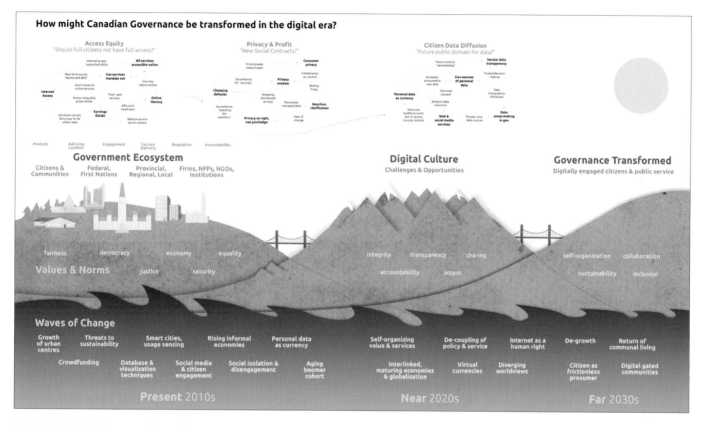

How might Canadian Governance be transformed in the digital era?

Access Equity
"Should full citizens not have full access?"

Privacy & Profit
"New Social Contracts?"

Citizen Data Diffusion
"Future public domain for data?"

Government Ecosystem — Digital Culture — Governance Transformed

Values & Norms

Waves of Change

Present 2010s — Near 2020s — Far 2030s

FIGURE 13-11. A Gigamap of Canadian governance in the digital era.

- A major symposium held in Ottawa collected ideas from participants, which were further developed in a subsequent workshop at the Institute on Governance.

Figure 13-12 shows a version of a Gigamap template used to engage participants during sessions at early stages of the project. The intent was to reveal to participants an understanding of the spectrum of changes influencing and transforming governance in the digital era.

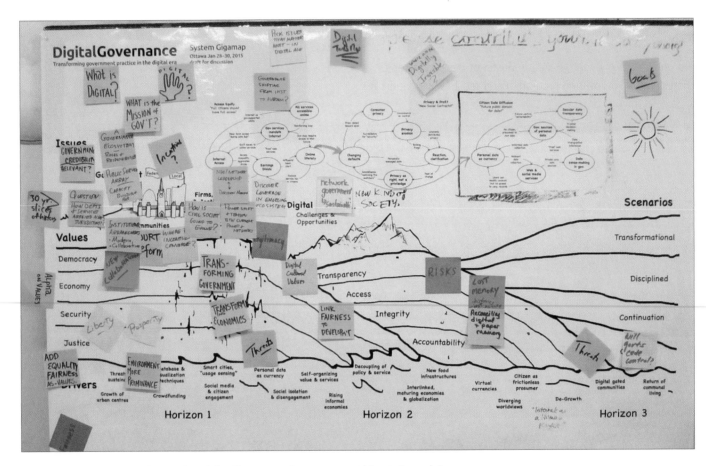

FIGURE 13-12. An interactive version of the Gigamap used to engage participants in workshops.

Overall, the issue is not one of "digital governance." Instead, our focus is on the systemic shifts anticipated within federal, provincial, and local governance and citizen experience driven by the rapid alterations brought on by *digital cultures*. We used the Gigamap as a primary means of cultivating a long-term perspective and guide multisector vision building.

About the Contributor

Dr. Peter Jones is an associate professor at OCAD University, Toronto, where he teaches in the Master of Design Strategic Foresight and Innovation program. Peter teaches innovation research and systemic design and guide research in the Strategic Innovation Lab (sLab). sLab contributors to the case project included SFI graduate Kelly Kornet and sLab director Greg van Alstyne.

Peter is managing partner of the Redesign Network (*redesign-network.com*) and the author of *Design for Care* (Rosenfeld Media, 2013). You can follow him on Twitter at *@redesign*.

Diagram and Image Credits

Figures 13-2 and 13-3: Consumer insight maps and template by Kim Erwin, appearing in her article "Consumer Insight Maps: The Map as Story Platform in the Design Process," *Parsons Journal for Information Mapping* (Winter 2011). *http://piim.newschool.edu/journal/issues/2011/01/pdfs/ParsonsJournalForInformationMapping_Erwin-Kim.pdf*

Figures 13-4 and 13-5: Diagrams of Collaboratonia created by Patrick Kovacich, used with permission

Figure 13-6: Diagram by Chiara Diana and Roberta Tassi, used with permission

Figures 13-7a through 13-7d: Isometric maps created by Paul Kahn, Julia Moisand Egea, and Laurent Kling, used with permission, originally appearing in Paul Kahn and Julia Moisand. "Patterns That Connect: The Value of Mapping Complex Data Networks," *Information Design Journal* (2009)

Figure 13-8: Diagram created by Mark Simmons and Aaron Lewis, CC BY-SA 3.0, used with permission

Figure 13-9: Photos of the Cloudwash prototype by Timo Arnall, copyright Berg, used with permission. I'd like to thank Sofia Hussain for pointing the example out in her presentation at the UX STRAT 2014 conference.

Figure 13-10: Ecosystem diagram by Andy Polaine, Lavrans Løvlie, and Ben Reason, appearing in *Service Design* (Rosenfeld Media, 2013), used with permission

Figures 13-11 and 13-12: Example of a Gigamap diagram thanks to Peter Jones, Greg van Alsty, and Evert Lindquist, used with permission

References

Abilla, Pete. "Lean Service: Customer Value and Don't Waste the Customer's Time" (Schmula.com, 2010). *http://www.shmula.com/lean-consumption-dont-waste-the-customers-time/2760/*.

Anthony, Scott et al. The Innovator's Guide To Growth (Harvard Business Press, 2008).

Berkun, Scott. *The Myths of Innovation* (O'Reilly, 2007).

Sterling, Bruce. "Cloudwash: The Berg Cloud-Connected Washing Machine," Wired (Feb, 2014).

Berners-Lee, Tim, James Hendler and Ora Lassila. "The Semantic Web," *Scientific American* (2001). *http://www.sciam.com/article.cfm?articleID=00048144-10 D2-1C70-84A9809EC588EF21andsc=I100322*.

Bitner, Mary Jo, Amy L. Ostrom and Felicia N. Morgan. "Service Blueprinting: A Practical Technique for Service Innovation," Working Paper, Center for Leadership Services, Arizona State University (2007). *http://files.g51studio.com/parsons/ServiceBlueprinting.pdf*.

Bettencourt, Lance and Anthony W. Ulwick. "The Customer-Centered Innovation Map," Harvard Business Review (May 2008).

Beyer, Hugh and Karen Holtzblatt. *Contextual Design* (Morgan Kaufmann, 1997).

Bodine, Kerry. "How To Map Your Customer Experience Ecosystem," Forrester Reports (May, 2013).

Booz and Co. "Executives Say They're Pulled in Too Many Directions and That Their Company's Capabilities Don't Support Their Strategy" (Feb 2011).

Bringhurst, Robert. *The Elements of Typographic Style*, version 3.2 (Hartley and Marks, 2008).

British Standards Institution. "BS 7000-3:1994 Design management systems. Guide to managing service design" (BSI, 1994).

Brown, David. "Hugh Dubberly. Supermodeler," *GAIN : AIGA Journal of Design for the Network Economy* (2000) *http://www.aiga.org/supermodeler-hugh-dubberly/*.

Brown, Tim. *Change by Design* (Harper, 2009).

Browne, Jonathan with John Dalton and Carla O'Connor. "Case Study: Emirates Uses Customer Journey Maps To Keep The Brand On Course" (Forrester Reports, 2013).

Brugnoli, Gianluca. "Connecting the Dots of User Experience," *Journal of Information Architecture* (Spring 2009) *http://journalofia.org/volume1/issue1/02-brugnoli/jofia-0101-02-brugnoli.pdf*.

Carbone, Lewis and Stephan Haeckel. "Engineering Customer Experiences," Marketing Management (1994). *http://www.expeng.com/articles/MM_Winter1994_EngineeringCustomerExperiences.pdf*.

Card, Stuart, Jock Mackinlay and Ben Shneiderman (Eds.) *Readings in Information Visualization: Using Vision to Think* (Morgan Kaufmann, 1999).

Carlzon, Jan. *Moments of Truth* (Reed Business, 1987).

Charan, Ram. *What The Customer Wants You To Know* (Portfolio, 2007).

Cheng, Kevin. *See What I Mean* (Rosenfeld Media, 2012).

Christensen, Clayton. *The Innovator's Dilemma* (Harvard Business Press, 1997)

Christensen, Clayton. *The Innovator's Solution* (Harvard Business School Press, 2003).

Christensen, Clayton, Scott Cook and Taddy Hall. "Marketing Malpractice: The Cause and the Cure," *Harvard Business Review* (Dec 2005).

Christensen, Clayton and Derek van Beyer. "The Capitalist's Dilemma," *Harvard Business Review* (Jun 2014).

Claro Partners. "A guide to succeeding in the Internet of Things" (2014). *http://www.claropartners.com/IoTGuide/Guide-to-succeeding-in-the-IoT_Claro%20Partners.pdf*.

Colley, Russell. *Defining Advertising Goals for Measured Advertising Results.* (Association of National Advertisers, 1961).

Constable, Giff. *Talking to Humans* (2014).

Constantine, Larry. "Essential Modeling: Use Cases for User Interfaces," *ACM Interactions* (Apr 1995).

Craik, Kenneth. *The Nature of Explanation* (Cambridge University Press, 1943).

Danielson, David. "Transitional Volatility in Web Navigation," *IT and Society* (1/3, 2003). *http://citeseerx.ist.psu.edu/viewdoc/download?doi=10.1.1.58.845andrep=rep1andtype=pdf*.

David Court, Dave Elzinga, Susan Mulder and Ole Jørgen Vetvik. "The consumer decision journey," *McKinsey Quarterly* (Jun 2009). *http://www.mckinsey.com/insights/marketing_sales/the_consumer_decision_journey*.

Desmet, Pieter. *Designing Emotions* (2002).

Denning, Steve. "Why Building A Better Mousetrap Doesn't Work Anymore," *Forbes* (Feb 2014). *http://www.forbes.com/sites/stevedenning/2014/02/28/why-building-a-better-mousetrap-doesnt-work-any-more/*.

Denning, Steve. "The Copernican Revolution In Management," *Forbes* (2013). *http://www.forbes.com/sites/stevedenning/2013/07/11/the-copernican-revolution-in-management/*.

"Designing CX." *http://designingcx.com*.

Diana Chiara, Elena Pacenti, and Roberta Tassi. "Visualtiles: Communication tools for (service) design," First Nordic Conference on Service Design and Service Innovation (2009). *http://servdes.org/pdf/2009/diana-pacenti-tassi.pdf*.

Diller, Steve, Nathan Shedroff and Darrel Rhea. *Making Meaning: How Successful Businesses Deliver Meaningful Customer Experiences* (New Riders, 2005).

Drucker, Peter. *The Practice of Management* (Harper and Brothers, 1954).

Dubberly, Hugh. "A System Perspective on Design Practice" [Video talk at Carnegie Melon] (2012). *http://vimeo.com/51132200*.

Edelman, David. "Branding in the Digital Age: You're Spending Your Money in All the Wrong Places," *Harvard Business Review* (Dec, 2010).

Erwin, Kim. "Consumer Insight Maps: The Map as Story Platform in the Design Process," *Parsons Journal for Information Mapping* (Winter, 2011). *http://pjim.newschool.edu/issues/2011/01/pdfs/ParsonsJournalForInformationMapping_Erwin-Kim.pdf*.

Flom, Joel. "The Value of Customer Journey Maps: A UX Designer's Personal Journey," *UX Matters* (Sept 2011). *http://www.uxmatters.com/mt/archives/2011/09/the-value-of-customer-journey-maps-a-ux-designers-personal-journey.php*.

Frishberg, Leo and Charles Lambdin. *Presumptive Design: Design Provocations for Innovation* (Morgan Kaufmann, 2015).

Furr, Nathan and Jeff Dyer. *The Innovator's Method* (Harvard Business Review Press, 2014).

Gilmore, James and B. J. Pine II. *The Experience Economy* (Harvard Business School Press, 1999).

Gilmore, James and B.J. Pine II. *Authenticity: What Consumers Really Want* (Harvard Business School Press, 2007).

Golub, Harvey, Jane Henry, John L. Forbis, Nitin T. Mehta, Michael J. Lanning, Edward G. Michaels, and Kenichi Ohmae. "Delivering value to customers," *McKinsey Quarterly* (Jun 2000). *http://www.mckinsey.com/insights/strategy/delivering_value_to_customers*.

GfK. "UX Score" *http://www.gfk.com/solutions/ux/our-products/ux-measurement/Pages/UX-Score.aspx*.

Gothelf, Jeff. "Using Proto-Personas for Executive Alignment," *UX Magazine* (May 2012).

Gothelf, Jeff. *Lean UX* (O'Reilly, 2013).

Gray, Dave et al. *Gamestorming* (O'Reilly, 2010).

Grocki, Megan. "How to Create a Customer Journey Map," *UX Mastery* (Sep 2014). *http://uxmastery.com/how-to-create-a-customer-journey-map/*.

Harrington, Richard and Anthony Tjan. "Transforming Strategy One Customer at a Time," *Harvard Business Review* (Mar, 2008).

Hobber, Steven and Eric Berkman. *Designing Mobile Interfaces* (O'Reilly, 2011).

Hohmann, Luke. *Innovation Games* (Addison-Wesley, 2006).

Holtzblatt, Karen, Jessamyn Burns Wendell and Shelley Wood. *Rapid Contextual Design* (Morgan Kaufmann, 2004).

Hubert, Lis and Donna Lichaw. "Storymapping: A MacGyver Approach to Content Strategy, Part 2," *UX Matters* (Mar 2014). *http://www.uxmatters.com/mt/archives/2014/03/storymapping-a-macgyver-approach-to-content-strategy-part-2.php*.

Hussain, Sofia. "Designing Digital Strategies, Part 1: Cartography," *UX Booth* (Feb 2014). *http://www.uxbooth.com/articles/designing-digital-strategies-part-1-cartography/*.

Hussain, Sofia. "Designing Digital Strategies, Part 2: Connected User Experiences," *UX Booth* (Jan 2015). *http://www.uxbooth.com/articles/designing-digital-strategies-part-2-connected-user-experiences/*.

Jenkins, John R.G. *Marketing and Customer Behaviour* (Pergamon Press, 1971).

Kahn, Paul and Julia Moisand. "Patterns that Connect: the Value of Mapping Complex Data Networks," *Information Design Journal* (2009). *http://www.madpow.com/insights/2013/12/patterns-that-connect-the-value-of-mapping-complex-data-networks*.

Kahn, Paul. "Information Architecture for the Web: Applied IA" [presentation] *http://www.slideshare.net/pauldavidkahn/04-appled-ia*.

Kalbach, James. *Designing Web Navigation* (O'Reilly, 2007).

Kalbach, James. "Strategy Blueprint" (2015).

Kaplan, Robert and David Norton. "Having Trouble with Your Strategy? Then Map It," *Harvard Business Review* (Sep, 2000). *http://www.hbs.edu/faculty/Pages/item.aspx?num=6720*.

Kaplan, Robert and David Norton. *Strategy Maps* (Harvard Business Review Press, 2004).

Kaplan, Robert and David Norton, "Linking the Balanced Scorecard to Strategy," (1996). *http://www.hbs.edu/faculty/Pages/item.aspx?num=3294*.

Katz, Joel. *Designing Information* (Wiley, 2012).

Kempton, Willett. "Two theories of home heat control," *Cognitive Science* (1986).

Kolko, John. "Dysfunctional Products Come from Dysfunctional Organizations," *Harvard Business Review* (Jan 2015). *https://hbr.org/2015/01/dysfunctional-products-come-from-dysfunctional-organizations*.

Kyle, Elizabeth. "With Child: Personal Informative and Pregnancy." *http://www.bethkyle.com/EKyle_Workbook3_Final.pdf*.

Philip Johnson-Laird. *Mental Models* (Harvard University Press, 1983).

Lafley, A.G. and Roger Martin. *Playing To Win* (Harvard Business Review Press, 2013).

Lavidge, Robert and Gary Steiner. "A Model for Predictive Measurements of Advertising Effectiveness," *Journal of Marketing 25/4* (1961).

Lazonick, William. "Profits Without Prosperity," *Harvard Business Review* (Sep 2014).

Lecinski, Jim. *ZMOT: Winning the Zero Moment of Truth* (Google, 2011). *http://ssl.gstatic.com/think/docs/2011-winning-zmot-ebook_research-studies.pdf*.

Leinwand, Paul and Cesare Mainardi. *The Essential Advantage* (Harvard Business Review Press, 2010).

Levitt, Theodore. "Marketing Myopia," *Harvard Business Review* (1960). *https://hbr.org/2004/07/marketing-myopia*.

Lichaw, Donna. *Storylines* (Rosenfeld Media, 2015).

Løvlie, Lavrans. "Customer Journeys and Customer Lifecycles," Customer Blah [live|work blog] (Dec 2013). *http://liveworkstudio.com/the-customer-blah/customer-journeys-and-customer-lifecycles/*.

Manning, Harley and Kerry Bodine. *Outside In: The Power of Putting Customers at the Center of Your Business* (New Harvest, 2012).

Martin, Karin and Mike Osterling. *Value Steam Mapping* (McGraw Hill, 2014).

Maurya, Ash. *Running Lean* (O'Reilly, 2012).

McGrath, Rita Gunther. *The End of Competitive Advantage* (Harvard Business Review Press, 2013).

Meirelles, Isabel. *Design for Information* (Rockport, 2013).

Merchant, Nilofer. *The New How* (O'Reilly, 2009).

McMullin, Jess. "Searching For The Center of Design," *Boxes and Arrows* (Sep 2003).

Mintzberg, Henry, Joseph Lampel and Bruce Ahlstrand. *Strategy Safari* (Free Press, 1998).

Norman, Don. *The Design of Everyday Things* (1988).

Ogilvie, Tim and Jeanne Liedtka. "Journey Mapping," Ch. 4 in *Designing for Growth* (Columbia Business School Publishing, 2011).

O'Reilly, Charles and Michael Tushman. "The Ambidextrous Organization," *Harvard Business Review* (Apr 2004). *https://hbr.org/2004/04/the-ambidextrous-organization*.

Osterwalder, Alexander. *Business Model Generation* (Wiley, 2010).

Patton, Jeff. *User Story Mapping* (O'Reilly, 2014).

Polaine, Andy, Lavrans Løvlie and Ben Reason. *Service Design* (Rosenfeld Media, 2013).

Polaine, Andy. "Blueprint+: Developing a Tool for Service Design" (Service Design Network Conference, 2009). *http://www.slideshare.net/apolaine/blueprint-developing-a-tool-for-service-design*.

Porter, Michael and Mark R. Kramer. "Creating Shared Value," *Harvard Business Review* (Jan 2011). *https://hbr.org/2011/01/the-big-idea-creating-shared-value*.

Porter, Michael. "Creating Shared Value, an HBR interview with Michael Porter," *Harvard Business IdeaCasts* (Apr 2011) Part 1: *https://www.youtube.com/watch?v=F44G4B2uVh4*; Part 2: *https://www.youtube.com/watch?v=3xwpF1Ph22U*.

Rawson, Alex, Ewan Duncan and Conor Jones. "The Truth About Customer Experience," *Harvard Business Review* (Sep 2013). *https://hbr.org/2013/09/the-truth-about-customer-experience/ar/1*.

Fred Reichheld. *The Ultimate Question: Driving Good Profits and True Growth* (Harvard Business School Press, 2006).

Reis, Eric. *Lean Startup* (O'Reilly, 2011).

Reynolds, Thomas and Jonathan Gutman. "Laddering theory, method, analysis, and interpretation," *Journal of Advertising Research* (1988).

Richardson, Adam. "*Using Customer Journey Maps to Improve Customer Experience*," Harvard Business Blog (Nov 2010); and "*Touchpoints Bring the Customer Experience to Life*," Harvard Business Blog (Dec 2010).

Risdon, Chris. "The Anatomy of an Experience Map," *Adaptive Path Blog* (Nov 2011). *http://www.adaptivepath.com/ideas/the-anatomy-of-an-experience-map/*.

Risdon, Chris. "Unsucking The Touchpoint." *Adaptive Path Blog* (2013). *http://www.uie.com/articles/un-sucking-the-touchpoint/.*

Rogers, Everett. *Diffusion of Innovations*, 5th ed. (Free House, 2003).

Sauro, Jeff. "Measuring Usability with the System Usability Scale (SUS)," *Measuring U* (Feb 2011). *http://www.measuringu.com/sus.php.*

Schauer, Brandon. "Exploratorium: Mapping the Experience of Experiments," Adaptive Path Blog (Apr 2013). *http://adaptivepath.org/ideas/exploratorium-mapping-the-experience-of-experiments.*

Schrage, Michael. *Who Do You Want Your Customers To Become?* (Harvard Business Review Press, Jul 2012).

Schrage, Michael. *The Innovator's Hypothesis* (MIT Press, 2014).

Service Design Tools, *http://www.servicedesigntools.org.*

Shaw, Colin and John Ivens. *Building Great Customer Experiences* (Palgrave Macmillan, 2002).

Shaw, Colin. *The DNA of Customer Experience: How Emotions Drive Value* (Palgrave Macmillan, 2007).

Shedroff, Nathan. "Bridging Strategy with Design: How Designers Create Value for Businesses," Interaction South America [presentation] (Nov 2014). *https://www.youtube.com/watch?v=64-HpMC1tCw.*

Sheth, Jagdish, Bruce Newman and Barbara Gross. *Consumption Values and Market Choices* (South-Western Publishing, 1991).

Shostack, G. Lynn. "How to Design a Service," *European Journal of Marketing* 16/1 (1982).

Shostack, G. Lynn. "Designing Services That Deliver," *Harvard Business Review* (1984).

Bjørndal Skjelten, Elisabeth. *Complexity and Other Beasts* (Oslo School of Architecture and Design, 2014).

Smith, Gene. "Experience Maps: Understanding Cross-Channel Experiences for Gamers," nForm Blog (Feb 2010). *http://nform.com/blog/2010/02/experience-maps-cross-channel-experiences-deliverable-for-gamers.*

SUMI, *http://sumi.ucc.ie.*

Susan Spraragen and Carrie Chan. "Service Blueprinting: When Customer Satisfaction Numbers are not enough." (International DMI Education Conference, 2008).

Susan Spraragen. "Enabling Excellence in Service with Expressive Service Blueprinting," Case Study 9 in Design for Services by Anna Meroni and Daniela Sangiorgi (Gower, 2011).

Spengler, Christoph, Werner Wirth and Renzo Sigrist. "360° Touchpoint Management—How important is Twitter for our brand?" Marketing Review St. Gallen (Feb 2010). *http://www.accelerom.com/en/wp-content/uploads/2012/10/2010_Marketing-Review_360-degree-Touchpoint-Management.pdf.*

Stickdorn, Marc and Jakob Schneider. *This is Service Design Thinking: Basics-Tools-Cases* (BIS Publishers, 2012).

Tate, Tyler. "Cross-Channel Blueprints: A tool for modern IA," Tyler Tate blog (Feb 2012). *http://tylertate.com/blog/2012/02/21/cross-channel-ia-blueprint.html.*

Temkin, Bruce. "Mapping the Customer Journey," Forrester Reports (Feb 2010).

Temkin, Bruce. "It's All About Your Customer's Journey," *Customer Experience Matters* (2010). *http://experiencematters.wordpress.com/2010/03/04/its-all-about-your-customers-journey/*.

Thompson, Ed and Esteban Kolsky. "How to Approach Customer Experience Management" (Gartner Research Reports, 2004). *https://www.gartner.com/doc/466017/approach-customer-experience-management*.

Tufte, Edward. *Envisioning Information* (Graphics Press, 1990).

Tufte, Edward. *Visual Explanations: Images and Quantities, Evidence and Narrative* (Graphics Press, 1997).

Ulwick, Anthony. *What Customers Want* (McGraw Hill, 2005).

Ulwick, Anthony. "Turn Customer Input into Innovation," *Harvard Business Review* (2003). *https://hbr.org/2002/01/turn-customer-input-into-innovation/ar/1*.

Unger, Russ, Brad Nunnally and Dan Willis. *Designing the Conversation* (New Riders, 2013).

Walters, Jeannie. "What IS a Customer Touchpoint?" Customer Think blog (Oct 2014). *http://360connext.com/customer-touchpoint/*.

Williams, Luke. *Disrupt* (FT Press, 2011).

Womack, James and Daniel Jones. "Lean Consumption,'' *Harvard Business Review* (March 2005). *https://hbr.org/2005/03/lean-consumption/ar/1*.

Womack, James and Daniel Jones. *Lean Thinking*, 2nd Ed. (Simon and Schuster, 2010).

Wreiner, T., Mårtensson, I., Arnell, O., Gonzalez, N., Holmlid, S, and Segelström, F. "Exploring Service Blueprints for Multiple Actors" (First Nordic Conference on Service Design and Service Innovation, 2009). *http://www.ep.liu.se/ecp/059/017/ecp09059017.pdf*.

Young, Indi. *Mental Models* (Rosenfeld Media, 2008).

Young, Indi. *Practical Empathy* (Rosenfeld Media, 2015).

Young, Indi. "Try the 'Lightning Quick' Mental Model Method," Indi Young Blog (Mar 2010). *http://indiyoung.com/the-lightening-quick-method/*.

Zeithaml, Valarie, Mar Jo Bitner and Dwayne Gremler. *Services Marketing-Integrating Customer Focus Across the Firm*, 6th Ed. (McGraw-Hill, 2012).

Index